S0-AQL-171

THE CHARLTON STANDARD CATALOGUE OF

BESWICK ANIMALS

FOURTH EDITION

DIANA CALLOW
JOHN CALLOW

MARILYN SWEET
PETER SWEET

PUBLISHER
W. K. CROSS

The Charlton Press

TORONTO, ONTARIO ❖ PALM HARBOR, FLORIDA

COPYRIGHT NOTICE AND TRADEMARK NOTICE

Copyright © 1999 Charlton International Inc. All Rights Reserved
Photographs © Charlton International Inc.
The terms Charlton, Charlton's, The Charlton Press and abbreviations thereof, are trademarks of Charlton International Inc. and shall not be used without written consent from Charlton International Inc.

No part of this publication, except the various numbering systems, may be reproduced, stored in a retrieval system, or transmitted in any form or by any means, electronic, mechanical, photocopying, recording, or otherwise, without the prior written permission of the copyright owner.

No copyright material may be used without written permission in each instance from Charlton International Inc. Permission is hereby given for brief excerpts to be used in newspapers, magazines, periodicals and bulletins, other than in the advertising of items for sale, providing the source of the material so used is acknowledged in each instance.

While every care has been taken to ensure accuracy in the compilation of the data in this catalogue, the publisher cannot accept responsibility for typographical errors.

DISCLAIMER

Products listed or shown were manufactured by Royal Doulton (UK) Limited. This book has been produced independently and neither the authors nor the publisher has any connection whatsoever with either Royal Doulton (UK) Limited or the Royal Doulton International Collectors Club. Royal Doulton is a registered trade mark and is used in this book with the permission of Royal Doulton (UK) Limited. Any opinions expressed are those of the authors and not necessarily endorsed by Royal Doulton (UK) Limited.

Canadian Cataloguing In Publication Data

The National Library of Canada has catalogued this publication as follows:

Main entry under title:

The Charlton standard catalogue of Beswick animals
2nd ed. (1996)-
Continues: Charlton price guide to Beswick animals, ISSN 1202-9831
ISSN 1203-8318
ISBN 0-88968-213-5 (4th ed.)

1. Porcelain animals - Catalogs. 2. Royal Doulton figurines - Catalogs. 3. Beswick (Firm) - Catalogs. I. Charlton Press. II. Title: Beswick animals.

NK4660.C48   738.8'2'0294   C96-900264-5

EDITORIAL

Editor	Jean Dale
Assistant Editor	Cindy Raycroft
Graphic Technician	Davina Rowan

ACKNOWLEDGMENTS

The Charlton Press wishes to thank those who have helped and assisted with the fourth edition of *The Charlton Standard Catalogue of Beswick Animals*.

SPECIAL THANKS

Our thanks go to the staff at Royal Doulton (U.K.) Limited who helped with additional technical information and photography, especially Valerie Baynton, Joan Barker, Ian Howe, Julie McKeown, Maria Murtagh and Gill Walters.

CONTRIBUTORS TO THE FOURTH EDITION

The Publisher would like to thank the following individuals or companies who graciously supplied pricing, direct mail lists, photographs or allowed us access to their collections for photographic purposes. We offer sincere thanks to:

Steve Anderson; Pottery Specialist Auctions; **Frances Allington**, Bucks., England; **Sandra Cheetham**, Hants., England; **John Fornaszewski**, Missouri; **E.M. Holland**, Warrington, England; **Mavis Kelly**, Pickering, England; **Jill Livesey**, Brentwood Bay, B.C.; **Harvey May**, Essex, England; **Margaret Mitchell**, England; **Linda J. Pointer**, Columbus, Ohio; **Laura Rock-Smith**, Sayville, New York; **Joe Schenberg**, St. Louis, Missouri; **Evelyn M. Speak**, Somerset, England; **Linda Walter**, Troy, Alabama; **P. R. Whitelock**, Bucks., England

A SPECIAL NOTE TO COLLECTORS

We welcome and appreciate any comments or suggestions in regard to *The Charlton Standard Catalogue of Beswick Animals*. If you would like to participate in pricing or supply previously unavailable data or information, please contact Jean Dale at (416) 488-1418, or e-mail us at chpress@charltonpress.com.

Printed in Canada
in the Province of Ontario

The Charlton Press

Editorial Office
2040 Yonge Street, Suite 208
Toronto, Ontario, Canada M4S 1Z9
Telephone (416) 488-1418 Fax: (416) 488-4656
Telephone (800) 442-6042 Fax: (800) 442-1542
www.charltonpress.com

HOW TO USE THIS CATALOGUE

THE FOURTH EDITION

Published in the final month of the second millennium *The Charlton Standard Catalogue of Beswick Animals* has seen tremendous growth in the area of collecting Beswick models. With over 25,000 copies of this guide in print, we would like to feel that in some small way we have contributed to this growth.

We have seen the Beswick backstamp on hundreds of models in the mid-part of this century fall to a few by 1989, created by the transference of many Beswick models to the Royal Doulton backstamp. With the return of many of these models to the Beswick backstamp in September 1999, we hope to see a revival in the Beswick collecting field. This change will give the Beswick collector the needed optimism to enter the new millennium.

THE LISTINGS

The main body of the book, chapters one to eight, which contain the majority of the animal figures, is first listed alphabetically by chapter, i.e. birds, butterflys, cats, dogs, farm animals, etc.; within each of these chapters, the listings are in Beswick model number order. The remaining chapters are devoted to specialty items such as resin sculptures, whisky flasks and commissioned models. Each chapter has a short introduction and index by model number located on the chapter title page.

THE PURPOSE

The third edition of this price guide covers the complete range of animals produced at the John Beswick Studios.

As with other catalogues in Charlton's Royal Doulton/Beswick reference library, this publication has been designed to serve two specifc purposes. First, to furnish the collector with accurate and detailed listings that provide the essential information needed to build a rewarding collection. Second, to provide collectors and dealers with an indication of current market prices for the complete line of Beswick animal figures.

VARIETY CLASSIFICATIONS

In developing the series of Royal Doulton/Beswick catalogues, we found it necessary to divide the model changes into three classifications based on the degree of complexity.

STYLES: When two or more animal figures have the same name - but different physical modelling characteristics - they are listed as **Style One, Style Two** and so after their names. Such figures will also have different model numbers.

VERSIONS: Versions are modifications in a minor style element, such as the Siamese Cat, model 1559. In the first version, the head of the cat shows puffed out cheeks, with the body being fleshy and having a short neck. The second version shows the cat with a sleek tapering face, a long neck and a lean body. Another example of a version change is model 1014 the Welsh Cob (rearing) where the first version has the tail of the horse attached the the ceramic base whilst in the second version the tail of the horse hangs loose.

VARIATIONS: A change in colour is a variation; for example, almost any of the horses or cats with the lists of colourways and finishes are variations.

A WORD ON PRICING

The purpose of this catalogue is to give readers the most accurate, up-to-date retail prices for Beswick animal figures in the United States, Canada and the United Kingdom.

To accomplish this, The Charlton Press continues to access an international pricing panel of experts who submit prices based on both dealer and collector retail-price activity, as well as current auction results in the U.S., Canada, and the U.K. These market prices are carefully averaged to reflect accurate valuations for figures in each of these markets.

The prices published herein are for models in mint condition. Collectors are cautioned that a repaired or restored piece may be worth as little as 25 percent of the value of the same figure in mint condition.

Current models are priced according to the manufacturers suggested retail price in each of the market regions. Please be aware that price or promotional sales discounting is always possible and can result in lower prices than those listed.

One exception, however, occurs in the case of current models or recent limited editions issued in only one of the three markets. Since such items were priced by Doulton only in the country in which they were to be sold, prices for the other markets are not shown.

A further word on pricing: As mentioned previously, this is a catalogue giving prices for models in the currency of a particular market (U.S. dollars for the American market and sterling for the U.K. market). The bulk of the prices given herein are not determined by currency exchange calculations, but by actual market activity in the market concerned.

Please see the section on internet pricing, for now little stands in the way of a universal price.

In some cases the number of models produced is so small that market activity does not exist; there is no price activity on which to base a price. An example of this is the Spirit of Whitfield with only four existing models. The price in this instance is purely between the buyer and the seller. We have therefore listed the last known auction price for this model. If this model was to be offered for sale at a future date, the price may be higher or lower than the auction price listed, depending on the demand for the model at that time. For models with little or no market data due to the limited number of figures produced,we have reverted to the following rarity table:

Rare	26 - 50 figures known
Very rare	11 - 25 figures known
Extremely rare	5 - 10 figures known
Auction results	1 - 4 figures known

When prices are italicized in the pricing tables, for example, the Galloway Bull (Model No. 1746A), this indicates that the price is only an indication. The prices are too high and too volatile to establish a solid market price. Once again, the final price determination must be made between buyer and seller.

THE INTERNET AND PRICING

The internet is changing the way business is being done in the collectable marketplace. Linking millions of collectors around the world through chat rooms, antique and collector malls, internet auctions and producer web sites, e-commerce has become big business.

Some of the effects caused by the internet and e-commerce on the collectable business are as follows:

1. Collectors deal directly with other collectors, changing the dynamics of the traditional customer/dealer relationship.

2. Information concerning new issues, finds and varieties is readily available, twenty-four hours a day. Collectors' wants are made known instantly to a wide spectrum of dealers and collectors.

3. Prices:

    (a) Price differentials dissappear between global market areas as collectors and the delivery services team up to stretch the purchasing power of the collectable dollar/pound.

    (b) Prices of common to scarce items will adjust downward to compensate for the temporary increase in merchandise supply. Conversely, prices of rare and extremely rare items will increase, a result of their increased exposure to demand.

    (c) After a time even the prices of the common items will increase due to the worldwide increase in demand for collectables.

4. Internet auction sites listing millions of items for sale on a daily basis continue to grow as more and more collectors discover the viability of using this method to buy and sell merchandise.

5. Traditional marketing strategies (retail stores, direct mail retailers, collectable shows and fairs, and collectable magazines and papers) face increased pressure in a more competitive environment.

The internet is user-friendly: no travelling required, twenty-four hour accessibility, no face-to-face contact or other pressure to buy or sell. Without a doubt, the arrival of e-commerce will change the way a collector collects.

FURTHER READING

Storybook Figures

The Charlton Standard Catalogue of Bunnykins, by Jean Dale and Louise Irvine
The Charlton Standard Catalogue of Royal Doulton Storybook Figurines, by Jean Dale
Collecting Cartoon Classics and other Character Figures, by Louise Irvine
Royal Doulton Bunnykins Figures, by Louise Irvine
Bunnykins Collectors Book, by Louise Irvine
Beatrix Potter Figures and Giftware, edited by Louise Irvine
The Beswick Price Guide, by Harvey May

Animals, Figures and Character Jugs

Royal Doulton Figures, by Desmond Eyles, Louise Irvine and Valerie Baynton
The Charlton Standard Catalogue of Beswick Animals, by Diane & John Callow and Marilyn & Peter Sweet
The Charlton Standard Catalogue of Royal Doulton Animals, by Jean Dale
The Charlton Standard Catalogue of Royal Doulton Beswick Figurines, by Jean Dale
The Charlton Standard Catalogue of Royal Doulton Beswick Jugs, by Jean Dale
Collecting Beswick - A Guide to Horses, Ponies and Foals, by Marilyn Sweet
Collecting Character and Toby Jugs, by Jocelyn Lukins
Collecting Doulton Animals, by Jocelyn Lukins
Doulton Flambé Animals, by Jocelyn Lukins
The Character Jug Collectors Handbook, by Kevin Pearson
The Doulton Figure Collectors Handbook, by Kevin Pearson

General

The Charlton Standard Catalogue of Beswick Pottery, by Diane and John Callow
Discovering Royal Doulton, by Michael Doulton
The Doulton Story, by Paul Atterbury and Louise Irvine
Royal Doulton Series Wares, by Louise Irvine (Vols. 1-5)
Limited Edition Loving Cups and Jugs, by Louise Irvine and Richard Dennis
Doulton for the Collector, by Jocelyn Lukins
Doulton Kingsware Flasks, by Jocelyn Lukins
Doulton Burslem Advertising Wares, by Jocelyn Lukins
Doulton Lambeth Advertising Wares, by Jocelyn Lukins
The Doulton Lambeth Wares, by Desmond Eyles
The Doulton Burslem Wares, by Desmond Eyles
Hannah Barlow, by Peter Rose
George Tinworth, by Peter Rose
Sir Henry Doulton Biography, by Edmund Gosse
Phillips Collectors Guide, by Catherine Braithwaite
Royal Doulton, by Jennifer Queree
John Beswick: A World of Imagination. Catalogue reprint (1950-1996)
Royal Doulton, by Julie McKeown

Magazines and Newsletters

Rabbiting On (Bunnykins Newsletter) Contact Leah Selig: 2 Harper Street, Merrylands 2160
    New South Wales, Australia. Tel./Fax 61 2 9637 2410 (International), 02 637 2410 (Australia)
Collect it! (Contact subscription department at: P.O. Box 3658, Bracknell, Berkshire RG12 7XZ.
    Telephone: (1344) 868280 or e-mail: collectit@dialpipex.com
Collecting Doulton Magazine, contact Doug Pinchin, P.O. Box 310, Richmond, Surrey TW9 1FS, England
Doulton News, published by Thorndon Antiques & Fine China Ltd., edited by David Harcourt
    P.O. Box 12-076 (109 Molesworth Street), Wellington, New Zealand
Beswick Quarterly (Beswick Newsletter) Contacr Laura Rock-Smith: 10 Holmes Court, Sayville
    N.Y. 11782-2408, U.S.A. Tel./Fax (516) 589-9027

TABLE OF CONTENTS

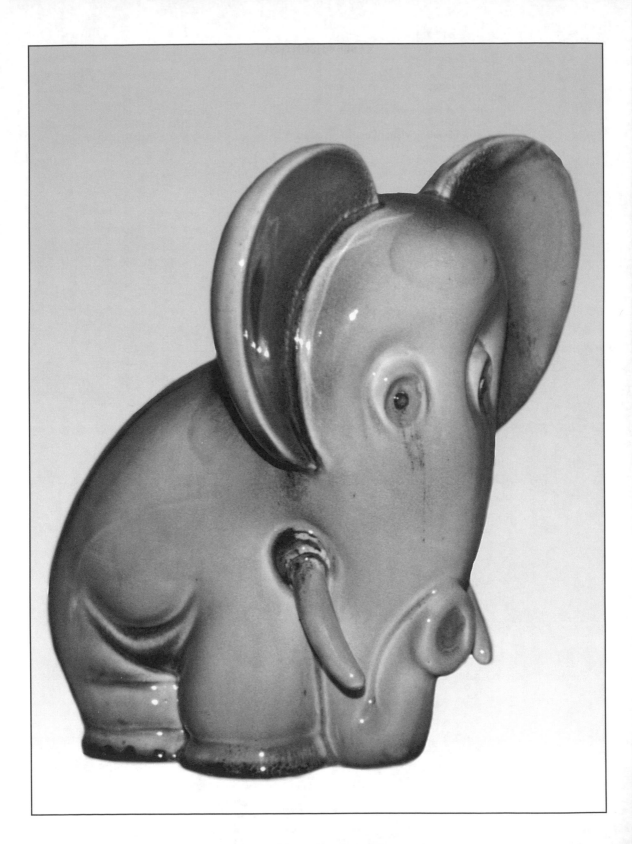

INTRODUCTION

An article entitled "Equestrian Figures for Collectors —Growth of the House of Beswick," in the *Pottery Gazette and Glass Trade Review* of September 1961, ended with this paragraph: "Among the potters of the present day yet to reach the one hundred-year mark, and whose products are already highly prized, none is more likely to be of future interest to collectors and antique dealers than the House of Beswick." How prophetic this has proved to be. In 1985 the Beswick Collector's Circle was formed as interest in the products of the Beswick factory was aroused. The circle has flourished as more and more people worldwide have joined the search to add to their collections and to seek information in order to enjoy their finds to the full. This book represents the most comprehensive attempt to date to form as complete a guide as possible to the Beswick animal collection.

In 1994 the John Beswick factory celebrated its centenary—a hundred years of producing an unbelievably wide variety of pottery items, from mundane household earthenware right through to the intricate ornamental ware and pure ornaments of all shapes and sizes.

Initially the factory produced plain and decorated ware. An advertisement from about 1900 lists "jugs, tea ware, dinner ware, toilet ware, flower pots, pedestals, novelties, vases, figures, bread trays, cheese dishes, etc., etc." The figures included the traditional Old Staffordshire dogs, but hares and hounds, horses, generals, a cow and calf, milkmaids, gardeners and Puss in Boots are also mentioned. Unfortunately many of these pieces were not marked Beswick.

From the start the Beswick factory was very much a family-run firm. James Wright Beswick, the founder, and his sons, John and Gilbert, and John's son, John Ewart, were all very committed to the factory's success. In 1934 ,when John Ewart Beswick became chairman and managing director and his uncle, Gilbert Beswick, was sales manager, several new pieces were introduced to the range, and recorded in the "shape book."

Arthur Gredington in his studio

This was the start of shape numbers being impressed into the base whenever possible and also the more widespread use of a Beswick backstamp.

Five years later Arthur Gredington took up his appointment as the first full-time modeller. His influence was enormous, for he had a great talent for modelling not only accurate and realistic animals of all kinds , but also ones of the comical variety, for example the very appealing "Grebie," number 1006. Consequently his name appears more than that of any other person in this book, and it is a tribute to his skill that many of his models are still in production in 1996 as *Doulton Animals*.

James Hayward also made an outstanding contribution to the high quality associated with the Beswick name. As decorating manager from 1934 and art director from 1957, he was responsible for designing almost three thousand different decorations and patterns. He also designed new shapes, such as the 720 "Panda Cub," and was an outstanding glaze chemist. His experience with glazes was fundamental in the development of the matt glaze used initially on the top of the range *Connoisseur Series*.

Mould making

When a complex model, such as an animal, is being manufactured, the mould it will be produced from is of vital importance. In this department Albert Hallam had exceptional skill. He joined Beswick in 1926 at age 14 as an apprentice mouldmaker and went on to become head of the mouldmaking department and also a modeller. The series of butterflies are Albert Hallam's creations, as are a number of horses, dogs and cats, which were modelled after Arthur Gredingtons retirement. These include at least one model that is very sought after today, number 2282 "Norwegian Fjord Horse."

There are several other modellers whose work is featured in this book. Very little is known about some of them as they tended to be employed on a freelance basis, for example, Miss Catford, who modelled character-type animals like the 663 "Elephant" holding a five-ton weight and Mr. Garbet, who contributed cats, dogs and a sheep. Although small in number, significant contributions were also made by Alan Maslankowski, whose 2578 "Shire Horse" is quite magnificent, Colin Melbourne, who besides the unique "C.M." series also modelled most of the Peter Scott ducks, Graham Orwell whose models included the 1374 "Galloping Horse" and 1391 "Mounted Indian," and Pal Zalman whose one equine model, the 1549 "Horse, Head tucked," is still in production.

By the late 1960s, Ewart and Gilbert Beswick were nearing retirement, and as there was not another generation to follow them into the family business, the decision was made in 1969 to sell to Royal Doulton. Beswick animals continued to be produced, and although much rationalization took place, such as reducing the number of colourways of the horses and withdrawing many pieces, the ranges were also expanded by the regular introduction of new pieces.

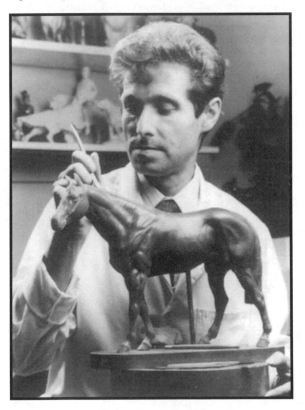

Graham Tongue at work

Then in August 1989, the decision was implemented to make the vast majority of the remaining animals produced at the Beswick factory into *Doulton Animals*, and the pieces were all issued with DA numbers. At the same time, grey and palomino matts were withdrawn from the horses' colourways, and only a few continued to be available in grey and palomino glosses.

Currently the modelling team at Beswick is headed by design manager Graham Tongue and includes the young team of Warren Platt, Amanda Hughes-Lubeck and Martyn Alcock. Graham Tongue has worked at Beswick since 1966 and became head modeller in 1973, when Albert Hallam retired. He has concentrated on the modelling of animals, and his modelling skill is apparent in almost all the sections here.

Graham Tongue has the distinction of modelling the piece which holds the world-record price for a piece of Beswick, appropriately an equine model entitled the "Spirit of Whitfield." In 1987 he was commissioned by the Chatterley Mining Museum to model Kruger, the last pit pony used at the Staffordshire mine. The resulting model, based on the 2541 "Welsh Mountain Pony," was considerably adapted with incredible attention to detail. The result was superb. Only four models were made, one each for the Beswick and Chatterley Whitfield museums, one presented to HRH Princess Anne when she visited the museum, and one was auctioned in aid of the Princesss favourite charity. In April 1994 the mining museum was closed and everything was auctioned. The "Spirit of Whitfield" sold for £2,750, a far cry from one hundred years ago when Beswick was advertising pieces for 6 1/2d.

Although very few animals now carry the Beswick backstamp, this book illustrates the animal kingdom as seen through the eyes of the Beswick designers since the early 1930s. Cats and kittens with appealing eyes, birds and butterflies to fly across walls, a well-stocked zoo with animals from all over the world, everyday farm animals, animals which make you laugh, champion dogs, sleek horses and fish leaping from their pools are all lasting reminders of the Beswick story. The story will continue as more information emerges and the elusive models are discovered.

NOTE

In September 1999, Royal Doulton moved their complete range of animals (with the exception of the limited edition models) to the Beswick backstamp. Confusion in pricing will exist for a while until the secondary market catches up.

BESWICK BACKSTAMPS
1890-1999

Backstamp 1 - Beswick Ware ENGLAND

Backstamp 1 is of the earliest printed backstamp. It may also be found with "ENGLAND" replaced by "MADE IN ENGLAND" and with the addition of "MADE IN ENGLAND" impressed in the base.

Backstamp 2 - Beswick Handcraft ENGLAND

Backstamp 2 shows a version used on more highly decorated pieces, in this case on a jug, "Ruth." The colours used to decorate the piece are strong, in the style of deco flowers and leaves.

Backstamp 3 - Impressed name and MADE IN ENGLAND

Backstamp 3 illustrated a style which gave the name of the decoration as well as the decoration number. The shape name, in this case "Rome" is impressed, together with "Made in England."

Backstamp 4 - "H.M. THE QUEEN"

Backstamp 4 shows a backstamp announcing royal patronage. The Queen mentioned here is Queen Mary, the wife of King George V.

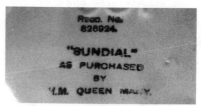

Backstamp 5 - "H.M. QUEEN MARY"

Backstamp 5 is the backstamp which can be found on items of the "Sundial" pattern. The form of words was necessary because after the death of King George V, Queen Mary became the Queen Mother. The registration number corresponds with the year 1938.

Backstamp 6 - TRENTHAM ART WARE

Backstamp 6 is the backstamp used for Trentham Art Wares. A gummed label with similar wording was also used.

Backstamp 7 - Circular BESWICK ENGLAND

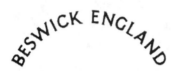

Backstamp 8 - Oval BESWICK ENGLAND

Backstamp 9 - BESWICK ENGLAND

Backstamp 9 may be found with "ENGLAND" or with "MADE IN ENGLAND" in either a straight line or a semi-circle.

Backstamp 10 - BESWICK CREST ENGLAND

SEALS

In addition to the first small gummed seal, green with gold lettering, an alternative oval style with gold lettering on a green background was used. The small green seal was replaced by the large oval style.

Seal 1 - Small gummed seal (first style) green with gold lettering

Seal 2 - Small gummed seal (second style) green with gold lettering

Seal 3 - Large gummed seal

ROYAL DOULTON COLLECTORS CLUB AND GUILD

Royal Doulton International Collectors Club

Founded in 1980, the Royal Doulton International Collectors Club provides an information service on all aspects of the company's products, past and present. A club magazine, *Gallery*, is published four times a year with information on new products and current events that will keep the collector up-to-date on the happenings in the world of Royal Doulton. Upon joining the club, each new member will receive a free gift and invitations to special events and exclusive offers throughout the year.

To join the Royal Doulton Collectors Club, please contact your local stockist, or contact the club directly at the address or telephone numbers below:

Royal Crown Derby Collectors Guild

The Royal Crown Derby Collectors Guild was established in 1994 to establish closer contact with Royal Crown Derby Collectors. Membership entitles the collector to a yearly subscription to the quarterley *Gallery* magazine, *Royal Crown Derby News*, membership gifts and free admission to the Royal Crown Derby Visitor Centre.

To join the Royal Crown Derby Collectors Guild, please contact the guild at the address or telephone number below:

Minton House
London Road, Stoke-on-Trent
Staffordshire ST4 7QD, England

Telephone:
U.K.: (01782) 292127
U.S.A. and Canada: 1-800-747-3045 (toll free)
Australia: 011-800-142624 (toll free)
Fax: U.K.: (01782) 292099
Attn: Maria Murtagh

Caithness Glass Paperweight Collectors Society
Cathness Glass International
Paperweight Collectors Society

Formed in 1997, by Colin Terris, the society is the clearing house for all information on Caithness Glass Paperweights. Membership of the society entitles the collector to receive *Reflections*, the society's twice yearly magazine, plus three newsletters and a personal tour of the paperweight studios in Perth, Scotland, if you are ever in the area. An annual International Convention is held in Scotland in October.

To join the Caithness Glass Paperweight Collectors Society, please contact the society at one of the addresses or telephone numers below:

In the U.K. and International
Caithness Glass Paperweight Collectors Society
Caithness Glass Inc.
Inveralmond, Perth PH1 3TZ, Scotland
Tel.: (44) (0)1738 637373
Fax: (44) (0)1738 622494

In the U.S.A.

Caithness Glass Paperweight Collectors Society
Caithness Glass Inc.
141 Lanza Avenue, Building No. 12
Garfield, N.J. 07026, U.S.A.
Tel.: 973-340-3330
Fax: 973-340-9415

COLLECTOR CLUB CHAPTERS

Chapters of the RDICC have formed across North America and are worthy of consideration in those areas.

Detroit Chapter
Frank Americk, President
1771 Brody, Allen Park, MI 48101

Edmonton Chapter
Mildred's Collectibles
6813 104 Street, Edmonton, AB

New England Chapter
Charles Wood, President
Charles Briggs, Secretary
21 Walpole Street, Norwood, MA 02062
Tel.: (781) 784-8121

Northern California Chapter
Donald A. Blubaugh, President
P.O. Box 3665, Walnut Creek, CA 94598
Tel.: (925) 945-1687 Fax: (925) 938-6674
e-mail: Blubaugh@usa.net

Northwest, Bob Haynes, Chapter
Alan Matthew, President
15202 93rd Place N.E., Bothell, WA 98011
Tel.: (425) 488-9604

Ohio Chapter
Reg Morris, President
Dick Maschmeier, Treasurer
5556 White Haven Avenue
North Olmstead, Ohio 44070
Tel.: (216) 779 5554

Rochester Chapter
Judith L. Trost, President
103 Garfield Street, Rochester, N.Y. 14611
Tel.: (716) 436-3321

Western Pennsylvania Chapter
John Re, President
9589 Parkedge Drive, Allison Park, PA 15101
Tel.: (412) 366-0201 Fax: (412) 366-2558

ROYAL DOULTON VISITOR CENTRES

Royal Doulton Visitor Centre

Opened in the summer of 1996, the Royal Doulton Visitor Centre houses the largest collection of Royal Doulton figurines in the world. The centre also is home to the Minton Fine Art Studio, which specializes in hand painting and gilding. Demonstration areas offer the collector a first hand insight on how figurines are assembled and decorated. Also at the Visitor Centre is a cinema showing a 20 minute video on the history of Royal Doulton, plus a restaurant, and a retail shop offering both the best quality ware and slight seconds.

Factory tours may be booked, Monday to Friday, at the Visitor Centre.

Nile Street, Burslem
Stoke-on-Trent ST6 2AJ, England
Tel.: (01782) 292434
Fax: (01782) 292424
Attn: Yvonne Wood

Royal Doulton John Beswick Studios

Tours of the John Beswick Factory and Museum are available Monday to Thursday by appointment only. Please book in advance.

Gold Street, Longton
Stoke-on-Trent ST3 2JP, England
Tel.: (01782) 291213
Fax: (01782) 291279
Attn: Joan Barker

Royal Crown Derby Visitor Centre

Opened in the spring of 1998, the Visitor Centre was created to provide an insight into the tradition, history and skills that go into making Royal Crown Derby collectables. The centre houses the largest collection of Royal Crown Derby seen anywhere in the world, a demonstration area for skilled Royal Crown Derby artists and crafts people, restaurants, and shops.

Factory tours may be booked Monday to Friday at the centre, with advance bookings suggested.

194 Ormastson Road
Derby DE23 8JZ, England
Tel.: (01332) 712841
Fax: (01332) 712899
Attn: Stella Birks

Caithness Glass Visitor Centre

The Visitor Centre is home to the largest public display of Caithness Glass paperweights. Over 1200 designs are on display. A special viewing gallery enables visitors to watch the complete paperweight making process.

Inveralmond
Perth PH1 3TZ, Scotland
Tel.: (44) (0)1738 637373
Fax: (44) (0)1738 622494

Factory Shops

Royal Doulton Visitor Centre
Nile Street, Burslem
Stoke-on-Trent ST6 2AJ, England
Tel.: (01782) 292451

Royal Doulton Group Factory Shop
Lawley Street, Longton
Stoke-on-Trent ST3 2PH, England
Tel.: (01782) 291172

Royal Doulton Factory Shop
Minton House, London Road
Stoke-on-Trent ST4 7QD, England
Tel.: (01782) 292121

Royal Doulton Factory Shop
Leek New Road, Baddeley Green
Stoke-on-Trent ST2 7HS, England
Tel.: (01782) 291700

Royal Doulton Factory Shop
Victoria Road, Fenton
Stoke-on-Trent ST4 2PJ, England
Tel.: (01782) 291869

Beswick Factory Shop
Barford Street, Longton
Stoke-on-Trent ST3 2JP, England
Tel.: (01782) 291237

Web Site and E-mail Address

Sites: www.royal-doulton.com
www.caithnessglass.co.uk
E-mail:
Clubs: iss@royal-doulton.com
Visitor Centre: visitor@royal-doulton.com
Consumer Enquiries: enquiries@royal-doulton.com
Museum Curator: heritage@royal-doulton.com
Lawleys by Post: lbp@royal-doulton.com

WHERE TO BUY

Discontinued Doulton collectables can be found in Antique shops, markets, auctions, shows and fairs. Specialist dealers in Royal Doulton collectables attend many of the events listed below.

For auction happenings it is necessary to subscribe to Auction Houses that hold 20th Century or Doulton Auctions.

UNITED KINGDOM
Auction Houses

BBR Auctions
Elsecar Heritage Centre
Nr. Barnsley
South Yorkshire S74 8HJ, England
Te.: (01226) 745156
Fax: (01226) 351561
Attn: Alan Blakeman

Bonhams
65-69 Lots Road, Chelsea
London SW10 0RN, England
Tel.: (0171) 393-3900
Fax: (0171) 393-3906
www.bonhams.com
Attn: Neil Grenyer

Christie's South Kensington
85 Old Bromtpon Road
London SW7 3LD, England
Tel.: (0171) 581-7611
Fax.: (0171) 321-3321
www.christies.com
Attn: Michael Jeffrey

Potteries Specialist Auctions
271 Waterloo Road
Stoke-on-Trent ST6 3HR
Staffordshire, England
Tel.: (01782) 286622
Fax: (01782) 213777
Attn: Steve Anderson

Louis Taylor
Britannia House
10 Town Road, Hanley
Stoke-on-Trent ST1 2QG, England
Tel.: (01782) 21411
Fax: (01782) 287874
Attn: CLive Hillier

Phillips
101 New Bond Street
London W1Y 0AS, England
Tel.: (0171) 629-6602
Fax: (0171) 629-8876
www.phillips-auctions.com
Attn: Mark Oliver

Sotheby's
34-35 New Bond Street
London W1A 2AA, England
Tel.: (0171) 293-5000
Fax: (0171) 293-5989
www.sothebys.com
Attn: Christina Donaldson

Sotheby's Sussex
Summers Place
Billinghurst, Sussex RH14 9AF
England
Tel.: (01403) 833500
Fax: (01403) 833699

Thomson Roddick & Laurie
60 Whitesands
Dumfries DG1 2RS, Scotland
Tel.: (01387) 255366
Fax: (01387) 266236
Attn: Sybelle Medcalf

Peter Wilson Auctioneers
Victoria Gallery, Market Street
Nantwich, Cheshire CW5 5DG
England
Tel.: (01270) 623878
Fax: (01270) 610508
Attn: Stella Ashbrook or Robert Stone

Antique Fairs

Doulton and Beswick Collectors Fair
National Motorcycle Museum, Meriden, Birmingham
Usually March and August.
For information on times and dates:
Doulton and Beswick Dealers Association
Te.: (0181) 303 3316

Doulton and Beswick Collectors Fair
The Queensway Hall Civic Centre, Dunstable
Bedforshire. Usually in October.
For information on times and location:
UK Fairs Ltd., 10 Wilford Bridge Spur,
Melton, Woodbridge, Suffolk, 1P12 1RJ
Tel.: (01394) 386663

20th Centry Fairs
266 Glossop Road, Sheffield S10 2HS, England
Usually the last week in May, or the first week in June.
For information on times and dates:
Tel.: (0114) 275-0333
Fax: (0114) 275-4443

International Antique & Collectors Fair
Newark, Nottinghamshire
Usually six fairs annually. For information on times and dates:
International Antique & Collectors Fair Ltd.
P.O. Box 100, Newark, Nottinghamshire NG2 1DJ
Tel.: (01636) 702326

West London Wade Beswick & Doulton Fair
Brunel University, Kingston Lane
Uxbridge, Middlesex
For information on times and dates:
B & D Fairs, P.O. Box 273, Uxbridge
Middlesex, UB9 4LP
Tel.: (01895) 834694 or 834357

Yesterdays Doulton Fair
Usually November.
For information on times and dates:
Doulton and Beswick Dealers Association
Tel.: (0181) 303-3316

London Markets

Alfie's Antique Market
13-25 Church Street, London
Tuesday - Saturday

Camden Passage Market
London
Wednesday and Saturday

New Caledonia Market
Bermondsey Square, London
Friday Morning

Portobello Road Market
Portobello Road, London
Saturday

UNITED STATES
Auction Houses

Christie's East
219 East 67th Street
New York, NY 10021
Tel.: (212) 606-0400
www.christies.com
Attn: Timothy Luke

Sotheby's Arcade Auctions
1334 York Avenue
New York, NY 10021
Tel.: (212) 606-7000
www.sothebys.com
Attn: Andrew Cheney

Collectable Shows

Atlantique City
New Atlantic City Convention Centre
Atlantic City, NJ
Usually March and October.
For information on times and dates:
Brimfield and Associates
P.O. Box 1800, Ocean City, NJ 08226
Tel.: (609) 926-1800
www.atlantiquecity.com

Florida Doulton Convention & Sale
Sheraton Inn
1825 Griffin Road, Dania, Florida
Usually mid-January
For information on times and dates:
Pascoe & Company
932 Ponce De Leon Blvd., Coral Gables, FL
Tel.: (305) 445-3229
Charles Dombeck, 9720 Ridge Walk Court
Davie, Florida 33328 Tel.: (954) 452-9174

O'Hare National Antiques Show & Sale
Rosemont Convention Centre, Chicago, Illinois
Usually April, August and November.
For information on times and dates:
Manor House Shows Inc.
P.O. Box 7320, Fort Lauderdale, FL 33338
Tel.: (954) 563-6747

Royal Doulton Convention & Sale
John S. Knight Convention Centre
77 E. Mill Street, Akron, OH 44308
Usually August.
For information on times and dates:
Colonial House Productions
182 Front Street, Berea, Ohio 44017
Tel.: (800) 344-9299

CANADA
Auction Houses

Maynards
415 West 2nd Avenue
Vancouver, BC. V5Y 1E3
Tel.: (604) 876-1311

Ritchie's
288 King Street East, Toronto, Ontario M5A 1K4
Tel.: (416) 364-1864 Fax: (416) 364-0704
Attn: Caroline Kaiser

Collectable Shows

Canadian Art & Collectible Show & Sale
Kitchener Memorial Auditorium, Kitchener, Ontario
Usually early May.
For information on times and location:
George or Jackie Benninger
P.O. Box 130, Durham, Ontario, N0G 1R0
Tel.: (519) 369-6950

Canadian Doulton & Collectable Fair
Toronto, Ontario
Usually early September.
For information on times and location:
George or Jackie Benninger
P.O. Box 130, Durham, Ontario N0G 1R0
Tel.: (519) 369-6950

Chapter One

BIRDS

The models of our "feathered friends" are a delight for any bird enthusiast, and there are plenty here to choose from.

They come in all sizes, from very small birds, such as the little wren, to the impressive and large pheasant from the Connoisseur Series. Some are expensive, some are not, and quite a few are still in production. The figures cover a wide range from the comic Fun Models to wall plaques to the precise realism of the Peter Scott Wildfowl collection. When displayed in groups, the colours of their plumage create an impressive display.

Among the birds in this group are species that you could see any day of the week in your garden and also more exotic or rare varieties, such as the bald eagle, penguin and kookaburra.

INDEX BY MODEL NUMBER

Model No. 317
DUCK - On pottery base

Designer:	Miss Greaves
Height:	8 ¼", 21.0 cm
Colours:	See below
Issued:	c.1936-1954
Series:	Fun Models

Colourway	U.K. £	U.S. $	Can. $
1. Blue - gloss	135.00	225.00	325.00
2. Blue/green - matt	115.00	185.00	300.00
3. Green - gloss	115.00	185.00	300.00
4. Natural - satin	135.00	225.00	325.00
5. White - gloss	100.00	165.00	250.00

Model No. 370
DUCKS - Candleholder

Designer:	James Hayward
Height:	3 ½", 8.9 cm
Colours:	1. Various - satin matt
	2. White - matt
Issued:	1935-by 1954

Colourway	U.K. £	U.S. $	Can. $
1. Various - satin matt	45.00	75.00	100.00
2. White - matt	25.00	40.00	60.00

Model No. 450
PENGUIN

Designer:	Mr. Owen
Height:	Large - 8", 20.3 cm
	Small - 3 ½", 8.9 cm
Colours:	1. Black and white - gloss
	2. Blue - gloss
Issued:	1936-by 1954

Description	U.K. £	U.S. $	Can. $
1. Large - black	135.00	225.00	350.00
1. Small - black	85.00	135.00	200.00
2. Large - blue	160.00	265.00	400.00
2. Small - blue	100.00	165.00	250.00

Model No. 497
PELICAN - Match holder and ash-bowl

Designer:	Mr. Watkin
Height:	4", 10.1 cm
Colours:	1. Blue - gloss
	2. Various - satin matt
	3. White - matt
Issued:	1937- by 1954

Colourway	U.K. £	U.S. $	Can. $
1. Blue - gloss	75.00	125.00	185.00
2. Various - satin matt	65.00	115.00	100.00
3. White - matt	60.00	100.00	150.00

Model No. 617
DUCK - Ashtray

Designer:	Mr. Watkin
Height:	3", 7.6 cm
Colours:	1. Blue - gloss
	2. Various - satin matt
	3. White - matt
Issued:	1938-by 1954

Colourway	U.K. £	U.S. $	Can. $
1. Blue	85.00	150.00	200.00
2. Various	75.00	125.00	185.00
3. White	50.00	85.00	125.00

Model No. 618
PUFFIN

Designer:	Mr. Owen
Height:	9", 22.9 cm
Colours:	Blue - gloss
Issued:	1938-by 1954

Colourway	U.K. £	U.S. $	Can. $
Blue - gloss	200.00	300.00	425.00

Model No. 749
MALLARD DUCK - Rising

Designer:	Arthur Gredington
Height:	6 ½", 16.5 cm
Colours:	Browns, teal green and white - gloss
Issued:	1939-by 1965

Description	U.K. £	U.S. $	Can. $
Gloss	125.00	225.00	350.00

Model No. 750
MALLARD DUCK - Settling

Designer:	Arthur Gredington
Height:	6 ½", 16.5 cm
Colours:	Browns, teal green and white - gloss
Issued:	1939-by 1965

Description	U.K. £	U.S. $	Can. $
Gloss	125.00	225.00	350.00

Model No. 754
PHEASANT - Ashtray

Designer:	Mr. Watkin
Height:	3 ½", 8.9 cm
Colours:	Teal green and brown - gloss
Issued:	1939-1970

Description	U.K. £	U.S. $	Can. $
Gloss	25.00	45.00	50.00

Note: Model no. 767A was used for this ashtray.

Model No. 755
DUCK - Ashtray

Designer:	Mr. Watkin
Height:	4", 10.1 cm
Colours:	Teal green, brown and white - gloss
Issued:	1939-1969

Description	U.K. £	U.S. $	Can. $
Gloss	25.00	45.00	50.00

Note: Model no. 756/3 was used for this ashtray.

Model No. 756
MALLARD DUCK - Standing

Designer:	Mr. Watkin
Height:	756/1 - 7", 17.8 cm
	756/2 - 5 ¾", 14.6 cm
	756/2A - 4 ½", 11.9 cm
	756/3 - 3 ½", 8.9 cm
Colours:	1. Brown, teal green and white - gloss
	2. Blue - gloss
Issued:	1939-1973

Colourway	U.K. £	U.S. $	Can. $
1. 756/1 Brown	55.00	90.00	140.00
2. 756/1 Blue	115.00	190.00	275.00
3. 756/2 Brown	40.00	65.00	100.00
4. 756/2 Blue	85.00	135.00	200.00
5. 756/2A Brown	30.00	50.00	75.00
6. 756/2A Blue	75.00	125.00	175.00
7. 756/3 Brown	20.00	30.00	50.00
8. 756/3 Blue	65.00	100.00	150.00

Note: Model no. 756/3 has grass around feet.
Model no. 902 makes a set of five pieces.

Model No. 760
DUCK WITH LADYBIRD ON BEAK

Designer: Mr. Watkin
Height: 3 ¾", 9.5 cm
Colours: White with yellow beak,
ladybird on beak - gloss
Issued: 1939-1971
Series: Fun Models

Description	U.K. £	U.S. $	Can. $
Gloss	45.00	85.00	135.00

Model No. 762
DUCK ON SKIS

Designer: Mr. Watkin
Height: 3 ¼", 8.3 cm
Colours: White with orange beak - gloss
Issued: 1939-1969
Series: Fun Models

Description	U.K. £	U.S. $	Can. $
Gloss	45.00	85.00	135.00

Model No. 765
DUCK FAMILY

Designer: Arthur Gredington
Height: 2 ¾" x 7", 7.0 x 17.8 cm
Colours: White with yellow beaks - gloss
Issued: 1939-1971

Description	U.K. £	U.S. $	Can. $
Gloss	45.00	85.00	125.00

Model No. 767A
PHEASANT
First Version - Curved tail

Designer: Mr. Watkin
Height: 3", 7.6 cm
Colours: Red brown, teal green - gloss
Issued: 1939-1971

Description	U.K. £	U.S. $	Can. $
Gloss	25.00	35.00	45.00

Note: This model was used on 754 (pheasant ashtray).

Model No. 767B
PHEASANT
Second Version - Straight tail

Designer:	Mr. Watkin
Height:	3″, 7.6 cm
Colours:	Red, brown and teal green - gloss or matt
Issued:	1. Gloss - 1971-1995
	2. Matt - 1983-1989

Description	U.K. £	U.S . $	Can. $
1. Gloss	15.00	25.00	40.00
2. Matt	20.00	40.00	60.00

Model No. 768
SEAGULL ON ROCK

Designer:	Arthur Gredington
Height:	8 ½″, 21.6 cm
Colours:	Cream and dark brown, green and yellow base - gloss
Issued:	1939-by 1954

Description	U.K. £	U.S. $	Can. $
Gloss	300.00	500.00	700.00

Model No. 769
DUCK - Night light holder

Designer:	Mr. Watkin
Height:	6″, 20.3 cm
Colours:	Yellow and white duck, orange beak - gloss
Issued:	1939-by 1954

Description	U.K. £	U.S. $	Can. $
Gloss		Rare	

Model No. 800
PENGUIN - Chick

Designer:	Arthur Gredington
Height:	2″, 5.0 cm
Colours:	Black and white with yellow markings - gloss
Issued:	1940-1973
Set:	801, 802, 803

Description	U.K. £	U.S. $	Can. $
Gloss	15.00	25.00	40.00

Model No. 801
PENGUIN - Chick

Designer:	Arthur Gredington
Height:	2″, 5.0 cm
Colours:	Black and white with yellow markings - gloss
Issued:	1940-1973
Set:	800, 802, 803

Description	U.K. £	U.S. $	Can. $
Gloss	15.00	25.00	40.00

Model No. 802
PENGUIN - With umbrella

Designer:	Arthur Gredington
Height:	4 ¼″, 10.8 cm
Colours:	1. Black and white, red umbrella - gloss
	2. Black and white, green umbrella - gloss
Issued:	1940-1973
Set:	800, 801, 803

Colourway	U.K. £	U.S. $	Can. $
1. Red umbrella	30.00	50.00	75.00
2. Green umbrella	70.00	115.00	150.00

Note: Model 802 was altered in 1956.

Model No. 803
PENGUIN - With walking stick

Designer:	Arthur Gredington
Height:	3 ¾″, 9.5 cm
Colours:	Black and white with yellow markings, black walking stick - gloss
Issued:	1940-1973
Set:	800, 801, 802

Description	U.K. £	U.S. $	Can. $
Gloss	30.00	40.00	50.00

Note: Model 802 was altered in 1956.

Photograph not
available at press time

Model No. 817/1
MALLARD DUCK - Squatting

Designer:	Mr. Watkin
Height:	7 ½″, 19.1 cm
Colours:	Brown, teal green and white - gloss
Issued:	1940-1954
Set:	817/2

Description:	U.K. £	U.S. $	Can. $
Gloss	200.00	325.00	375.00

Model No. 817/2
MALLARD DUCK - Squatting

Designer: Mr. Watkin
Height: 6 ¾", 17.2 cm
Colours: Brown, teal green and white - gloss
Issued: 1940-1970
Set: 817/1

Description	U.K. £	U.S. $	Can. $
Gloss	135.00	225.00	300.00

Model No. 820
GEESE (Pair)

Designer: Arthur Gredington
Height: 4", 10.1 cm
Colours: White with orange feet and beaks - gloss
Issued: 1940-1971
Series: Fun Models
Set: 821, 822

Description	U.K. £	U.S. $	Can. $
Gloss	30.00	50.00	75.00

Model No. 821
GOSLING - Facing left

Designer: Arthur Gredington
Height: 2 ¼", 5.7 cm
Colours: White with orange beak - gloss
Issued: 1940-1971
Series: Fun Models
Set: 820, 822

Description	U.K. £	U.S. $	Can. $
Gloss	15.00	25.00	40.00

Model No. 822
GOSLING - Facing right

Designer: Arthur Gredington
Height: 1 ¾", 4.3 cm
Colours: White with orange beak - gloss
Issued: 1940-1971
Series: Fun Models
Set: 820, 821

Description	U.K. £	U.S. $	Can. $
Gloss	15.00	25.00	40.00

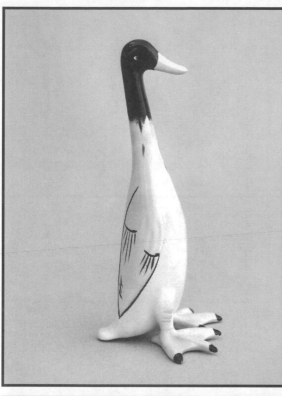

Model No. 827
HARDY'S DUCK - Standing

Designer:	Mr. Watkin
Height:	Large - 7 ½", 19.1 cm
	Medium - 6", 15.0 cm
	Small - 5", 12.7 cm
Colours:	1. White; brown and yellow - gloss
	2. White; solid decorated wing - gloss
	3. White; solid decorated neck, wing - gloss
	4. White; yellow bill, feet - gloss
Issued:	1940-by 1954

Description	U.K. £	U.S. $	Can. $
1. Large	110.00	200.00	275.00
2. Large	110.00	200.00	275.00
3. Large	110.00	200.00	275.00
4. Large	110.00	200.00	275.00
1. Medium	90.00	150.00	225.00
2. Medium	90.00	150.00	225.00
3. Medium	90.00	150.00	225.00
4. Medium	90.00	150.00	225.00
1. Small	80.00	135.00	200.00
2. Small	80.00	135.00	200.00
3. Small	80.00	135.00	200.00
4. Small	80.00	135.00	200.00

Model No. 849
PHEASANT ON BASE - Flying upwards

Designer:	Arthur Gredington
Height:	6", 15.0 cm
Colours:	Browns, teal green and yellow - gloss
Issued:	1940-1971

Description	U.K. £	U.S. $	Can. $
Gloss	110.00	200.00	300.00

Model No. 850
PHEASANT ON BASE - Settling

Designer:	Arthur Gredington
Height:	5 ¾", 14.6 cm
Colours:	Browns, teal green and yellow - gloss
Issued:	1940-1971

Description	U.K. £	U.S. $	Can. $
Gloss	110.00	200.00	300.00

Photograph not
available at press time

Model No. 862
FANTAIL PIGEON

Designer: Miss Joachin
Height: Unknown
Colours: Unknown
Issued: 1940-Unknown

Description	U.K. £	U.S. $	Can. $
Fantail Pigeon		Extremely Rare	

Note: Possibly not produced.

Model No. 902
MALLARD DUCK - Standing

Designer: Arthur Gredington
Height: 10", 25.4 cm
Colours: 1. Brown and teal green - gloss
             2. Brown, teal green or white - gloss
Issued: 1940-1970

Colourway	U.K. £	U.S. $	Can. $
1. Brown	125.00	200.00	275.00
2. Brown/white	125.00	200.00	275.00

Note: Makes a set of five with 756/1, 756/2, 756/2A, 756/3.

Model No. 919A
DUCK - Large

Designer: Mr. Watkin
Height: 3 ¾", 9.5 cm
Colours: 1. Brown, teal green, white and pink
                - gloss
             2. White with yellow beak and feet - gloss
Issued: 1941-1971

Colourway	U.K. £	U.S. $	Can. $
1. Brown	30.00	45.00	65.00
2. White	30.00	45.00	65.00

Model No. 919B
DUCK - Medium

Designer: Mr. Watkin
Height: 2 ½", 6.4 cm
Colours: 1. Brown, teal green, white and pink - gloss
             2. White with yellow beak and feet - gloss
Issued: 1941-1971

Colourway	U.K. £	U.S. $	Can. $
1. Brown	20.00	30.00	45.00
2. White	20.00	30.00	45.00

Model No. 919C
DUCK - Small

Designer:	Mr. Watkin
Height:	2", 5.0 cm
Colours:	1. Brown, teal green, white and pink - gloss
	2. White with yellow beak and feet - gloss
Issued:	1941-1971

Colourway	U.K. £	U.S. $	Can. $
1. Brown	20.00	35.00	45.00
2. White	20.00	35.00	45.00

Model No. 925
AMERICAN BLUE JAYS

Designer:	Arthur Gredington
Height:	5", 12.7 cm
Colours:	Blue and white - gloss
Issued:	1941-by 1965

Description	U.K. £	U.S. $	Can. $
Gloss	125.00	200.00	275.00

Model No. 926
BALTIMORE ORIOLES

Designer:	Arthur Gredington
Height:	5", 12.7 cm
Colours:	1. Golden and dark brown with blue markings - gloss
	2. Chestnut brown, green claws - gloss
Issued:	1941-by 1965

Colourway	U.K. £	U.S. $	Can. $
1. Golden	100.00	175.00	250.00
2. Chestnut	100.00	175.00	250.00

Model No. 927
CARDINAL

Designer:	Arthur Gredington
Height:	5 ¾", 14.6 cm
Colours:	Dark red - gloss
Issued:	1941-by 1959

Description	U.K. £	U.S. $	Can. $
Gloss	85.00	150.00	225.00

Model No. 928
TANAGER

Designer: Arthur Gredington
Height: 5 ¾", 14.6 cm
Colours: 1. Red - gloss
2. Various - gloss
3. Yellow, green and orange - gloss
Issued: 1941-1959

Colourway	U.K. £	U.S. $	Can. $
1. Red	75.00	115.00	165.00
2. Various	75.00	115.00	165.00
3. Yellow/green	75.00	115.00	165.00

Model No. 929
CHICKADEE

Designer: Arthur Gredington
Height: 5 ¾", 14.6 cm
Colours: Dark and light blue, white and yellow - gloss or lustre
Issued: 1941-1968

Description	U.K. £	U.S. $	Can. $
1. Gloss	60.00	95.00	145.00
2. Lustre	75.00	125.00	175.00

Model No. 930
PARAKEET

Designer: Arthur Gredington
Height: 6", 15.0 cm
Colours: Green and yellow - gloss
Issued: 1941-1975

Description	U.K. £	U.S. $	Can. $
Gloss	60.00	100.00	150.00

Model No. 980A
ROBIN
First Version - Base is a green mound

Designer: Arthur Gredington
Height: 3", 7.6 cm
Colours: Brown and red - gloss
Issued: 1942-1973

Description	U.K. £	U.S. $	Can. $
Gloss	25.00	40.00	60.00

Model No. 980B
ROBIN
Second Version - Base is a branch and leaf

Designer:	Arthur Gredington
Remodelled:	Albert Hallam
Height:	3", 7.6 cm
Colours:	Brown and red - gloss or matt
Issued:	1. Gloss - 1973 to the present
	2. Matt - 1983-1992

Description	U.K. £	U.S. $	Can. $
1. Gloss	15.00	N/A	N/A
2. Matt	15.00	30.00	45.00

Model No. 991A
CHAFFINCH
First Version - Base is a green mound

Designer:	Arthur Gredington
Height:	2 ¾", 7.0 cm
Colours:	Pink, brown and black - gloss
Issued:	1943-1973

Description	U.K. £	U.S. $	Can. $
Gloss	25.00	40.00	60.00

Model No. 991B
CHAFFINCH
Second Version - Base is a branch

Designer:	Arthur Gredington
Remodelled:	Albert Hallam
Height:	2 ¾", 7.0 cm
Colours:	Pink, brown, black - gloss or matt
Issued:	1. Gloss - 1973 to the present
	2. Matt - 1983-1992

Description	U.K. £	U.S. $	Can. $
1. Gloss	15.00	N/A	N/A
2. Matt	15.00	30.00	45.00

Model No. 992A
BLUE TIT
First Version - Base is a green mound

Designer:	Arthur Gredington
Height:	2 ½", 6.4 cm
Colours:	White, blue and green - gloss
Issued:	1943 - 1973

Description	U.K. £	U.S. $	Can. $
Gloss	30.00	50.00	75.00

Model No. 992B
BLUE TIT
Second Version - Base is branch and leaves with ladybug

Designer:	Arthur Gredington
Remodelled:	Unknown
Height:	2 ¼", 5.7 cm
Colours:	White, blue and green - gloss or matt
Issued:	1. Gloss - 1973 to the present
	2. Matt - 1983-1992

Description	U.K. £	U.S. $	Can. $
1. Gloss	15.00	N/A	N/A
2. Matt	15.00	30.00	45.00

Model No. 993A
WREN
First Version - Base is a green mound

Designer:	Arthur Gredington
Height:	2 ¼", 5.7 cm
Colours:	Light brown, pink breast - gloss
Issued:	1943-1973

Description	U.K. £	U.S. $	Can. $
Gloss	25.00	40.00	60.00

Model No. 993B
WREN
Second Version - Base is a green leaf

Designer:	Arthur Gredington
Remodelled:	Graham Tongue
Height:	2 ¼", 5.7 cm
Colours:	Dark and light brown - gloss or matt
Issued:	1. Gloss - 1973 to the present
	2. Matt - 1983-1992

Description	U.K. £	U.S. $	Can. $
1. Gloss	15.00	N/A	N/A
2. Matt	15.00	30.00	45.00

Model No. 994
SHELLDRAKE - Beak closed

Designer:	Arthur Gredington
Height:	6", 15.0 cm
Colours:	White, brown and green - gloss
Issued:	1943-1965

Description	U.K. £	U.S. $	Can. $
Gloss	150.00	250.00	350.00

Model No. 995
SHELLDRAKE - Beak open

Designer: Arthur Gredington
Height: 6 ¼", 15.9 cm
Colours: White, brown and green - gloss
Issued: 1943-1965

Description	U.K. £	U.S. $	Can. $
Gloss	150.00	250.00	350.00

Model No. 1001
COCKEREL

Designer: Arthur Gredington
Height: 5 ¾", 14.6 cm
Colours: Green, red and yellow - gloss
Issued: 1944-by 1959
Series: Stylistic Models

Description	U.K. £	U.S. $	Can. $
Gloss	200.00	325.00	450.00

Model No. 1004
ROOSTER

Designer: Arthur Gredington
Height: 7", 17.8 cm
Colours: White, green, red, blue and black - gloss
Issued: 1944-by 1959
Series: Stylistic Model

Description	U.K. £	U.S. $	Can. $
Gloss	175.00	325.00	450.00

Model No. 1006
GREBIE

Designer: Arthur Gredington
Height: 5 ¼", 13.3 cm
Colours: Green and browns - gloss
Issued: 1945-by 1954
Series: Stylistic Model

Description	U.K. £	U.S. $	Can. $
Gloss	300.00	475.00	675.00

Model No 1015
COURTING PENGUINS

Designer:	Arthur Gredington
Height:	5 ½", 14.0 cm
Colours:	1. Black and white with yellow markings - gloss
	2. Blue - gloss
Issued:	1945-1965

Colourway	U.K. £	U.S. $	Can. $
1. Black/white	200.00	325.00	475.00
2. Blue	225.00	350.00	500.00

Model No. 1018
BALD EAGLE

Designer:	Arthur Gredington
Height:	7 ¼", 18.4 cm
Colours:	1. Brown and white - gloss or matt
	2. Bronze with black - satin
Issued:	1a. Gloss - 1945-1995
	1b. Matt - 1983-1989
	2. Britannia Collection - 1989-1992

Description	U.K. £	U.S. $	Can. $
1a. Gloss	70.00	125.00	200.00
1b. Matt	80.00	125.00	200.00
2. Satin	60.00	100.00	150.00

Model No. 1022
TURTLE DOVES

Designer:	Arthur Gredington
Height:	7 ½", 19.1 cm
Colours:	Browns, pale blue and pink, light brown and green base - gloss
Issued:	1945-1970

Description	U.K. £	U.S. $	Can. $
Gloss	175.00	300.00	450.00

Model No. 1041A
GREY WAGTAIL
First Version - Head down, light green base

Designer:	Arthur Gredington
Height:	2 ½", 6.4 cm
Colours:	Yellow, grey and black - gloss
Issued:	1945-1973

Description	U.K. £	U.S. $	Can. $
Gloss	25.00	40.00	55.00

Model No. 1041B
GREY WAGTAIL
Second Version - Head up, dark blue and green base

Designer:	Arthur Gredington
Remodelled:	Albert Hallam
Height:	2 ½", 6.4 cm
Colours:	Yellow, grey and black - gloss or matt
Issued:	1. Gloss - 1973 to the present
	2. Matt - 1983-1989

Description	U.K. £	U.S. $	Can. $
1. Gloss	15.00	N/A	N/A
2. Matt	15.00	35.00	50.00

Model No. 1042A
BULLFINCH
First Version - Yellow base and flowers

Designer:	Arthur Gredington
Height:	2 ½", 6.4 cm
Colours:	Red breast, dark brown feathers, yellow flowers and base - gloss
Issued:	1945-1973

Description	U.K. £	U.S. $	Can. $
Gloss	25.00	40.00	60.00

Model No. 1042B
BULLFINCH
Second Version - Base is a twig

Designer:	Arthur Gredington
Remodelled:	Graham Tongue
Height:	2 ½", 6.4 cm
Colours:	Red, dark brown - gloss or matt
Issued:	1. Gloss - 1973-1998
	2. Matt - 1983-1989

Description	U.K. £	U.S. $	Can. $
1. Gloss	14.00	25.00	40.00
2. Matt	15.00	35.00	50.00

Model No. 1046A
BARN OWL
First Version - Split tail feathers

Designer:	Arthur Gredington
Height:	7 ¼", 18.4 cm
Colours:	Golden brown and white - gloss
Issued:	1946-Unknown

Description	U.K. £	U.S. $	Can. $
Gloss	100.00	175.00	250.00

Model No. 1046B
BARN OWL
Second Version - Closed tail feathers

Designer:	Arthur Gredington
Height:	7 ¼", 18.4 cm
Colours:	Golden brown and white - gloss or matt
Issued:	1. Gloss - Unknown-1997
	2. Matt - 1983-1989

Description	U.K. £	U.S. $	Can. $
1. Gloss	35.00	60.00	85.00
2. Matt	40.00	70.00	100.00

Model No. 1052
BARNACLE GOOSE

Designer:	Arthur Gredington
Height:	6 ½", 16.5 cm
Colours:	Dark grey-blue and white - gloss
Issued:	1943-1968

Description	U.K. £	U.S. $	Can. $
Gloss	525.00	850.00	1,200.00

Model No. 1099
COCK AND HEN - Salt and Pepper

Designer:	Unknown
Height:	2", 5.0 cm
Colours:	Teal green, brown, yellow and red - gloss
Issued:	1947-1959

Description	U.K. £	U.S. $	Can. $
Pair	35.00	60.00	90.00

Model No. 1159
KOOKABURRA

Designer:	Arthur Gredington
Height:	5 ¾", 14.6 cm
Colours:	Brown, blue and fawn - gloss
Issued:	1949-1976

Description	U.K. £	U.S. $	Can. $
Gloss	100.00	160.00	250.00

Model No. 1178
GOULDIAN FINCH - Wings out

Designer:	Arthur Gredington		
Height:	4", 10.1 cm		
Colours:	Purple, green and yellow - gloss		
Issued:	1949-by 1959		

Description	U.K. £	U.S. $	Can. $
Gloss	125.00	200.00	300.00

Model No. 1179
GOULDIAN FINCH - Wings in

Designer:	Arthur Gredington		
Height:	4 ½", 11.9 cm		
Colours:	Purple, green and yellow - gloss		
Issued:	1949-by 1959		

Description	U.K. £	U.S. $	Can. $
Gloss	125.00	200.00	300.00

Model No. 1180
COCKATOO - Small

Designer:	Arthur Gredington	
Height:	8 ½", 21.6 cm	
Colours:	1. Pink and grey - gloss	
	2. Turquoise and yellow - gloss	
Issued:	1949-1975	

Colourway	U.K. £	U.S. $	Can. $
1. Pink/grey	115.00	185.00	275.00
2. Turquoise/yellow	125.00	200.00	300.00

Note: Large version is model no. 1818.

Model No. 1212
DUCKS (Three) - Ashtray

Designer:	Arthur Gredington	
Height:	2 ¾", 7.0 cm	
Colours:	1. Blue - gloss	
	2. Teal green, white and brown - gloss	
Issued:	1. 1951-1965	
	2. 1951-1970	

Colourway	U.K. £	U.S. $	Can. $
1. Blue	30.00	50.00	65.00
2. Teal green	30.00	50.00	65.00

Model No. 1216A
BUDGERIGAR - Facing left
First Version - Flowers in high relief on base

Designer: Arthur Gredington
Height: 7", 17.8 cm
Colours: 1.   Blue with dark brown markings - gloss
            2.   Green with yellow markings - gloss
            3.   Yellow - gloss
Issued: 1951-1967

Colourway	U.K. £	U.S. $	Can. $
1. Blue	175.00	300.00	470.00
2. Green	375.00	550.00	900.00
3. Yellow		Rare	

Model No. 1216B
BUDGERIGAR - Facing left
Second Version - No flowers on base

Designer: Arthur Gredington
Height: 7", 17.8 cm
Colours: Blue, green or yellow - gloss
Issued: 1.   Blue - 1967-1975
            2.   Green - 1967-1972
            3.   Yellow - 1970-1972

Colourway	U.K. £	U.S. $	Can. $
1. Blue	125.00	200.00	350.00
2. Green	150.00	250.00	375.00
3. Yellow	175.00	275.00	425.00

Model No. 1217A
BUDGERIGAR - Facing right
First Version - Flowers in high relief on base

Designer: Arthur Gredington
Height: 7", 17.8 cm
Colours: 1.   Blue - gloss
            2.   Green - gloss
Issued: 1951-1967

Colourway	U.K. £	U.S. $	Can. $
1. Blue	175.00	325.00	500.00
2. Green	200.00	350.00	525.00

Model No. 1217B
BUDGERIGAR - Facing right
Second Version - No flowers on base

Designer: Arthur Gredington
Height: 7", 17.8 cm
Colours: 1.   Blue - gloss
            2.   Green - gloss
Issued: 1967-1970

Colourway	U.K. £	U.S. $	Can. $
1. Blue	125.00	200.00	300.00
2. Green	150.00	250.00	375.00

Model No. 1218A
GREEN WOODPECKER
First Version - Flowers in high relief on base

Designer:	Arthur Gredington
Height:	9", 22.9 cm
Colours:	Green, red and white - gloss
Issued:	1951-1967

Description	U.K. £	U.S. $	Can. $
Gloss	200.00	350.00	500.00

Model No. 1218B
GREEN WOODPECKER
Second Version - No flowers on base

Designer:	Arthur Gredington
Height:	9", 22.9 cm
Colours:	Green, red and white - gloss or matt
Issued:	1. Gloss - 1967-1989
	2. Matt - 1983-1988

Description	U.K. £	U.S. $	Can. $
1. Gloss	85.00	150.00	200.00
2. Matt	85.00	150.00	200.00

Model No. 1219A
JAY
First Version - Flowers in high relief on base

Designer:	Arthur Gredington
Height:	6", 15.0 cm
Colours:	Pink , blue and white - gloss
Issued:	1951-1967

Description	U.K. £	U.S. $	Can. $
Gloss	250.00	425.00	525.00

Model No. 1219B
JAY
Second Version - No flowers on base

Designer:	Arthur Gredington
Height:	6", 15.0 cm
Colours:	Pink, blue and white - gloss
Issued:	1967-1971

Description	U.K. £	U.S. $	Can. $
Gloss	185.00	300.00	450.00

Model No. 1225A
PHEASANT
First Version - Flowers in high relief on base

Designer:	Arthur Gredington
Height:	7 ¾", 19.7 cm
Colours:	Red-brown, teal green, green base - gloss
Issued:	1951-1967

Description	U.K. £	U.S. $	Can. $
Gloss	175.00	300.00	425.00

Model No. 1225B
PHEASANT
Second Version - No flowers on base

Designer:	Arthur Gredington
Height:	7 ¾", 19.7 cm
Colours:	Red-brown, teal green, green base - gloss
Issued:	1967-1977

Description	U.K. £	U.S. $	Can. $
Gloss	125.00	200.00	300.00

Model No. 1226A
PHEASANT
First Version - Flowers in high relief on base

Designer:	Arthur Gredington
Height:	6", 15.0 cm
Colours:	Red-brown, teal green, green base - gloss
Issued:	1951-1967

Description	U.K. £	U.S. $	Can. $
Gloss	150.00	250.00	350.00

Model No. 1226B
PHEASANT
Second Version - No flowers on base

Designer:	Arthur Gredington
Height:	6", 15.0 cm
Colours:	Red-brown, teal green, green base - gloss
Issued:	1967-1977

Description	U.K. £	U.S. $	Can. $
Gloss	125.00	200.00	300.00

Model No. 1383A
PIGEON
First Version - Three stripes on wings

Designer:	Mr. Orwell
Height:	5 ½", 14.0 cm
Colours:	1. Blue - gloss
	2. Red - gloss
Issued:	1955-1972

Colourway	U.K. £	U.S. $	Can. $
1. Blue - gloss	80.00	150.00	200.00
2. Red - gloss	80.00	150.00	200.00

Model No. 1383B
PIGEON
Second Version - Two stripes on wings

Designer:	Mr. Orwell
Height:	5 ½", 14.0 cm
Colours:	Blue or red - gloss or matt
Issued:	1. Gloss - 1955-1989
	2. Matt - 1983-1988

Colourway	U.K. £	U.S. $	Can. $
1a. Blue - gloss	90.00	150.00	225.00
1b. Blue - matt	85.00	140.00	200.00
2a. Red - gloss	90.00	150.00	225.00
2b. Red - matt	85.00	140.00	200.00

Model No. 1518

MALLARD DUCK

Designer:	Arthur Gredington
Length:	See below
Colours:	Teal green, brown, white, yellow beak - gloss
Issued:	See below
Series:	Peter Scott Wildfowl

Description	Issued	Length	U.K. £	Price U.S. $	Can. $
1. Large	1958-1971	6 ½", 16.5 cm	110.00	175.00	275.00
2. Medium	1958-1971	5 ½", 14.0 cm	85.00	135.00	225.00
3. Small - First Version	1958-1962	4 ½", 11.9 cm	90.00	145.00	225.00
4. Small - Second Version	1962-1971	3 ¾", 11.9 cm	65.00	100.00	165.00

Model No. 1519

MANDARIN DUCK

Designer: Arthur Gredington
Length: See below
Colours: Tan-brown and blue with red beak - gloss
Issued: 1958-1971
Series: Peter Scott Wildfowl

| | | | Price | |
Description	Length	U.K. £	U.S. $	Can. $
1. Large	4 ½", 11.9 cm	110.00	175.00	275.00
2. Medium	3 ¾", 9.5 cm	85.00	135.00	225.00
3. Small	3", 7.6 cm	65.00	100.00	165.00

Model No. 1520

POCHARD DUCK

Designer: Arthur Gredington
Length: See below
Colours: Brown, grey and black - gloss
Issued: 1958-1971
Series: Peter Scott Wildfowl

| | | | Price | |
Description	Length	U.K. £	U.S. $	Can. $
1. Large	5 ½", 14.0 cm	100.00	165.00	250.00
2. Medium	4 ½", 11.9 cm	65.00	100.00	165.00
3. Small	3 ½", 8.9 cm	60.00	95.00	150.00

Model No. 1521
KING EIDER DUCK

Designer: Colin Melbourne
Length: 4", 10.1 cm
Colours: Dark grey with tan, brown, green
           and white - gloss
Issued: 1958-1971
Series: Peter Scott Wildfowl

Description	U.K. £	U.S. $	Can. $
Gloss	65.00	100.00	160.00

Model No. 1522
SMEW DUCK

Designer: Colin Melbourne
Length: 3", 7.6 cm
Colours: Grey, black and white - gloss
Issued: 1958-1971
Series: Peter Scott Wildfowl

Description	U.K. £	U.S. $	Can. $
Gloss	75.00	125.00	185.00

Model No. 1523
TUFTED DUCK

Designer: Colin Melbourne
Length: 2 ¾", 7.0 cm
Colours: Black and white - gloss
Issued: 1958-1971
Series: Peter Scott Wildfowl

Description	U.K. £	U.S. $	Can. $
Gloss	75.00	125.00	185.00

Model No. 1524
GOLDENEYE DUCK

Designer: Colin Melbourne
Length: 3 ½", 8.9 cm
Colours: Black, white and green - gloss
Issued: 1958-1971
Series: Peter Scott Wildfowl

Description	U.K. £	U.S. $	Can. $
Gloss	85.00	135.00	200.00

Model No. 1525
GOOSANDER

Designer: Colin Melbourne
Length: 4 ½", 11.9 cm
Colours: Pink, black and white, orange
beak - gloss
Issued: 1958-1971
Series: Peter Scott Wildfowl

Description	U.K. £	U.S. $	Can. $
Gloss	75.00	125.00	185.00

Model No. 1526
WIDGEON DUCK

Designer: Colin Melbourne
Length: 3 ½", 8.9 cm
Colours: Pink, brown yellow, black and
white - gloss
Issued: 1958-1971
Series: Peter Scott Wildfowl

Description	U.K. £	U.S. $	Can. $
Gloss	85.00	135.00	200.00

Model No. 1527
SHELDUCK

Designer: Colin Melbourne
Length: 4", 10.1 cm
Colours: Dark grey, tan, white, green and
brown - gloss
Issued: 1958-1971
Series: Peter Scott Wildfowl

Description	U.K. £	U.S. $	Can. $
Gloss	75.00	125.00	185.00

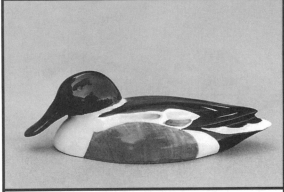

Model No. 1528
SHOVELER

Designer: Colin Melbourne
Length: 3 ½", 8.9 cm
Colours: Tan, blue, white and dark brown - gloss
Issued: 1958-1971
Series: Peter Scott Wildfowl

Description	U.K. £	U.S. $	Can. $
Gloss	75.00	125.00	185.00

Model No. 1529
TEAL DUCK

Designer:	Colin Melbourne
Length:	2 ¾", 7.0 cm
Colours:	Tan, yellow, black, white with blue beak - gloss
Issued:	1958-1971
Series:	Peter Scott Wildfowl

Description	U.K. £	U.S. $	Can. $
Gloss	75.00	125.00	185.00

Model No. 1614
FANTAIL PIGEON

Designer:	Arthur Gredington
Height:	5", 12.7 cm
Colours:	White - gloss
Issued:	1959-1969

Description	U.K. £	U.S. $	Can. $
Gloss	300.00	500.00	750.00

Model No. 1684
SWAN - Head up

Designer:	Arthur Gredington
Height:	3", 7.6 cm
Colours:	White - gloss
Issued:	1960-1973
Set:	1685, 1686, 1687

Description	U.K. £	U.S. $	Can. $
Gloss	75.00	125.00	150.00

Model No. 1685
SWAN - Head down

Designer:	Arthur Gredington
Height:	2", 5.0 cm
Colours:	White - gloss
Issued:	1960-1973
Set:	1684, 1686, 1687

Description	U.K £	U.S. $	Can. $
Gloss	75.00	125.00	150.00

Model No. 1686
CYGNET - Facing left

Designer:	Arthur Gredington
Height:	1", 2.5 cm
Colours:	Grey - gloss
Issued:	1960-1971
Set:	1684, 1685, 1687

Description	U.K. £	U.S. $	Can. $
Gloss	35.00	55.00	85.00

Model No. 1687
CYGNET - Facing right

Designer:	Arthur Gredington
Height:	1", 2.5 cm
Colours:	Grey - gloss
Issued:	1960-1971
Set:	1684, 1685, 1686

Description	U.K. £	U.S. $	Can. $
Gloss	35.00	55.00	85.00

Model No. 1774
PHEASANT - On pottery base

Designer:	Albert Hallam
Height:	4 ¾", 12.1 cm
Colours:	Red-brown, teal green and beige - gloss
Issued:	1961-1975

Description	U.K. £	U.S. $	Can. $
Gloss	75.00	125.00	175.00

Model No. 1818
COCKATOO - Large

Designer:	Albert Hallam
Height:	11 ½", 29.2 cm
Colours:	1. Pink and grey - gloss
	2. Turquoise and yellow - gloss
Issued:	1962-1973

Colourway	U.K. £	U.S. $	Can. $
1. Pink/grey	165.00	275.00	375.00
2. Turquoise/yellow	175.00	300.00	425.00

Model No. 1892
LEGHORN COCKEREL

Designer: Arthur Gredington
Height: 9", 22.9 cm
Colours: Teal green, red, orange and yellow - gloss
Issued: 1963-1983

Description	U.K. £	U.S. $	Can. $
Gloss	190.00	325.00	475.00

Model No. 1899
SUSSEX COCKEREL

Designer: Arthur Gredington
Height: 7", 17.8 cm
Colours: Black, white and pink - gloss
Issued: 1963-1971

Description	U.K. £	U.S. $	Can. $
Gloss	300.00	500.00	675.00

Model No. 1957
TURKEY

Designer: Albert Hallam
Height: 7 ¼", 18.4 cm
Colours: 1. Bronze - gloss
2. White - gloss
Issued: 1964-1969

Colourway	U.K. £	U.S. $	Can. $
1. Bronze	250.00	400.00	625.00
2. White	450.00	700.00	1,100.00

Model No. 2026
OWL

Designer: Albert Hallam
Height: 4 ½", 11.9 cm
Colours: Golden brown and white - gloss
Issued: 1965 to the present

Description	U.K. £	U.S. $	Can. $
Gloss	17.50	N/A	N/A

Model No. 2059
GAMECOCK

Designer: Arthur Gredington
Height: 9 ½", 24.0 cm
Colours: Brown, teal green, cream and red - gloss
Issued: 1966-1975

Description	U.K. £	U.S. $	Can. $
Gloss	600.00	900.00	1,500.00

Model No. 2062
GOLDEN EAGLE

Designer: Graham Tongue
Height: 9 ½", 24.0 cm
Colours: Dark brown - gloss, matt, or satin matt
Issued: 1. 1966-1974 - Gloss
2. 1970-1972 - Matt
3. 1973-1989 - Satin matt
Series: 3. Connoisseur

Description	U.K. £	U.S. $	Can. $
1. Gloss	125.00	200.00	300.00
2. Matt	100.00	175.00	250.00
3. Satin matt	75.00	125.00	175.00

Model No. 2063
GROUSE (Pair)

Designer: Albert Hallam
Height: 5 ½", 14.0 cm
Colours: Red-brown - gloss
Issued: 1966-1975

Description	U.K. £	U.S. $	Can. $
Gloss	275.00	450.00	600.00

Model No. 2064
PARTRIDGE (Pair)

Designer: Albert Hallam
Height: 5 ½", 14.0 cm
Colours: Brown and blue - gloss
Issued: 1966-1975

Description	U.K. £	U.S. $	Can. $
Gloss	250.00	425.00	600.00

Model No. 2067
TURKEY

Designer:	Albert Hallam
Height:	2 ½", 6.4 cm
Colours:	1. White and red - gloss
	2. Bronze - gloss
Issued:	1966-1969

Colourway	U.K. £	U.S. $	Can. $
1. White	90.00	150.00	225.00
2. Bronze	90.00	150.00	225.00

Photograph not
available at press time

Model No. 2071
OWL (Contemporary)

Designer:	Graham Tongue
Height:	5", 12.7 cm
Colours:	Unknown
Issued:	1966-Unknown
Series:	Contemporary Models

Description	U.K. £	U.S. $	Can. $
Owl		Extremely Rare	

Model No. 2078
PHEASANTS (Pair)

Designer:	Arthur Gredington
Height:	6 ¾", 17.2 cm
Colours:	Red-brown and teal green with
	yellow markings - gloss
Issued:	1966-1975

Description	U.K. £	U.S. $	Can. $
Gloss	275.00	450.00	700.00

Model No. 2105A
GREENFINCH
First Version - With flower on base

Designer:	Graham Tongue
Height:	3", 7.6 cm
Colours:	Green and yellow - gloss
Issued:	1967-1973

Description	U.K. £	U.S. $	Can. $
Gloss	30.00	50.00	75.00

Model No. 2105B
GREENFINCH
Second Version - Wthout flower on base

Designer: Graham Tongue
Remodelled: Albert Hallam
Height: 3", 7.6 cm
Colours: Natural - gloss or matt
Issued: 1.   Gloss - 1973-1998
                    2.   Matt - 1983-1992

Description	U.K. £	U.S. $	Can. $
1. Gloss	15.00	25.00	40.00
2. Matt	15.00	25.00	40.00

Model No. 2106A
WHITETHROAT
First Version - Mouth open, base is a green mound

Designer: Graham Tongue
Height: 3", 7.6 cm
Colours: Dark grey, white and pink - gloss
Issued: 1967-1973

Description	U.K. £	U.S. $	Can. $
Gloss	30.00	50.00	75.00

Model No. 2106B
WHITETHROAT
Second Version - Mouth closed, base is a leaf

Designer: Graham Tongue
Remodelled: Albert Hallam
Height: 3", 7.6 cm
Colours: Natural - gloss or matt
Issued: 1.   Gloss - 1973-1996
                    2.   Matt - 1983-1992

Description	U.K. £	U.S. $	Can. $
1. Gloss	15.00	25.00	40.00
2. Matt	15.00	25.00	40.00

Model No. 2183
BALTIMORE ORIOLE

Designer: Albert Hallam
Height: 3 ½", 8.9 cm
Colours: Black and red - gloss or matt
Issued: 1.   Gloss - 1968-1973
                    2.   Matt - 1970-1972

Description	U.K. £	U.S. $	Can. $
1. Gloss	75.00	125.00	175.00
2. Matt	75.00	125.00	175.00

Model No. 2184
CEDAR WAXWING

Designer: Graham Tongue
Height: 4 ½", 11.9 cm
Colours: Brown, black and yellow - gloss or matt
Issued: 1.   Gloss - 1968-1973
              2.   Matt - 1970-1972

Description	U.K. £	U.S. $	Can. $
1. Gloss	100.00	160.00	250.00
2. Matt	100.00	160.00	250.00

Model No. 2187
AMERICAN ROBIN

Designer: Graham Tongue
Height: 4", 10.1 cm
Colours: Dark grey and red - gloss or matt
Issued: 1.   Gloss - 1968-1973
              2.   Matt - 1970-1972

Description	U.K. £	U.S. $	Can. $
1. Gloss	110.00	175.00	275.00
2. Matt	75.00	125.00	175.00

Model No. 2188
BLUE JAY

Designer: Albert Hallam
Height: 4 ½", 11.9 cm
Colours: Blue and white - gloss or matt
Issued: 1.   Gloss - 1968-1973
              2.   Matt - 1970-1972

Description	U.K. £	U.S. $	Can. $
1. Gloss	125.00	200.00	300.00
2. Matt	100.00	165.00	250.00

Model No. 2189
BLACK CAPPED CHICADEE

Designer: Graham Tongue
Height: 4 ½", 11.9 cm
Colours: Yellow, white, grey, green
              and black - gloss or matt
Issued: 1.   Gloss - 1968-1973
              2.   Matt - 1970-1972

Description	U.K. £	U.S. $	Can. $
1. Gloss	100.00	160.00	250.00
2. Matt	85.00	150.00	225.00

Model No. 2190
EVENING GROSBEAK

Designer: Albert Hallam
Height: 4", 10.1 cm
Colours: Black and yellow - gloss or matt
Issued: 1. Gloss - 1968-1973
2. Matt - 1970-1972

Description	U.K. £	U.S. $	Can. $
1. Gloss	125.00	200.00	300.00
2. Matt	100.00	165.00	250.00

Model No. 2191
QUAIL

Designer: Albert Hallam
Height: 5", 12.7 cm
Colours: Browns, black and white - gloss or matt
Issued: 1. Gloss - 1968-1971
2. Matt - 1970-1972

Description	U.K. £	U.S. $	Can. $
1. Gloss	150.00	250.00	375.00
2. Matt	125.00	200.00	300.00

Model No. 2200
CHICKEN - Running

Designer: Graham Tongue
Height: 1 ¼", 3.2 cm
Colours: Yellow - gloss
Issued: 1968-1973
Set: 2201, 2202

Description	U.K. £	U.S. $	Can. $
Gloss	125.00	200.00	300.00

Model No. 2201
CHICKEN - Pecking

Designer: Graham Tongue
Height: 1", 2.5 cm
Colours: Yellow - gloss
Issued: 1968-1973
Set: 2200, 2202

Description	U.K. £	U.S. $	Can. $
Gloss	100.00	165.00	250.00

Model No. 2202
CHICKEN - Seated

Designer:	Graham Tongue
Height:	1 ½", 3.8 cm
Colours:	Yellow - gloss
Issued:	1968-1973
Set:	2200, 2201

Description	U.K. £	U.S. $	Can. $
Gloss	125.00	200.00	300.00

Photograph not
available at press time

Model No. 2238
OWL

Designer:	Harry Sales
Height:	6 ¾", 17.2 cm
Colours:	Unknown
Issued:	1968-1971
Series:	Moda Range

Description	U.K. £	U.S. $	Can. $
Owl		Very Rare	

Photograph not
available at press time

Model No. 2239
BIRD

Designer:	Harry Sales
Height:	5", 12.7 cm
Colours:	Unknown
Issued:	1968-1971
Series:	Moda Range

Description	U.K. £	U.S. $	Can. $
Bird		Very Rare	

Model No. 2240
COCKEREL

Designer:	Harry Sales
Height:	6", 15.0 cm
Colours:	1. Blue - gloss
	2. Brown - matt
Issued:	1968-1971
Series:	Moda Range

Colourway	U.K. £	U.S. $	Can. $
1. Blue	150.00	250.00	375.00
2. Brown	125.00	200.00	300.00

Model No. 2273
GOLDFINCH

Designer:	Graham Tongue
Height:	3", 7.6 cm
Colours:	Brown, white, red and yellow
	- gloss or matt
Issued:	1. Gloss - 1969-1995
	2. Matt - 1983-1992

Description	U.K. £	U.S. $	Can. $
1. Gloss	15.00	25.00	40.00
2. Matt	15.00	25.00	40.00

Model No. 2274
STONECHAT

Designer:	Albert Hallam
Height:	3", 7.6 cm
Colours:	Dark brown and white, red breast
	- gloss or matt
Issued:	1. Gloss - 1969-1997
	2. Matt - 1983-1992

Description	U.K. £	U.S. $	Can. $
1. Gloss	15.00	25.00	40.00
2. Matt	15.00	25.00	40.00

Model No. 2305
MAGPIE

Designer:	Albert Hallam
Height:	5", 12.7 cm
Colours:	Black and white - gloss
Issued:	1970-1982

Description	U.K. £	U.S. $	Can. $
Gloss	125.00	200.00	300.00

Model No. 2307
EAGLE ON ROCK

Designer:	Graham Tongue
Height:	3 ¾", 9.5 cm
Colours:	Browns - gloss
Issued:	1970-1975

Description	U.K. £	U.S. $	Can. $
Gloss	125.00	200.00	300.00

Model No. 2308
SONGTHRUSH

Designer: Albert Hallam
Height: 5 ¾", 14.6 cm
Colours: Brown with yellow speckled breast
 - gloss and matt
Issued: 1. Gloss - 1970-1989
 2. Matt - 1983-1989

Description	U.K. £	U.S. $	Can. $
1. Gloss	65.00	100.00	175.00
2. Matt	35.00	60.00	100.00

Model No. 2315
CUCKOO

Designer: Albert Hallam
Height: 5", 12.7 cm
Colours: Blue - gloss
Issued: 1970-1982

Description	U.K. £	U.S. $	Can. $
Gloss	100.00	165.00	250.00

Model No. 2316
KESTREL

Designer: Graham Tongue
Height: 6 ¾", 17.2 cm
Colours: Browns, white and blue - gloss or matt
Issued: 1. Gloss - 1970-1989
 2. Matt - 1983-1989

Description	U.K. £	U.S. $	Can. $
1. Gloss	65.00	115.00	175.00
2. Matt	50.00	80.00	125.00

Model No. 2357
PENGUIN

Designer:	Albert Hallam
Height:	12", 30.5 cm
Colours:	Black and white - gloss
Issued:	1971-1976
Series:	Fireside Model

Description	U.K. £	U.S. $	Can. $
Gloss	350.00	575.00	850.00

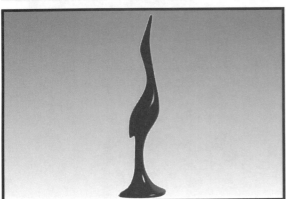

Model No. 2359
HERON - Stylistic

Designer:	Albert Hallam
Height:	10 ½", 26.7 cm
Colours:	Black - satin
Issued:	1971-Unknown

Description	U.K. £	U.S. $	Can. $
Satin	75.00	125.00	200.00

Model No. 2371
KINGFISHER

Designer:	Albert Hallam
Height:	5", 12.7 cm
Colours:	Blue and brown - gloss or matt
Issued:	1. Gloss - 1971-1991
	2. Matt - 1983-1989

Description	U.K. £	U.S. $	Can. $
1. Gloss	35.00	60.00	85.00
2. Matt	45.00	75.00	100.00

Model No. 2398
PENGUIN CHICK - Standing

Designer:	Graham Tongue
Height:	7", 17.8 cm
Colours:	Blue, black and white - gloss
Issued:	1971-1976

Description	U.K. £	U.S. $	Can. $
Gloss	250.00	375.00	575.00

Photograph not available at press time

Model No. 2399
PENGUIN CHICK

Designer:	Albert Hallam
Height:	6 ¾", 17.2 cm
Colours:	Black and white - gloss
Issued:	1972-Unknown

Description	U.K. £	U.S. $	Can. $
Gloss		Extremely Rare	

Note: Probably not put into production.

Model No. 2413
NUTHATCH

Designer:	Graham Tongue
Height:	3", 7.6 cm
Colours:	Dark blue and white - gloss or matt
Issued:	1. Gloss - 1972-1995
	2. Matt - 1983-1989

Description	U.K. £	U.S. $	Can. $
1. Gloss	15.00	25.00	40.00
2. Matt	15.00	25.00	40.00

Model No. 2415
GOLDCREST

Designer:	Graham Tongue
Height:	3", 7.6 cm
Colours:	Green, yellow and grey - gloss or matt
Issued:	1. Gloss - 1972 to the present
	2. Matt - 1983-1989

Description	U.K. £	U.S. $	Can. $
1. Gloss	15.00	N/A	N/A
2. Matt	35.00	60.00	75.00

Model No. 2416A
LAPWING
First Version - Tail feathers split

Designer:	Albert Hallam
Height:	5 ½", 14.0 cm
Colours:	Black, dark green and white - gloss
Issued:	1972-Unknown

Description	U.K. £	U.S. $	Can. $
Gloss	125.00	200.00	300.00

Model No. 2416B
LAPWING
Second Version - Tail feathers together

Designer:	Albert Hallam
Height:	5 ½", 14.0 cm
Colours:	Black, dark green and white - gloss
Issued:	Unknown-1982

Description	U.K. £	U.S. $	Can. $
Gloss	100.00	165.00	250.00

Model No. 2417
JAY

Designer:	Graham Tongue
Height:	5", 12.7 cm
Colours:	Brown, white and blue - gloss
Issued:	1972-1982

Description	U.K. £	U.S. $	Can. $
Gloss	100.00	165.00	250.00

Model No. 2420
LESSER SPOTTED WOODPECKER

Designer:	Graham Tongue
Height:	5 ½", 14.0 cm
Colours:	Red, white and black - gloss
Issued:	1972-1982

Description	U.K. £	U.S. $	Can. $
Gloss	100.00	165.00	250.00

Model No. 2434
PENGUIN CHICK - Sliding

Designer: Graham Tongue
Height: 3 ¾" x 8", 9.5 x 20.3 cm
Colours: Blue, black and white - gloss
Issued: 1972-1976

Description	U.K. £	U.S. $	Can. $
Gloss	400.00	625.00	900.00

Model No. 3272
TAWNY OWL

Designer: Mr. Sutton
Height: 3 ¼", 8.3 cm
Colours: Brown and white - gloss
Issued: 1990 to the present

Description	U.K. £	U.S. $	Can. $
Gloss	15.00	N/A	N/A

Model No. 2760
PHEASANT

Designer: Graham Tongue
Height: 10 ½", 26.7 cm
Colours: 1. Tan and brown - satin matt
2. Bronze with black shading - satin
Issued: 1. Satin matt - 1982-1989
2. Matt - 1989-1992
Series: 1. Connoisseur
2. Britannia Collection

Description	U.K. £	U.S. $	Can. $
1. Connoisseur	150.00	300.00	425.00
2. Britannia	200.00	325.00	450.00

Note: Transferred to Royal Doulton backstamp
(DA 38 Open Ground) 08/89. Satin matt version.

Model No. 3273
BARN OWL

Designer:	Martyn Alcock
Height:	3 ¼", 8.3 cm
Colours:	Light brown and white - gloss
Issued:	1990-1998

Description	U.K. £	U.S. $	Can. $
Gloss	15.00	25.00	40.00

Model No. 3274
GREAT TIT

Designer:	Martyn Alcock
Height:	3", 7.6 cm
Colours:	Black, yellow, white and grey - gloss
Issued:	1990-1995

Description	U.K. £	U.S. $	Can. $
Gloss	15.00	25.00	40.00

Model No. 3275
KINGFISHER

Designer:	Mr. Sutton
Height:	2 ¾", 7.0 cm
Colours:	Blue head and wings, orange breast - gloss
Issued:	1990-1998

Description	U.K. £	U.S. $	Can. $
Gloss	15.00	25.00	40.00

BIRD WALL PLAQUES

INDEX BY MODEL NUMBER

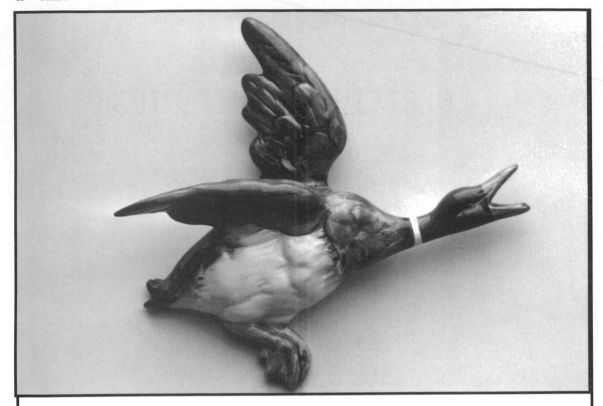

Model No. 596

MALLARD

Designer: Mr. Watkin
Length: See below
Issued: See below
Colours: 1. Brown, teal green and white - gloss
2. White with yellow beaks - matt

Model No.	Finish	Issued	Length	U.K. £	Price U.S. $	Can. $
1. 596/0	Gloss	1938-1971	11 ¾", 29.8 cm	65.00	100.00	130.00
2. 596/0	Matt	1938-1971	11 ¾", 29.8 cm	60.00	95.00	130.00
3. 596/1	Gloss	1938-1973	10", 25.4 cm	55.00	90.00	100.00
4. 596/1	Matt	1938-1973	10", 25.4 cm	50.00	80.00	100.00
5. 596/2	Gloss	1938-1973	8 ¾", 22.2 cm	45.00	75.00	85.00
6. 596/2	Matt	1938-1973	8 ¾", 22.2 cm	40.00	65.00	85.00
7. 596/3	Gloss	1938-1973	7", 17.8 cm	35.00	55.00	70.00
8. 596/3	Matt	1938-1973	7", 17.8 cm	30.00	50.00	70.00
9. 596/4	Gloss	1938-1971	5 ¾", 14.6 cm	25.00	40.00	60.00
10. 596/4	Matt	1938-1971	5 ¾", 14.6 cm	25.00	40.00	60.00

Note: These also exist with a small "pocket" between the wings.

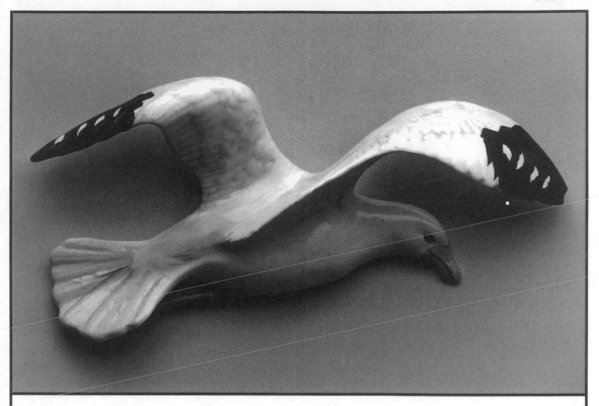

Model No. 658

SEAGULL
Style One - Wings up, apart

Designer: Mr. Watkin
Length: See below
Colours: 1. White, black and yellow - gloss
            2. White and yellow - matt
            3. White - matt
Issued: 1938-1967

Model No.	Finish	Length	U.K. £	Price U.S. $	Can. $
1. 658/1	Gloss	14", 35.5 cm	65.00	100.00	130.00
2. 658/1	Matt	14", 35.5 cm	60.00	95.00	130.00
3. 658/1	Matt	14", 35.5 cm	55.00	90.00	120.00
4. 658/2	Gloss	11 ¾", 29.8 cm	60.00	95.00	130.00
5. 658/2	Matt	11 ¾", 29.8 cm	50.00	80.00	110.00
6. 658/2	Matt	11 ¾", 29.8 cm	45.00	75.00	100.00
7. 658/3	Gloss	10", 25.4 cm	50.00	80.00	110.00
8. 658/3	Matt	10", 25.4 cm	40.00	65.00	90.00
9. 658/3	Matt	10", 25.4 cm	35.00	55.00	75.00
10. 658/4	Gloss	8", 20.3 cm	40.00	65.00	90.00
11. 658/4	Matt	8", 20.3 cm	30.00	50.00	70.00
12. 658/4	Matt	8", 20.3 cm	30.00	50.00	70.00

Model No. 661

PHEASANT

Designer: Mr. Watkin
Length: See below
Colours: 1. Teal green, browns and white - gloss
2. White - matt
Issued: 1938-1971

Model No./Size		Finish	Length	U.K. £	Price U.S. $	Can. $
1.	661/1 Large	Gloss	12", 30.5 cm	65.00	100.00	130.00
2.	661/1 Large	Matt	12", 30.5 cm	60.00	95.00	130.00
3.	661/2 Medium	Gloss	10 ¼", 26.0 cm	60.00	95.00	125.00
4.	661/2 Medium	Matt	10 ¼", 26.0 cm	50.00	80.00	125.00
5.	661/3 Small	Gloss	8 ½", 21.6 cm	50.00	80.00	100.00
6.	661/3 Small	Matt	8 ½", 21.6 cm	40.00	65.00	100.00

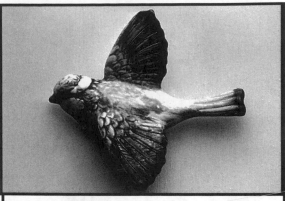

Model No. 705
BLUE TIT - Flying to the right

Designer:	Mr. Watkin
Height:	4 ½", 11.9 cm
Size:	Large
Colours:	Blue and browns - gloss
Issued:	1939-1967
Set:	706, 707

Description	U.K. £	U.S. $	Can. $
Gloss	100.00	165.00	250.00

Model No. 706
BLUE TIT - Flying to the left

Designer:	Mr. Watkin
Height:	4 ½", 11.9 cm
Size:	Medium
Colours:	Blue and browns - gloss
Issued:	1939-1967
Set:	705, 707

Description	U.K. £	U.S. $	Can. $
Gloss	100.00	165.00	250.00

Model No. 707
BLUE TIT - Wings up, flying to the left

Designer:	Mr. Watkin
Height:	4 ½", 11.9 cm
Size:	Small
Colours:	Blue and browns - gloss
Issued:	1939-1967
Set:	705, 706

Description	U.K. £	U.S. $	Can. $
Gloss	100.00	165.00	250.00

Model No. 729

KINGFISHER - Flying to the right

Designer: Arthur Gredington
Height: See below
Colours: 1. Green and yellow - gloss
           2. Blue - gloss
Issued: 1939-1971

Model No./Size	Colourway	Height	U.K. £	Price U.S. $	Can. $
1. 729/1 Large	Green	7 ½", 19.1 cm	65.00	125.00	175.00
2. 729/1 Large	Blue	7 ½", 19.1 cm	100.00	200.00	300.00
3. 729/2 Medium	Green	6", 15.0 cm	55.00	100.00	150.00
4. 729/2 Medium	Blue	6", 15.0 cm	100.00	200.00	300.00
5. 729/3 Small	Green	5", 12.7 cm	45.00	75.00	125.00
6. 729/3 Small	Blue	5", 12.7 cm	90.00	175.00	275.00

Note: Model no. 729/2 can be paired with no. 743 to make a facing pair.

Model No. 731
FLAMINGO

Designer: Mr. Watkin
Length: 15", 38.1 cm
Colours: 1.   Pearl orange and black - gloss
            2.   White, yellow and black wing
                 tips - satin
Issued: 1939-1954

Description	U.K. £	U.S. $	Can. $
1. Gloss	250.00	450.00	675.00
2. Satin	250.00	450.00	675.00

Model No. 743
KINGFISHER

Designer: Arthur Gredington
Height: 6", 15.0 cm
Colours: Greens and yellow - gloss
Issued: 1939-1954

Description	U.K. £	U.S. $	Can. $
Gloss	100.00	200.00	300.00

Note: Model no. 743 can be paired with no. 729/2
to make a facing pair.

Model No. 757

SWALLOW

Designer: Arthur Gredington
Height: See below
Colours: 1. Blues - gloss
2. Golden brown; yellow tail - gloss
Issued: 1939-1973

Model No./Colourway	Size	Height	U.K. £	Price U.S. $	Can. $
1. 757/1 Blue	Large	7 ½", 19.1 cm	80.00	130.00	200.00
2. 757/1 Brown	Large	7 ½", 19.1 cm		Extremely Rare	
3. 757/2 Blue	Medium	6 ¼", 15.9 cm	70.00	115.00	175.00
4. 757/2 Brown	Medium	6 ¼", 15.9 cm		Extremely Rare	
5. 757/3 Blue	Small	5", 12.7 cm	60.00	100.00	150.00
6. 757/3 Brown	Small	5", 12.7 cm		Extremely Rare	

Model No. 922
SEAGULL
Style Two - Wings up, together

Designer:	Arthur Gredington
Height:	Large - 12″, 30.5 cm
	Medium - 10 ½″, 26.7 cm
	Small - 9 ½″, 24.0 cm
Colours:	White, grey and black - gloss or matt
Issued:	1941-1971

Description	U.K. £	U.S. $	Can. $
1. Large - gloss	75.00	125.00	190.00
2. Large - matt	65.00	100.00	165.00
3. Medium - gloss	65.00	100.00	165.00
4. Medium - matt	60.00	95.00	150.00
5. Small - gloss	55.00	90.00	140.00
6. Small - matt	50.00	80.00	125.00

Model No. 1023
HUMMING BIRD

Designer:	Arthur Gredington
Height:	Large - 5 ¾″, 14.6 cm
	Medium - 5″, 12.7 cm
	Small - 4 ¾″, 12.1 cm
Colours:	Browns, grey and red - gloss
Issued:	1944-1967

Description	U.K. £	U.S. $	Can. $
1. Large - gloss	90.00	150.00	225.00
2. Medium - gloss	80.00	130.00	200.00
3. Small - gloss	70.00	120.00	175.00

Model No. 1188

PINK LEGGED PARTRIDGE

Designer: Arthur Gredington
Length: See below
Colours: Browns, white and grey - gloss
Issued: 1950-1967

Model No.	Size	Length	U.K. £	Price U.S. $	Can. $
1. 1188/1	Large	10 ½", 26.7 cm	100.00	165.00	250.00
2. 1188/2	Medium	9", 22.9 cm	85.00	140.00	200.00
3. 1188/3	Small	7 ½", 19.1 cm	70.00	125.00	175.00

Model No. 1344

GREEN WOODPECKER

Designer: Mr. Orwell
Length: See below
Colours: Greens and brown, red head - gloss
Issued: 1954-1968

	Model No.	Size	Length	U.K. £	Price U.S. $	Can. $
1.	1344/1	Large	7 ½", 19.1 cm	110.00	185.00	275.00
2.	1344/2	Medium	6", 15.0 cm	100.00	165.00	250.00
3.	1344/3	Small	5", 12.7 cm	80.00	130.00	200.00

Model No. 1530

TEAL

Designer: Arthur Gredington
Length: See below
Colours: Brown, grey and green - gloss
Issued: 1958-1968

Model No.	Size	Length	U.K. £	Price U.S. $	Can. $
1. 1530/1	Large	8 ¼", 21.0 cm	150.00	250.00	350.00
2. 1530/2	Medium	7 ¼", 18.4 cm	125.00	200.00	300.00
3. 1530/3	Small	6 ¼", 15.9 cm	100.00	165.00	250.00

Chapter Two
BUTTERFLY PLAQUES

Butterflies are an unusual choice for the medium of pottery, and these few wall plaques tend to be rare. It is also unusual to find them in perfect condition, as often the antennae have suffered from the passage of time. These butterfly wall plaques were modelled in large, medium and small sizes. The Beswick attention to detail is very apparent here.

At the present time, there have been no catalogues found in which these models are illustrated. Fortunately, each model is impressed on the back with the name of the butterfly and the shape number. If this were not the case, then identification would be a problem.

Model No. 1487

PURPLE EMPEROR BUTTERFLY

Designer: Albert Hallam
Height: 6 ¼" x 4", 15.9 x 10.1 cm
Size: Large

Colourway	Issued	U.K. £	Price U.S. $	Can. $
Blue and white - gloss	1957-by 1963	375.00	600.00	900.00

Model No. 1488
RED ADMIRAL BUTTERFLY

Designer:	Albert Hallam
Dimensions:	6 ¼" x 4", 15.9 x 10.1 cm
Size:	Large
Colours:	Browns, blue and white - gloss
Issued:	1957-by 1963

Description	U.K. £	U.S. $	Can. $
Gloss	350.00	550.00	800.00

Model No. 1489
PEACOCK BUTTERFLY

Designer:	Albert Hallam
Dimensions:	6 ¼" x 4", 15.9 x 10.1 cm
Size:	Large
Colours:	Browns, black and yellow - gloss
Issued:	1957-by 1963

Description	U.K. £	U.S. $	Can. $
Gloss	350.00	550.00	800.00

Model No. 1490
CLOUDED YELLOW BUTTERFLY

Designer:	Albert Hallam
Dimensions:	5 ¼" x 3 ½", 13.3 x 8.9 cm
Size:	Medium
Colours:	Yellow, black and red - gloss
Issued:	1957-by 1963

Description	U.K. £	U.S. $	Can. $
Gloss	325.00	500.00	750.00

Model No. 1491
TORTOISESHELL BUTTERFLY

Designer:	Albert Hallam
Dimensions:	5 ¼" x 3 ½", 13.3 x 8.9 cm
Size:	Medium
Colours:	Yellow, blue and black - gloss
Issued:	1957-by 1963

Description	U.K. £	U.S. $	Can. $
Gloss	325.00	500.00	750.00

Model No. 1492
SWALLOW-TAIL BUTTERFLY

Designer:	Albert Hallam
Dimensions:	5 ¼″ x 3 ½″, 13.3 x 8.9 cm
Size:	Medium
Colours:	Brown, green and blue wings - gloss
Issued:	1957-by 1963

Description	U.K. £	U.S. $	Can. $
Gloss	325.00	525.00	775.00

Model No. 1493
SMALL COPPER BUTTERFLY

Designer:	Albert Hallam
Dimensions:	3 ¾″ x 2 ¼″, 9.5 x 5.7 cm
Size:	Small
Colours:	Browns - gloss
Issued:	1957-by 1963

Description	U.K. £	U.S. $	Can. $
Gloss	275.00	475.00	700.00

Model No. 1494
PURPLE HAIRSTREAK BUTTERFLY

Designer:	Albert Hallam
Dimensions:	3 ¾″ x 2 ¼″, 9.5 x 5.7 cm
Size:	Small
Colours:	Browns and grey - gloss
Issued:	1957-by 1963

Description	U.K. £	U.S. $	Can. $
Gloss	300.00	475.00	700.00

Model No. 1495
SMALL HEATH BUTTERFLY

Designer:	Albert Hallam
Dimensions:	3 ¾″ x 2 ¼″, 9.5 x 5.7 cm
Size:	Small
Colours:	Browns - gloss
Issued:	1957-by 1963

Description	U.K. £	U.S. $	Can. $
Gloss	300.00	475.00	700.00

Chapter Three

CATS

Cat lovers will appreciate the variety of felines offered here. As well as realistic models, there are cats playing instruments and playing ball, zodiac cats and cats just clowning around.

These figures were also produced in a large selection of colours and finishes:

Colourways	Dates of Issue
Black gloss	Model No. 1897 only
Black matt	1984 - 1988
British Blue (lead grey gloss)	1964 - 1966
Chocolate point gloss	1953 - 1963
Copper lustre	1971 only
Ginger matt	1984 - 1988
Ginger (dark) gloss	1945 - 1970
Ginger (pale) gloss	1959 - 1963
Ginger striped gloss	1965 - 1989
Ginger Swiss roll gloss	1964 - 1966
Grey matt	1984 - 1988
Grey (shaded) gloss	1965 - 1989
Grey (smokey blue) gloss	1945 - 1970
Grey striped gloss	1962 - 1973
Grey Swiss roll gloss	1964 - 1966
Royal blue gloss	Only one example known
Seal point gloss	1963 - 1989
Seal point matt	1984 - 1988
White (large eyes) gloss	1963 - 1989
White (small eyes) gloss	1945 - 1963
White matt	1984 - 1988
White Zodiac cat	1958 - 1970

Colours listed under individual cats are those on which they could be found. The Swiss roll decoration has two Swiss roll patterns, one on the shoulder and one on the hip.

INDEX BY MODEL NUMBER

Model 1031 White gloss (large eyes) left, (small eyes) right

Model 1880
Persian Cat
Ginger (dark)

Model 1030
Cat
Grey (smokey blue)

Model 1880
Persian Cat
British Blue (lead grey)

Model 1867
Persian Cat
Grey (shaded)

Model 1031
Cat
Grey striped

Model 1031
Cat
Ginger striped

Model 1437
Cat
Grey striped

Model 1296
Siamese Kittens
Chocolate point, Seal point

Model 1885
Persian Kitten
Grey Swiss roll

Model 1436
Kitten
Ginger (pale)

Model 1883
Persian Cat
White (large eyes)

Top Row: Models 1877 and 1876 Grey Swiss roll
Bottom Row: Model 1886 Grey Swiss roll

Top Row: Models 1882, 2139, 1897 Seal Point
Middle Row: Model 1296 Chocolate Point; 1887 Seal Point
Bottom Row: Models 1559 and 1558 Chocolate Point

Top Row: Models 1885 Ginger (pale)
1436, 1031 Ginger (pale) and Ginger striped
Bottom Row: Models 1883 Ginger Swiss roll
1316, 1886 Ginger (dark), 1886 Ginger Swiss roll
and Ginger striped

Top Row: Model 1030 Grey striped, Grey (smokey blue)
Centre Row: Model 1031 White (large eyes), (small eyes)
Bottom Row: Model 1031 Grey striped
Ginger striped, Grey (smokey blue)

WHITE
Top Row: Models 1898, 1560, 1880
Middle Row: Models 1031, 1877, 1883, 1886
Bottom Row: Models 1559, 1436, 1885, 1876

BRITISH BLUE (lead grey)
Top Row: Models 1880, 1885
Bottom Row: Model 1883

GREY STRIPED
Top Row: Models 1438, 1435
Middle Row: Models 1437, 1316
Bottom Row: Models 1436, 1030, 1031, 1436

GREY STRIPED AND GREY SWISS ROLL
Top Row: Models 1898, 1885 Grey striped
Bottom Row: Model 1883 Grey striped
and Models 1867, 1876 Grey Swiss roll

Ayrshire Cow Ch. "Ickham Bessie" (1350)

Ayrshire Calf (1249b)

Guernsey Cow, First Version (1248a)

Guernsey Calf (1249a)

Hereford Calf - Roan Colourway (901a)

Hereford Calf - Brown Colourway (901b)

Hereford Bull (1363)

Polled Hereford Bull (2549a)

Friesian Calf (1249c)

Red Friesisn Calf (2690)

Aberdeen Angus Calf (1827a)

Friesian Cow "Claybury Leegwater" (1362a)

Red Friesenan Cow (1362b)

Aberdeen Angus Cow (1563)

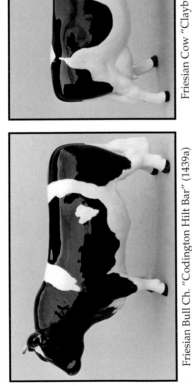

Friesian Bull Ch. "Codington Hilt Bar" (1439a)

Red Friesian Bull (1439c)

Aberdeen Angus Bull (1562)

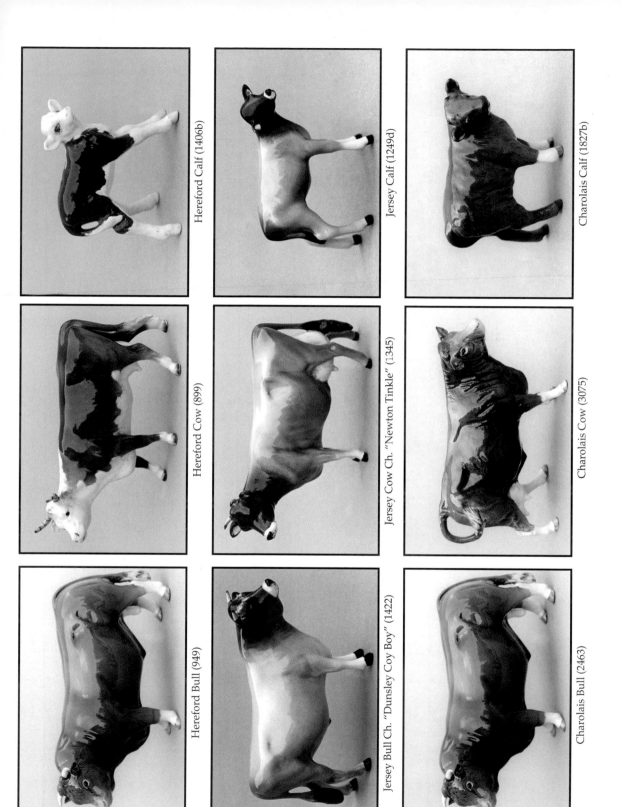

Hereford Calf (1406b)

Jersey Calf (1249d)

Charolais Calf (1827b)

Hereford Cow (899)

Jersey Cow Ch. "Newton Tinkle" (1345)

Charolais Cow (3075)

Hereford Bull (949)

Jersey Bull Ch. "Dunsley Coy Boy" (1422)

Charolais Bull (2463)

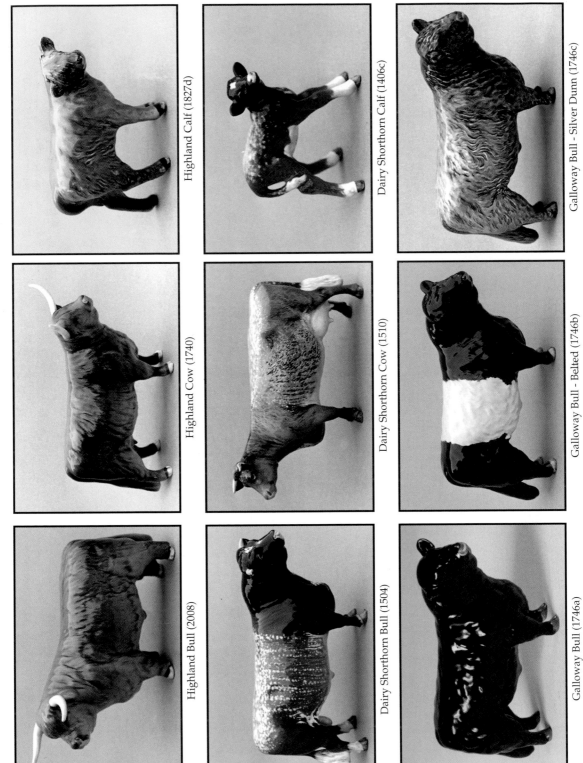

Highland Calf (1827d)

Dairy Shorthorn Calf (1406c)

Galloway Bull - Silver Dunn (1746c)

Highland Cow (1740)

Dairy Shorthorn Cow (1510)

Galloway Bull - Belted (1746b)

Highland Bull (2008)

Dairy Shorthorn Bull (1504)

Galloway Bull (1746a)

Model No. 1026
CAT CONDUCTOR

Designer:	Arthur Gredington
Height:	2", 5.0 cm
Colours:	Grey striped - gloss
Issued:	1945-1973
Series:	Cat Orchestra
Set:	1027, 1028, 1029

Description	U.K. £	U.S. $	Can. $
Gloss	50.00	85.00	125.00

Model No. 1027
CAT WITH CELLO

Designer:	Arthur Gredington
Height:	2", 5.0 cm
Colours:	Grey striped - gloss
Issued:	1945-1973
Series:	Cat Orchestra
Set:	1026, 1028, 1029

Description	U.K. £	U.S. $	Can. $
Gloss	50.00	85.00	125.00

Model No. 1028
CAT WITH FIDDLE

Designer:	Arthur Gredington
Height:	2", 5.0 cm
Colours:	Grey striped - gloss
Issued:	1945-1973
Series:	Cat Orchestra
Set:	1026, 1027, 1029

Description	U.K. £	U.S. $	Can. $
Gloss	50.00	85.00	125.00

Model No. 1029
CAT WITH SAXOPHONE

Designer:	Arthur Gredington
Height:	2", 5.0 cm
Colours:	Grey striped - gloss
Issued:	1945-1973
Series:	Cat Orchestra
Set:	1026, 1027, 1028

Description	U.K. £	U.S. $	Can. $
Gloss	50.00	85.00	125.00

Model No. 1030
CAT - Seated, head looks up

Designer: Arthur Gredington
Height: 6 ¼", 15.9 cm

Colourway	Finish	Intro.	Disc.	U.K. £	Price U.S. $	Can. $
1. British Blue (lead grey)	Gloss	1964	1966	200.00	375.00	550.00
2. Ginger (dark)	Gloss	1945	1970	85.00	150.00	200.00
3. Ginger (pale)	Gloss	1959	1963	75.00	135.00	195.00
4. Ginger striped	Gloss	1965	1973	100.00	165.00	185.00
5. Ginger Swiss roll	Gloss	1964	1966	180.00	300.00	425.00
6. Grey (shaded)	Gloss	1971	1973	75.00	135.00	195.00
7. Grey (smokey blue)	Gloss	1945	1970	60.00	95.00	145.00
8. Grey striped	Gloss	1962	1973	100.00	165.00	225.00
9. Grey Swiss roll	Gloss	1964	1966	200.00	425.00	600.00
10. Royal blue	Gloss				**Unique***	
11. White (small eyes)	Gloss	1945	1963	70.00	125.00	175.00
12. White (large eyes)	Gloss	1963	1973	65.00	100.00	150.00

Note: * Only one example known.

Model No. 1031
CAT - Seated, head looks forward

Designer: Arthur Gredington
Height: 4 ½", 11.9 cm

Colourway	Finish	Intro.	Disc.	U.K. £	Price U.S. $	Can. $
1. British Blue (lead grey)	Gloss	1964	1966	200.00	350.00	500.00
2. Ginger (dark)	Gloss	1945	1970	70.00	115.00	175.00
3. Ginger (pale)	Gloss	1959	1963	60.00	95.00	150.00
4. Ginger striped	Gloss	1965	1973	80.00	125.00	175.00
5. Ginger Swiss roll	Gloss	1964	1966	185.00	300.00	450.00
6. Grey (shaded)	Gloss	1971	1973	65.00	100.00	150.00
7. Grey (smokey blue)	Gloss	1945	1970	55.00	85.00	135.00
8. Grey striped	Gloss	1962	1973	85.00	145.00	225.00
9. Grey Swiss roll	Gloss	1964	1966	200.00	325.00	475.00
10. White (small eyes)	Gloss	1945	1963	60.00	95.00	145.00
11. White (large eyes)	Gloss	1963	1973	55.00	85.00	135.00

Model No. 1296
SIAMESE KITTENS - Curled together

Designer: Miss Granoska
Length: 2 ¾", 7.0 cm

Colours	DA#	Issued	U.K. £	Price U.S. $	Can. $
1. Chocolate point - gloss		1953-1963	55.00	95.00	125.00
2. Copper lustre - gloss (2)		1971	65.00	100.00	150.00
3. One white/one pale grey - gloss (3)				Unique	
4. Seal point - gloss (1)					
a. Original issue	122	1964-1989	14.00	25.00	35.00
b. Reissued	122	1999-Current	14.00	N/A	N/A
5. Seal point - matt		1984-1989	55.00	95.00	125.00

Note: 1. The Seal point model with a gloss finish was transferred to R.D. backstamp (DA122) in August 1989. It reverted to the Beswick backstamp in September 1999.
2. Copper lustre was produced for export only.
3. Only one example known.

Model No. 1316
PERSIAN KITTENS - Seated

Designer: Miss Granoska
Height: 3 ½", 8.9 cm

	Colourway	Finish	Intro.	Disc.	U.K. £	Price U.S. $	Can. $
1.	British Blue (lead grey)	Gloss	1964	1966	150.00	250.00	375.00
2.	Ginger (dark)	Gloss	1953	1970	50.00	85.00	125.00
3.	Ginger (pale)	Gloss	1959	1963	40.00	65.00	100.00
4.	Ginger striped	Gloss	1971	1973	60.00	100.00	150.00
5.	Ginger Swiss roll	Gloss	1964	1966	125.00	235.00	325.00
6.	Grey (shaded)	Gloss	1965	1973	40.00	65.00	100.00
7.	Grey striped	Gloss	1962	1973	60.00	95.00	145.00
8.	Grey Swiss roll	Gloss	1964	1966	165.00	250.00	375.00
9.	White (large eyes)	Gloss	1963	1973	40.00	65.00	100.00

Model No. 1435
CAT - Seated

Designer: Colin Melbourne
Height: 5 ¼″, 13.3 cm
Colours: Grey striped - gloss
Issued: 1956-1963

Colourway	Finish	Intro.	Disc.	U.K. £	Price U.S. $	Can. $
Grey striped	Gloss	1956	1963	200.00	350.00	450.00

Model No. 1436
KITTEN - Seated

Designer: Colin Melbourne
Height: 3 ¼″, 8.3 cm

Colourway	Finish	Intro.	Disc.	U.K. £	Price U.S. $	Can. $
1. Black	Matt	1984	1989	30.00	50.00	65.00
2. British Blue (lead grey)	Gloss	1964	1966	95.00	175.00	300.00
3. Ginger	Matt	1984	1989	25.00	40.00	55.00
4. Ginger (dark)	Gloss	1956	1970	30.00	50.00	65.00
5. Ginger (pale)	Gloss	1959	1963	20.00	35.00	45.00
6. Ginger striped	Gloss	1965	1989	40.00	65.00	90.00
7. Ginger Swiss roll	Gloss	1964	1966	95.00	175.00	300.00
8. Grey	Matt	1984	1989	35.00	60.00	80.00
9. Grey (shaded)	Gloss	1965	1989	25.00	40.00	55.00
10. Grey striped	Gloss	1962	1973	30.00	50.00	65.00
11. Grey Swiss roll	Gloss	1964	1966	100.00	200.00	350.00
12. White (small eyes)	Gloss	1956	1963	40.00	65.00	90.00
13. White (large eyes)	Gloss	1963	1989	30.00	50.00	65.00
14. White	Matt	1984	1989	40.00	65.00	90.00

Note: Transferred to the R.D. backstamp (DA123) August 1989 in ginger, grey, white - gloss.

Model No. 1437
CAT - Seated, looking up
Designer: Colin Melbourne
Height: 3 ¼", 8.3 cm
Colours: Grey striped - gloss
Issued: 1956-1963

Colourway	U.K. £	Price U.S. $	Can. $
Grey striped	200.00	350.00	475.00

Model No. 1438
CAT - Standing, looking back
Designer: Colin Melbourne
Height: 3 ¾", 9.5 cm
Colours: Grey striped - gloss
Issued: 1956-1963

Colourway	U.K. £	Price U.S. $	Can. $
Grey striped	250.00	425.00	600.00

Photograph not
available at press time

Model No. 1541
CAT - Seated

Designer: Mr. Garbet
Height: Unknown
Colours: Dark pewter - Satin gloss
Issued: 1958-1961

Description	U.K. £	U.S. $	Can. $
Satin gloss		Extremely Rare	

Model No. 1542
CAT - Lying, left front paw up

Designer: Mr. Garbet
Height: Unknown
Colours: Dark pewter - Satin gloss
Issued: 1958-1961

Description	U.K. £	U.S. $	Can. $
Satin gloss		Sold February 27th, 1999 at Potteries Antique Auction for £800.00.	

Model No. 1543
CAT - Seated, left front paw up

Designer: Mr. Garbet
Height: Unknown
Colours: Dark pewter- Satin gloss
Issued: 1958-1961

Description	U.K. £	U.S. $	Can. $
Satin gloss		Extremely Rare	

Model No. 1558A
SIAMESE CAT - Lying, facing left
First Version -
Puffed out cheeks, short neck, fleshy body

Designer: Pal Zalmen
Length: 7 ¼", 18.4 cm
Colours: Chocolate point - gloss
Issued: 1958-c.1963

Description	U.K. £	U.S. $	Can. $
Gloss	75.00	150.00	200.00

Model No. 1558B
SIAMESE CAT - Lying, facing left
Second Version -
Sleek, tapering face, long neck and body

Designer: Pal Zalmen
Remodelled: Albert Hallam
Length: 7 ¼", 18.4 cm
Colours: 1. Copper lustre - gloss
           2. Seal point - gloss or matt
Issued: 1. Copper lustre
               a. Gloss - 1971 (export only)
           2. Seal point - gloss
               a. Original issue - c.1963-1989
               b. Reissued - 1999 to the present
           3. Seal point
               a. Matt - 1984-1989

Description	U.K. £	U.S. $	Can. $
1. Copper lustre	100.00	175.00	125.00
2. Seal point - gloss			
a. Original issue	18.00	27.50	45.00
b. Reissued	18.00	N/A	N/A
3. Seal point - matt	50.00	85.00	115.00

Note: Transferred to R.D. backstamp (DA124) 08/89,
in seal point - gloss. Reverted to Beswick 09/99.

Model No. 1559A
SIAMESE CAT - Lying, facing right
Version One -
Puffed out cheeks, short neck, fleshy body

Designer: Pal Zalmen
Length: 7 ¼", 18.4 cm
Colours: Chocolate point - gloss
Issued: 1958-c.1963

Description	U.K. £	U.S. $	Can. $
Gloss	65.00	125.00	175.00

Model No. 1559B
SIAMESE CAT - Lying, facing right
Version Two -
Sleek, tapering face, long neck and body

Designer: Pal Zalmen
Remodelled: Albert Hallam
Length: 7 ¼", 18.4 cm
Colours: 1. Copper lustre - gloss
            2. Seal Point - gloss or matt
Issued: 1. Copper lustre
               a. Gloss - 1971 (export only)
           2. Seal point - gloss
               a. Original issue - c.1963-1989
               b. Reissued - 1999-to the present
           3. Seal point
               a. Matt - 1984-1989

Description	U.K. £	U.S. $	Can. $
1. Copper lustre	90.00	145.00	225.00
2. Seal point - gloss			
a. Original issue	18.00	27.50	45.00
b. Reissued	18.00	N/A	N/A
3. Seal point - matt	45.00	70.00	100.00

Note: Transferred to R.D. backstamp (DA125) 08/89, seal point - gloss. Reverted to Beswick 09/99.

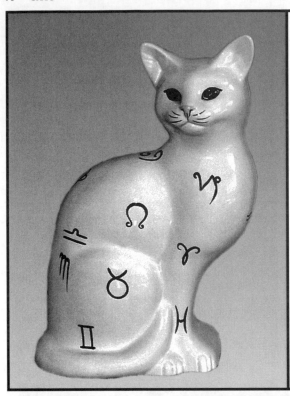

Model No. 1560
ZODIAC CAT - Seated, facing right

Designer: Pal Zalmen
Length: 11", 27.9 cm
Colours: 1. Black with gold details - gloss
           2. White with zodiac symbols - gloss
Issued: 1958-1967
Set: Stylized model forming a pair with 1561

Colourway	U.K. £	U.S. $	Can. $
1. Black	250.00	425.00	600.00
2. White	200.00	350.00	525.00

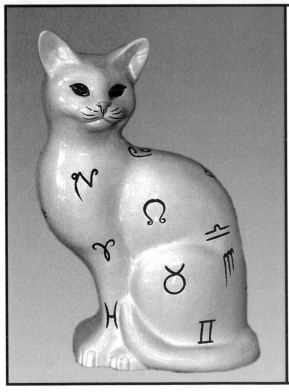

Model No. 1561
ZODIAC CAT - Seated, facing left

Designer: Pal Zalmen
Length: 11", 27.9 cm
Colours: 1. Black with gold details - gloss
           2. White with zodiac symbols - gloss
Issued: 1958-1967
Set: Stylized model forming a pair with 1560

Colourway	U.K. £	U.S. $	Can. $
1. Black	250.00	425.00	600.00
2. White	200.00	350.00	525.00

Model No. 1677
SIAMESE CAT - Climbing

Designer: Albert Hallam
Length: 6 ½", 16.5 cm
Colours: Seal point - gloss
Issued: 1960-1997

Description	U.K. £	U.S. $	Can. $
Gloss	15.00	30.00	40.00

Model No. 1803
CAT - Seated, looking up

Designer: Albert Hallam
Height: 1 ¼", 3.2 cm
Colours: Ginger striped - gloss
Issued: 1962-1971
Series: Bedtime Chorus

Description	U.K. £	U.S. $	Can. $
Gloss	50.00	85.00	135.00

Photograph not
available at press time

Model No. 1857
SIAMESE CAT - Climbing

Designer: Albert Hallam
Length: 5 ½", 14.0 cm
Colours: Seal point - gloss
Issued: 1962-Unknown

Description	U.K. £	U.S. $	Can. $
Gloss		Extremely Rare	

Note: Similar in shape to model no. 1677.

Model No. 1867
PERSIAN CAT - Seated, looking up

Designer: Albert Hallam
Height: 8 ½", 21.6 cm

Colourway	Finish	Intro.	Disc.	U.K. £	Price U.S. $	Can. $
1. Black	Matt	1984	1989	55.00	90.00	135.00
2. British Blue (lead grey)	Gloss	1964	1966	225.00	375.00	525.00
3. Ginger	Matt	1984	1989	65.00	100.00	150.00
4. Ginger (dark)	Gloss	1963	1970	65.00	100.00	150.00
5. Ginger striped	Gloss	1965	1989	125.00	200.00	300.00
6. Ginger Swiss roll	Gloss	1964	1966	150.00	250.00	350.00
7. Grey (shaded)	Gloss	1963	1989	50.00	85.00	125.00
8. Grey	Matt	1984	1989	65.00	100.00	150.00
9. Grey striped	Gloss	1963	1973	150.00	250.00	350.00
10. Grey Swiss roll	Gloss	1964	1966	175.00	275.00	425.00
11. White (large eyes)	Gloss	1963	1989	50.00	85.00	125.00
12. White	Matt	1984	1989	55.00	90.00	135.00

Note: Transferred to the R.D. backstamp (DA126) in August 1989, in ginger, grey and white gloss.

Model No. 1876
PERSIAN CAT - Lying

Designer: Albert Hallam
Height: 3 ½" x 6 ½", 8.0 x 6.5 cm

Colourway	Finish	Intro.	Disc.	U.K. £	Price U.S. $	Can. $
1. British Blue (lead grey)	Gloss	1964	1966	225.00	375.00	550.00
2. Ginger (dark)	Gloss	1963	1970	125.00	200.00	300.00
3. Ginger striped	Gloss	1965	1971	135.00	225.00	350.00
4. Ginger Swiss roll	Gloss	1964	1966	200.00	325.00	475.00
5. Grey (shaded)	Gloss	1963	1971	85.00	135.00	200.00
6. Grey striped	Gloss	1963	1971	140.00	235.00	350.00
7. Grey Swiss roll	Gloss	1964	1966	250.00	450.00	675.00
8. White (large eyes)	Gloss	1963	1971	85.00	135.00	200.00

Model No. 1877
CAT - Seated, scratching ear

Designer: Albert Hallam
Height: 6 ½", 16.5 cm

Colourway	Finish	Intro.	Disc.	U.K. £	Price U.S. $	Can. $
1. British Blue (lead grey)	Gloss	1964	1966	300.00	475.00	700.00
2. Ginger (dark)	Gloss	1963	1970	150.00	250.00	375.00
3. Ginger striped	Gloss	1965	1971	225.00	350.00	500.00
4. Ginger Swiss roll	Gloss	1964	1966	300.00	475.00	700.00
5. Grey (shaded)	Gloss	1963	1971	145.00	225.00	325.00
6. Grey striped	Gloss	1963	1971	250.00	400.00	600.00
7. Grey Swiss roll	Gloss	1964	1966	350.00	550.00	700.00
8. White (large eyes)	Gloss	1963	1971	125.00	200.00	300.00

Model No. 1880
PERSIAN CAT - Seated, looking up

Designer: Albert Hallam
Height: 5 ¼", 13.3 cm

Colourway	Finish	Intro.	Disc.	U.K. £	Price U.S. $	Can. $
1. British Blue (lead grey)	Gloss	1964	1966	200.00	325.00	475.00
2. Ginger (dark)	Gloss	1963	1970	135.00	225.00	325.00
3. Ginger striped	Gloss	1965	1971	150.00	250.00	375.00
4. Ginger Swiss roll	Gloss	1964	1966	175.00	275.00	425.00
5. Grey (shaded)	Gloss	1963	1971	125.00	200.00	300.00
6. Grey striped	Gloss	1963	1971	150.00	250.00	375.00
7. Grey Swiss roll	Gloss	1964	1966	200.00	325.00	475.00
8. White (large eyes)	Gloss	1963	1971	95.00	150.00	225.00

Model No. 1882
SIAMESE CAT - Seated, head forward

Designer:	Albert Hallam
Height:	9 ½", 24.0 cm
Series:	Fireside Model

Colourway	Finish	Intro.	Disc.	U.K. £	Price U.S. $	Can. $
1. Black	Gloss	1986	1989	65.00	100.00	150.00
2. Black	Matt	1986	1989	75.00	125.00	190.00
3. Copper lustre	Gloss	1971	1971	125.00	200.00	300.00
4. Seal point	Gloss	1963	1989	70.00	115.00	175.00
5. Seal point	Matt	1984	1989	80.00	135.00	200.00

Note: 1. Transferred to R.D. backstamp (DA127) in August 1989 in the seal point colourway (gloss).
2. Copper lustre issued for export only.

Model No. 1883
PERSIAN CAT - On hind legs

Designer: Albert Hallam
Height: 6", 15.0 cm

Colourway	Finish	Intro.	Disc.	U.K. £	Price U.S. $	Can. $
1. British Blue (lead grey)	Gloss	1964	1966	250.00	425.00	600.00
2. Ginger (dark)	Gloss	1963	1970	150.00	250.00	375.00
3. Ginger striped	Gloss	1965	1971	165.00	275.00	400.00
4. Ginger Swiss roll	Gloss	1964	1966	225.00	350.00	525.00
5. Grey (shaded)	Gloss	1963	1971	185.00	300.00	450.00
6. Grey striped	Gloss	1963	1971	165.00	275.00	400.00
7. Grey Swiss roll	Gloss	1964	1966	250.00	425.00	625.00
8. White (large eyes)	Gloss	1963	1971	100.00	165.00	250.00

Model No. 1885
PERSIAN KITTEN - Standing

Designer: Albert Hallam
Height: 4 ¾", 12.1 cm

Colourway	Finish	Intro.	Disc.	U.K. £	Price U.S. $	Can. $
1. British Blue (lead grey)	Gloss	1964	1966	225.00	375.00	525.00
2. Ginger (dark)	Gloss	1963	1970	100.00	165.00	250.00
3. Ginger striped	Gloss	1965	1973	125.00	200.00	300.00
4. Ginger Swiss roll	Gloss	1964	1966	175.00	300.00	450.00
5. Grey (shaded)	Gloss	1963	1973	100.00	165.00	250.00
6. Grey striped	Gloss	1963	1973	125.00	200.00	300.00
7. Grey Swiss roll	Gloss	1964	1966	225.00	375.00	525.00
8. White (large eyes)	Gloss	1963	1973	100.00	165.00	250.00

Model No 1886
PERSIAN KITTEN - Seated, looking up

Designer: Albert Hallam
Height: 4", 10.1 cm

Colourway	Finish	Intro.	Disc.	U.K. £	Price U.S. $	Can. $
1. Black	Matt	1984	1989	40.00	65.00	90.00
2. British Blue (lead grey)	Gloss	1964	1966	100.00	200.00	275.00
3. Ginger	Matt	1984	1989	35.00	60.00	75.00
4. Ginger (dark)	Gloss	1963	1970	35.00	60.00	75.00
5. Ginger striped	Gloss	1965	1989	55.00	95.00	125.00
6. Ginger Swiss roll	Gloss	1964	1966	100.00	175.00	250.00
7. Grey						
a. Original issue	Gloss	1965	1989	11.00	17.50	25.00
b. Reissued (DA128)	Gloss	1999	Current	11.00	N/A	N/A
8. Grey	Matt	1984	1989	50.00	80.00	110.00*
9. Grey striped	Gloss	1962	1973	60.00	100.00	125.00
10. Grey Swiss roll	Gloss	1964	1966	115.00	200.00	300.00
11. White						
a. Original issue	Gloss	1963	1989	11.00	17.50	25.00
b. Reissued (DA128)	Gloss	1999	Current	11.00	N/A	N/A
12. White	Matt	1984	1989	25.00	45.00	60.00

Note: Transferred to R.D. backstamp (DA128) in August 1989, in the ginger, grey and white colourways (gloss). The grey and white colourways reverted to Beswick backstamp in September 1999.

Model No. 1887
SIAMESE CAT - Seated, head turned back

Designer: Albert Hallam
Height: 4", 10.1 cm

Colourway	Finish	Intro.	Disc.	U.K. £	Price U.S. $	Can. $
1. Copper lustre	Gloss	1971	1971	75.00	125.00	175.00
2. Seal point						
a. Original issue	Gloss	1971	1989	11.00	17.50	25.00
b. Reissued (DA129)	Gloss	1999	Current	11.00	N/A	N/A
3. Seal point	Matt	1984	1989	30.00	60.00	75.00

Note: 1. Model 1887 was transferred to the R.D. backstamp (DA129) in August 1989, in the seal point
colourway (gloss). It reverted to Beswick backstamp in September 1999.
2. Copper lustre produced for export only.

Model No. 1897
SIAMESE CAT - Standing

Designer: Albert Hallam
Height: 6 ½", 16.5 cm
Series: Fireside Model

Colourway	Finish	Intro.	Disc.	U.K. £	Price U.S. $	Can. $
1. Black	Gloss	1987	1989	60.00	100.00	130.00
2. Black	Matt	1987	1989	65.00	110.00	150.00
3. Copper lustre	Gloss	1971	1971	150.00	250.00	375.00
4. Seal point	Gloss	1963	1980	35.00	60.00	80.00
5. Seal point	Matt	1984	1989	45.00	75.00	100.00

Note: 1. In 1987 introduced as "Lucky Black Cat."
2. Transferred to the R.D. backstamp in August 1989, in seal point (DA 130) and black (DA131) - gloss.
3. Copper lustre produced for export only.

Model No. 1898
PERSIAN CAT - Standing, tail erect

Designer: Albert Hallam
Height: 5", 12.7 cm

Colourway	Finish	Intro.	Disc.	U.K. £	Price U.S. $	Can. $
1. Black	Matt	1984	1989	35.00	60.00	80.00
2. British Blue (lead grey)	Gloss	1964	1966	175.00	275.00	425.00
3. Ginger	Matt	1984	1989	55.00	90.00	135.00
4. Ginger striped	Gloss	1965	1989	60.00	100.00	130.00
5. Ginger Swiss roll	Gloss	1964	1966	175.00	275.00	425.00
6. Grey	Matt	1984	1989	35.00	60.00	95.00
7. Grey (shaded)	Gloss	1963	1989	30.00	50.00	75.00
8. Grey Swiss roll	Gloss	1964	1966	200.00	325.00	500.00
9. White (large eyes)	Gloss	1963	1989	40.00	65.00	90.00
10. White	Matt	1984	1989	40.00	65.00	90.00

Note: Transferred to R.D. backstamp (DA132) 08/89, in ginger, grey and white - gloss.

Model No. 2100
CAT WITH MOUSE

Designer:	Albert Hallam
Height:	3", 7.6 cm
Colours:	Brown cat, white mouse - gloss
Issued:	1967-1973
Series:	Fun Models

Description	U.K. £	U.S. $	Can. $
Gloss	75.00	125.00	175.00

Model No. 2101
CAT - Laughing

Designer:	Albert Hallam
Height:	3", 7.6 cm
Colours:	Grey - gloss
Issued:	1967-1973
Series:	Fun Models

Description	U.K. £	U.S. $	Can. $
Gloss	75.00	125.00	175.00

Model No. 2139
SIAMESE CAT - Seated, head up

Designer:	Mr. Garbet
Height:	13 ¾", 34.9 cm
Colours:	See below
Issued:	1. Copper lustre - 1971 (export only)
	2. Seal point - 1967-1989
Series:	Fireside Models

Colourway	U.K. £	U.S. $	Can. $
1. Copper lustre	125.00	200.00	300.00
2. Seal point - gloss	75.00	125.00	200.00

Note: Transferred to (DA83) 08/89, in seal point - gloss.

Model No. 2156/2157
CAT CRUET, SALT AND PEPPER

Designer:	Unknown
Height:	5 ½", 14.0 cm
Colours:	Black cat (pepper), white cat (salt) - gloss
Issued:	1967-1969

Colourway	U.K.£	U.S.$	Can.$
Black	35.00	60.00	90.00
White	35.00	60.00	90.00

Model No. 2233
CAT AND DOG WALL PLAQUE
Cat left, dog right

Designer:	Graham Tongue
Height:	9" x 6 ¼", 23 x 15.9 cm (Concave)
Colours:	Unknown - gloss
Issued:	1968-Unknown
Series:	Wall Plaques

Description	U.K.£	U.S.$	Can.$
Gloss	65.00	100.00	150.00

Model No. 2236
CAT WALL PLAQUE

Designer:	Graham Tongue
Height:	9" x 6 ¼", 23 x 15.9 cm (Concave)
Colours:	Ginger cat with yellow eyes on dark pewter background - gloss
Issued:	1968-Unknown
Series:	Wall Plaques

Description	U.K.£	U.S.$	Can.$
Gloss	65.00	100.00	150.00

Photograph not
available at press time

Model No. 2301
CAT - Climbing

Designer:	Albert Hallam
Height:	4 ½", 11.9 cm
Colours:	Unknown
Issued:	1969-Unknown

Description	U.K. £	U.S. $	Can. $
Cat - Climbing		Extremely Rare	

Note: Similar to model no. 1677. Possibly not issued.

Photograph not
available at press time

Model No. 2311
SIAMESE CAT

Designer:	Graham Tongue
Length:	1 ½", 3.8 cm
Colours:	Unknown
Issued:	1970-Unknown

Description	U.K. £	U.S. $	Can. $
Siamese Cat		Extremely Rare	

Note: Similar to model no. 2139. Possibly not issued.

Model No. 2480
CHESHIRE CAT

Designer:	Graham Tongue
Height:	1 ½", 3.8 cm
Colours:	Tabby - gloss
Issued:	1973-1982
Series:	Alice in Wonderland

Description	U.K. £	U.S. $	Can. $
Gloss	400.00	650.00	950.00

Note: For the rest of the pieces in the Alice in Wonderland series see *The Charlton Standard Catalogue of Royal Doulton Beswick Storybook Figurines.*

Model No. 2761
CAT ON CHIMNEY POT - Salt and pepper

Designer:	Unknown
Height:	4", 10.1 cm
Colours:	White and gold - gloss
Issued:	1982-1985
Series:	Fun Models

Description	U.K. £	U.S. $	Can. $
Gloss	85.00	135.00	175.00

Model No. 2805
CAT ON POST BOX - Money Box

Designer:	Unknown
Height:	6 ¼", 15.9 cm
Colours:	White cat on red post box - gloss
Issued:	1983-1986
Series:	Fun Models

Description	U.K. £	U.S. $	Can. $
Gloss	75.00	125.00	150.00

Model No. 2810
CAT EGG CUP

Designer:	Unknown
Height:	2 ½", 6.4 cm
Colours:	Ginger kitten with white egg cup - gloss
Issued:	1983-1986
Series:	Fun Models

Description	U.K. £	U.S. $	Can. $
Gloss	40.00	65.00	100.00

Model No. 3012
SPORTING CAT

Designer:	Warren Platt
Length:	4 ¼", 10.8 cm
Colours:	1. Cat dressed as a soccer player with striped jersey; black, blue, burgundy, red, yellow
	2. Cat dressed as a soccer player with plain jersey; black, blue, burgundy, red, yellow
Modelled:	1986
Issued:	1987-1987
Series:	Fun Models

			Price	
Colourways	Finish	U.K. £	U.S. $	Can. $
1. Black stripe	Gloss	50.00	90.00	125.00
2. Black	Gloss	50.00	90.00	125.00
3. Blue stripe	Gloss	50.00	90.00	125.00
4. Blue	Gloss	50.00	90.00	125.00
5. Burgundy stripe	Gloss	50.00	90.00	125.00
6. Burgundy	Gloss	50.00	90.00	125.00
7. Red stripe	Gloss	50.00	90.00	125.00
8. Red	Gloss	50.00	90.00	125.00
9. Yellow stripe	Gloss	50.00	90.00	125.00
10. Yellow	Gloss	50.00	90.00	125.00

Note: Introduced as a trial in August 1987, but not put into general production, although many sets were sold from the factory shop.

Model No. FF2
MEE-OUCH

Designer: Andy Moss
Height: 3 ¼", 8.0 cm
Colour: Blue shirt; white shorts; black boots
Issued: 1998 in a limited edition of 1,500
Series: Footballing Felines

Colourway	U.K. £	U.S. $	Can. $
Blue/white	45.00	75.00	125.00

Note: Commissioned by Sinclairs.
FF1 not issued.

Model No. FF3
KITCAT

Designer: Andy Moss
Height: 4 ¼", 11.0 cm
Colour: Red shirt; white shorts; black boots
Issued: 1998 in a limited edition of 1,500
Series: Footballing Felines

Colourway	U.K. £	U.S. $	Can. $
Red/white	45.00	75.00	125.00

Note: Commissioned by Sinclairs.

Model No. FF4
DRIBBLE

Designer: Andy Moss
Height: 4 ¼", 11.0 cm
Colour: White shirt; black shorts and boots
Issued: 1998 in a limited edition of 1,500
Series: Footballing Felines

Colourway	U.K. £	U.S. $	Can. $
Black/white	45.00	75.00	125.00

Note: Commissioned by Sinclairs.

Model No. FF5
THROW IN

Designer: Andy Moss
Height: 6", 15.0 cm
Colour: Yellow shirt; white shorts; black boots
Issued: 1999 in a limited edition of 1,500
Series: Footballing Felines

Colourway	U.K. £	U.S. $	Can. $
Yellow/white	45.00	75.00	125.00

Note: Commissioned by Sinclairs.

Model No. FF6
REFEREE: RED CARD

Designer:	Andy Moss
Height:	6 ¼", 15.9 cm
Colour:	Black uniform; black and white socks
Issued:	1999 in a limited edition of 1,500
Series:	Footballing Felines

Colourway	U.K. £	U.S. $	Can. $
Black/white	45.00	75.00	125.00

Note: Commissioned by Sinclairs.

Model No. K194
CAT - Seated

Designer:	Marilyn C.R.Alcock
Height:	3 ¾", 9.5 cm
Colour:	Black and white
Issued:	1999 to the present

Colourway	U.K. £	U.S. $	Can. $
Black and white	15.00	N/A	N/A

Note: Transferred from the Royal Doulton backstamp (DA194) in September 1999.

Model No. K229
QUIET PLEASE

Designer:	Warren Platt
Height:	1 ¾", 4.4 cm
Colour:	Grey and white kitten - gloss
Issued:	1999 to the present

Colourway	U.K. £	U.S. $	Can. $
Grey and white	17.00	N/A	N/A

Note: Transferred from the Royal Doulton backstamp (DA229) in September 1999.

Chapter Four

DOGS

Beswick produced mantelpiece dogs of the old Staffordshire type from about 1898. In 1933, when the shape book was created — in which each model was illustrated by a sketch with details such as height, modeller and dates — these dogs, in various sizes, were the initial numbers. During the 1930s dogs of the novelty type were produced with several unrealistic-looking decorations, including blue and green gloss and mottled blue in a satin-type finish. In fact customers could order novelties in any decoration to match the domestic ware being made at the time. Then in 1941, Arthur Gredington, following his success with realistic models of horses, created the first of the champion dogs, the Dalmatian "Arnoldene," shape number 961. Seven other breeds were also produced in 1941, and four more the following year. These figures were all modelled in a show stance from champions of their particular breed, and almost all of them were modelled by Arthur Gredington.

Over the years most of the popular breeds joined the Beswick "kennel," and many were also produced in a smaller size. Action poses were added to the collection, such as the 1507 Spaniel running. This type of model was reintroduced with the Good Companions series in 1987, the same time several more medium-sized dogs were issued. These and the Good Companions, had a short production run with the Beswick backstamp (some for less than a year), as from August 1989 they were issued with Royal Doulton backstamps and given DA numbers. By 1994 all the Beswick medium-sized dogs had been withdrawn, leaving only the small dogs collection with Beswick backstamps. However, in September 1999 Royal Doulton announced that animal sculptures carrying their backstamp (except limited editions) would revert to the Beswick backstamp.

Many of the dogs share with the horses the distinction of being in continual production for four or five decades. During this time there has been a deterioration in the moulds and decorating processes; therefore, the quality of the models is variable. It is well worth looking out for the older figures that exhibit more mould detail and toning and shading in colour.

The dogs collection also includes some of Beswick's largest models; the seated Fireside models range from the 2377 Yorkshire Terrier at 10 ¼" to the 13 ½" 2314 Labrador. At the other extreme is the tiny 1 ½" singing dog from the Bedtime Chorus set, a very elusive little fellow.

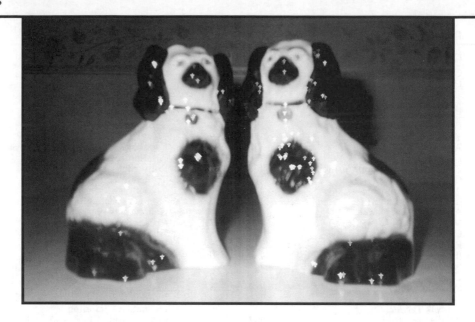

Model Nos. 1 to 6   **OLD STAFFORDSHIRE DOGS**

Designer:	Unknown
Colours:	Black and white
Issued:	1933-1955
Series:	Mantelpiece Dogs

Model No.	1	2	3	4	5	6
Height:	13 ¾", 34.9 cm	11 ½", 29.2 cm	10", 25.4 cm	9", 22.9 cm	7 ½", 19.1 cm	5 ½", 14.0 cm

Price	Model No. 1	Model No. 2	Model No. 3	Model No. 4	Model No. 5	Model No. 6
U.K. £	85.00	75.00	65.00	55.00	45.00	35.00
U.S. $	150.00	130.00	115.00	95.00	75.00	60.00
Can. $	200.00	175.00	150.00	125.00	100.00	80.00

Note: Prices above are for singles, they are available in pairs, left and right facing.

Model No. 87
DOG STANDING IN ARMCHAIR - Bookend

Designer:	Unknown
Height:	7", 18.0 cm
Colours:	See below
Issued:	1934-by 1966
Series:	Fun Models

Colourway	U.K. £	U.S. $	Can. $
1. Blue	125.00	200.00	300.00
2. Various	85.00	150.00	225.00
3. White	85.00	150.00	225.00

Note: Prices are for single bookends.

Model No. 88
SCOTTIE - Ashtray

Designer:	Unknown	
Height:	3 ¼", 8.3 cm	
Colours:	1.	Blue - gloss
	2.	Various - satin matt
	3.	White - matt
Issued:	1934-1965	

Colourway	U.K. £	U.S. $	Can. $
1. Blue	35.00	60.00	90.00
2. Various	25.00	50.00	75.00
3. White	30.00	50.00	75.00

Model No. 171
DOG - Begging

Designer:	Unknown
Height:	4 ¾", 12.1 cm
Colours:	White and tan - gloss
Issued:	1934-by 1954

Description	U.K. £	U.S. $	Can. $
Gloss	60.00	125.00	175.00

Model No. 286
DOG - Seated

Designer:	Mr. Watkin
Height:	6 ¼", 15.9 cm
Colours:	1. Blue - gloss
	2. White and tan - gloss
Issued:	1. 1934-1967
	2. 1934-by 1954

Colourway	U.K. £	U.S. $	Can. $
1. Blue	90.00	150.00	225.00
2. White/tan	50.00	100.00	125.00

Model No. 301
SEALYHAM PLAQUE - Bow on right

Designer:	Unknown
Height:	7 ½", 19.1 cm
Colours:	Cream; blue bow - satin finish
Issued:	1936-1940
Series:	Wall Plaques

Description	U.K. £	U.S. $	Can. $
Satin finish	200.00	400.00	600.00

Model No. 302
SEALYHAM - Standing

Designer:	Mr. Watkin
Height:	6", 15.0 cm
Colours:	1. Blue - gloss
	2. White with dark ears - gloss
Issued:	1. 1936-1967
	2. 1936-by 1964

Colourway	U.K. £	U.S. $	Can. $
1. Blue	150.00	325.00	475.00
2. White/dark ears	100.00	200.00	300.00

Model No. 307
SEALYHAM PLAQUE

Designer:	Mr. Watkin
Height:	7", 17.8 cm
Colours:	Cream - satin finish
Issued:	1935-1940
Series:	Wall Plaques

Description	U.K. £	U.S. $	Can. $
Satin finish	200.00	400.00	600.00

Model No. 308
PUPPY - Seated

Designer:	Mr. Watkin
Height:	6 ¼", 15.9 cm
Colours:	1. Blue - gloss
	2. White with brown ears - gloss
Issued:	1. 1935-1967
	2. 1935-by 1954

Colourway	U.K. £	U.S. $	Can. $
1. Blue	100.00	175.00	250.00
2. White/brown	75.00	125.00	175.00

Note: Also issued as a money-box.

Model No. 324
Character Dog - Begging

Designer:	Miss Greaves
Height:	7", 17.8 cm
Colours:	1. Blue - gloss
	2. Cream - gloss
Issued:	1. 1936-by 1954
	2. 1936-by 1954
Series:	Fun Models

Colourway	U.K. £	U.S. $	Can. $
1. Blue	125.00	200.00	300.00
2. Cream	75.00	125.00	225.00

Model No. 361
DACHSHUND - Standing

Designer: Mr. Watkin
Height: 5 ½", 14.0 cm
Colours: 1. Black/tan - gloss 2. Blue - gloss
          3. Tan - gloss
Issued: 1. 1936-1983 2. 1936-by 1954
          3. 1936-1983

Colourway	U.K. £	U.S. $	Can. $
1. Black/tan	40.00	95.00	150.00
2. Blue	100.00	150.00	225.00
3. Tan	40.00	95.00	150.00

Model No. 373
SEALYHAM PLAQUE

Designer: Unknown
Height: 7", 17.8 cm
Colours: White dog with blue bow - satin matt
Issued: 1936-1940
Series: Wall Plaques

Colourway	U.K. £	U.S. $	Can. $
White dog	250.00	400.00	600.00

Model No. 453
OLD ENGLISH SHEEPDOG - Seated

Designer: Unknown
Height: 8 ½", 21.6 cm
Colours: 1. Blue - gloss
          2. Grey and white - gloss
Issued: 1. 1936-by 1954
          2. 1936-1973

Colourway	U.K. £	U.S. $	Can. $
1. Blue	150.00	250.00	375.00
2. Grey/white	100.00	200.00	300.00

Model No. 454
LOLLOPY DOG - Seated Puppy

Designer: Miss Greaves
Height: 4 ¼", 10.8 cm
Colours: 1. Blue - gloss
          2. Various - satin matt
          3. White - matt
Issued: 1. 1936-1969 2. 1936-by 1954
          3. 1936-1969

Colourway	U.K. £	U.S. $	Can. $
1. Blue	30.00	55.00	75.00
2. Various	25.00	45.00	60.00
3. White	25.00	45.00	60.00

Model No. 624
DOG- Toothbrush holder

Designer:	Miss Catford
Height:	4", 10.1 cm
Colours:	1. Blue - gloss
	2. Various - satin matt
	3. White - matt
Issued:	1938-by 1954

Colourway	U.K. £	U.S. $	Can. $
1. Blue	100.00	175.00	250.00
2. Various	150.00	250.00	375.00
3. White	100.00	175.00	250.00

Model No. 668
DOG PLAQUE

Designer:	Mr. Symcox
Height:	11", 27.9 cm
Colours:	Deep red brown - gloss
Issued:	1938-1960
Series:	Wall Plaques

Description	U.K. £	U.S. $	Can. $
Gloss	100.00	200.00	300.00

Model No. 761
DOG WITH TOOTHACHE

Designer:	Mr. Watkin
Height:	4 ¼", 10.8 cm
Colours:	1. White dog with red kerchief - gloss
	2. White dog with green kerchief - gloss
Issued:	1939-1971
Series:	Fun Models

Colourway	U.K. £	U.S. $	Can. $
1. Red kerchief	60.00	95.00	150.00
2. Green kerchief	75.00	125.00	200.00

Model No. 804
DOG WITH LADYBIRD ON NOSE

Designer:	Mr. Watkin
Height:	4", 10.1 cm
Colours:	White with red ladybird - gloss
Issued:	1940-1969
Series:	Fun Models

Description	U.K. £	U.S. $	Can. $
Gloss	45.00	85.00	125.00

Model No. 805
DOG WITH LADYBIRD ON TAIL

Designer: Mr. Watkin
Height: 1. Large - 3 ¾", 9.5 cm
                 2. Small - 2 ½", 6.4 cm
Colours: White dog with red ladybird - gloss
Issued: 1940-1969
Series: Fun Models

Description	U.K. £	U.S. $	Can. $
1. Large	35.00	65.00	100.00
2. Small	25.00	45.00	60.00

Model No. 810
BULLDOG WITH SAILOR'S HAT - Ashtray

Designer: Arthur Gredington
Height: 4", 10.1 cm
Colours: White dog, white sailor cap with blue
               band, biscuit coloured base - gloss
Issued: 1940-by 1954

Description	U.K. £	U.S. $	Can. $
Gloss	175.00	300.00	400.00

Model No. 811
DOG PLAYING ACCORDION

Designer: Mr. Watkin
Height: 4", 10.1 cm
Colours: White dog with green and brown
               accordion - gloss
Issued: 1940-1970

Description	U.K. £	U.S. $	Can. $
Gloss	75.00	125.00	200.00

Model No. 812
DOG ASLEEP ON DRUM

Designer: Mr. Watkin
Height: 3", 7.6 cm
Colours: White dog, yellow, blue and red
               drum - gloss
Issued: 1940-1970
Series: Fun Models

Description	U.K. £	U.S. $	Can. $
Gloss	75.00	125.00	200.00

Model No. 813
DOG WITH LADYBIRD ON NOSE

Designer:	Mr. Watkin
Height:	4", 10.1 cm
Colours:	White dog, red ladybird - gloss
Issued:	1940-1970
Series:	Fun Models

Description	U.K. £	U.S. $	Can. $
Gloss	45.00	75.00	100.00

Model No. 831
DOG WITH GLASSES READING A BOOK

Designer:	Arthur Gredington
Height:	6 ¼", 15.9 cm
Colours:	White dog, yellow-red glasses, brown and white book - gloss
Issued:	1940-1970
Series:	Fun Models

Description	U.K. £	U.S. $	Can. $
Gloss	100.00	165.00	250.00

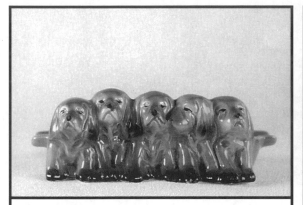

Model No. 869
FIVE PUPPY ASHTRAY

Designer:	Mr. Watkin	
Height:	2", 5.0 cm	
Colours:	1.	Brown puppies, green ashtray - gloss
	2.	Light tan puppies with black shading, green ashtray - gloss
Issued:	1940-1967	

Colourway	U.K. £	U.S. $	Can. $
1. Brown	35.00	60.00	85.00
2. Light tan	35.00	60.00	85.00

Model No. 907
DOG WITH LADYBIRD ON TAIL

Designer:	Mr. Watkin
Height:	3 ¾", 9.5 cm
Colours:	White dog, red ladybird - gloss
Issued:	1941-1971
Series:	Fun Models

Description	U.K. £	U.S. $	Can. $
Gloss	45.00	75.00	100.00

Model No. 916
THREE PUPPY ASHTRAY

Designer:	Mr. Watkin
Height:	2″, 5.0 cm
Colours:	1. Brown puppies, green ashtray - gloss
	2. Light brown puppies with black shading, green ashtray - gloss
Issued:	1941-1967

Colourway	U.K. £	U.S. $	Can. $
1. Brown	20.00	30.00	45.00
2. Light brown	20.00	30.00	45.00

Note: The three dogs are same as used in model no. 917.

Model No. 917
THREE PUPPIES

Designer:	Mr. Watkin
Height:	2″, 5.0 cm
Colours:	Brown puppies - gloss
Issued:	1941-1965

Description	U.K. £	U.S. $	Can. $
Gloss	20.00	30.00	45.00

Note: The three dogs are same as used in model no. 916.

Model No. 941
FOXHOUND
First Version - Thick legs and tail

Designer:	Mr. Watkin
Height:	2 ¾″, 7.0 cm
Colours:	White, tan and black - gloss
Issued:	1941-1969
Varieties:	2262

Description	U.K. £	U.S. $	Can. $
Gloss	35.00	60.00	85.00

Note: Remodelled in 1969 see also no. 2263.

Model No. 942
FOXHOUND
First Version - Thick legs and tail

Designer:	Mr. Watkin
Height:	2 ¾″, 7.0 cm
Colours:	White, tan and black - gloss
Issued:	1941-1969
Varieties:	2263

Description	U.K. £	U.S. $	Can. $
Gloss	35.00	60.00	85.00

Note: Remodelled in 1969 see also no. 2262.

Model No. 943
FOXHOUND
First Version - Thick legs and tail

Designer:	Mr. Watkin
Height:	2 ¾", 7.0 cm
Colours:	White, tan and black - gloss
Issued:	1941-1969
Varieties:	2265

Description	U.K. £	U.S. $	Can. $
Gloss	35.00	60.00	85.00

Note: Remodelled in 1969 see also no. 2265.

Model No. 944
FOXHOUND
First Version - Thick legs and tail

Designer:	Mr. Watkin
Height:	2 ¾", 7.0 cm
Colours:	White, tan and black - gloss
Issued:	1941-1969
Varieties:	2264

Description	U.K. £	U.S. $	Can. $
Gloss	35.00	60.00	85.00

Note: Remodelled in 1969 see also no. 2264.

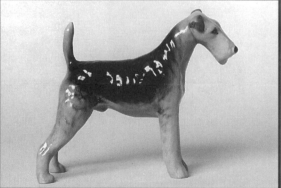

Model No. 961
DALMATION "ARNOLDENE" - Large

Designer:	Arthur Gredington
Height:	5 ¾", 14.6 cm
Colours:	White with black spot - gloss; matt
Issued:	1. Gloss - 1941-1994
	2. Matt - 1970-1994

Description	U.K. £	U.S. $	Can. $
1. Gloss	40.00	100.00	150.00
2. Matt	40.00	100.00	150.00

Note: For the small size see no. 1763.

Model No. 962
AIREDALE TERRIER "CAST IRON MONARCH"

Designer:	Arthur Gredington
Height:	5 ½", 14.0 cm
Colours:	Black and tan - gloss; matt
Issued:	1. Gloss - 1941-1989
	2. Matt - 1987-1989

Description	U.K. £	U.S. $	Can. $
1. Gloss	40.00	100.00	150.00
2. Matt	40.00	100.00	150.00

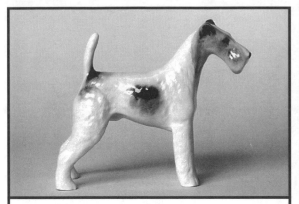

Model No. 963
WIRED-HAIRED TERRIER
"TALAVERA ROMULUS"

Designer:	Arthur Gredington
Height:	5 ¾", 14.6 cm
Colours:	White, light sandy brown and black - gloss
Issued:	1941-1984

Description	U.K. £	U.S. $	Can. $
Gloss	65.00	125.00	200.00

Model No. 964
SMOOTH-HAIRED TERRIER
"ENDON BLACK ROD"

Designer:	Arthur Gredington
Height:	5 ½", 14.0 cm
Colours:	White with black patches - gloss
Issued:	1941-1973

Description	U.K. £	U.S. $	Can. $
Gloss	225.00	400.00	600.00

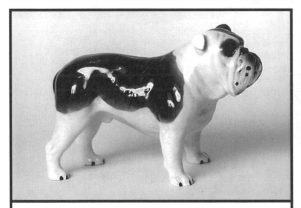

Model No. 965
BULLDOG "BASFORD BRITISH MASCOT" - Large

Designer:	Arthur Gredington
Height:	5 ½", 14.0 cm
Colours:	Brindle, tan and white - gloss; matt
Issued:	1. Gloss - 1941-1990
	2. Matt - 1987-1989

Description	U.K. £	U.S. $	Can. $
1. Gloss	50.00	100.00	135.00
2. Matt	45.00	95.00	125.00

Note: For small size see no. 1731.

Model No. 966
IRISH SETTER "SUGAR OF WENDOVER"

Designer:	Arthur Gredington
Height:	5 ¾", 14.6 cm
Colours:	Red brown - gloss; matt
Issued:	1. Gloss - 1941-1989
	2. Matt - 1987-1989

Description	U.K. £	U.S. $	Can. $
1. Gloss	45.00	90.00	125.00
2. Matt	40.00	90.00	125.00

Model No. 967

COCKER SPANIEL "HORSESHOE PRIMULA"

Designer: Arthur Gredington
Height: 5 ¾", 14.6 cm

Colourway	Issued	U.K. £	Price U.S. $	Can. $
1. Black - gloss	1965-1982	55.00	90.00	150.00
2. Black and white - gloss	1970-1982	65.00	100.00	150.00
3. Golden brown - gloss	1941-1994	35.00	65.00	100.00
4. Golden brown - matt	1987-1994	30.00	60.00	100.00
5. Liver and white - gloss	1970-1994	45.00	75.00	125.00
6. Liver and white - matt	1987-1994	40.00	75.00	125.00

Model No. 968
GREAT DANE "RULER OF OUBOURGH"

Designer:	Arthur Gredington
Height:	7", 17.8 cm
Colours:	Light sandy brown - gloss; matt
Issued:	1. Gloss - 1941-1994
	2. Matt - 1987-1994

Description	U.K. £	U.S. $	Can. $
1. Gloss	50.00	95.00	145.00
2. Matt	45.00	85.00	125.00

Model No. 969
ALSATIAN "ULRICA OF BRITTAS" - Large

Designer:	Arthur Gredington
Height:	5 ¾", 14.6 cm
Colours:	Black and light brown - gloss; matt
Issued:	1. 1942-1994
	2. 1970-1994

Description	U.K. £	U.S. $	Can. $
1. Gloss	45.00	90.00	125.00
2. Matt	40.00	80.00	100.00

Note: For small size see no. 1762.

Model No. 970
BULL TERRIER "ROMANY RHINESTONE" - Large

Designer:	Arthur Gredington
Height:	6 ½", 16.5 cm
Colours:	1. Brindle and white - gloss
	2. White - gloss; matt
Issued:	1. Gloss - 1942-1975
	2a. Gloss - 1942-1994
	2b. Matt - 1987-1994

Colourway	U.K. £	U.S. $	Can. $
1. Brindle/white	175.00	300.00	425.00
2a. White - gloss	45.00	85.00	125.00
2b. White - matt	45.00	85.00	125.00

Model No. 971
SEALYHAM "FORESTEDGE FOXGLOVE"

Designer:	Arthur Gredington
Height:	4 ¼", 10.8 cm
Colours:	White - gloss
Issued:	1942-1967

Description	U.K. £	U.S. $	Can. $
Gloss	125.00	225.00	325.00

Model No. 972
GREYHOUND "JOVIAL ROGER"

Designer:	Arthur Gredington
Height:	6", 15.0 cm
Colours:	Light sandy brown - gloss; matt
Issued:	1. Gloss - 1942-1990
	2. Matt - 1970-1990

Description	U.K. £	U.S. $	Can. $
1. Gloss	55.00	95.00	135.00
2. Matt	45.00	85.00	125.00

Model No. 973
ENGLISH SETTER "BAYLDONE BARONET"

Designer:	Arthur Gredington
Height:	5 ½", 14.0 cm
Colours:	Speckled grey - gloss; matt
Issued:	1. Gloss - 1942-1989
	2. Matt - 1987-1989

Description	U.K. £	U.S. $	Can. $
1. Gloss	45.00	85.00	125.00
2. Matt	40.00	75.00	100.00

Model No. 1002
PUPPIT DOG

Designer:	Arthur Gredington
Height:	4 ¾", 12.1 cm
Colours:	White with black markings - gloss
Issued:	1944-1969
Series:	Fun Models

Description	U.K. £	U.S. $	Can. $
Gloss	60.00	100.00	150.00

Model No. 1054
SPANIEL HOLDING "MY PLATE"

Designer:	Arthur Gredington	
Height:	4 ¼", 12.1 cm	
Colours:	White and brown - gloss	
Issued:	1947-1967	
Series:	Fun Models	

Description	U.K. £	U.S. $	Can. $
Gloss	85.00	135.00	200.00

Model No. 1055A
CAIRN TERRIER
First Version - With ball on left leg

Designer:	Arthur Gredington
Height:	4", 10.1 cm
Colours:	Beige with brown "stripes," red ball - gloss
Issued:	1946-1969

Description	U.K. £	U.S. $	Can. $
With ball	85.00	200.00	275.00

Note: Also found with ball on right leg.

Model No. 1055B
CAIRN TERRIER
Second Version - Without ball

Designer:	Arthur Gredington
Height:	4", 10.1 cm
Colours:	Beige with brown "stripes" - gloss
Issued:	1946-1969

Description	U.K. £	U.S. $	Can. $
Without ball	100.00	225.00	300.00

Model No. 1057
SPANIEL - Running
Designer: Arthur Gredington
Height: 3 ¾", 9.5 cm
Colours: White with golden tan patches - gloss
Issued: 1946-1967

Description	U.K. £	U.S. $	Can. $
Gloss	60.00	135.00	175.00

Model No. 1058
DOG WITH COLLAR "SCAMP"
Designer: Arthur Gredington
Height: 4 ½", 11.9 cm
Colours: Tan - gloss
Issued: 1948-1973
Seies: Fun Models

Description	U.K. £	U.S. $	Can. $
Gloss	55.00	85.00	150.00

Model No. 1059
PEKINESE - Begging
Designer: Arthur Gredington
Height: 4 ¼", 10.8 cm
Colours: Golden tan - gloss
Issued: 1946-1967

Description	U.K. £	U.S. $	Can. $
Gloss	60.00	135.00	175.00

Model No. 1060
RED SETTER - Lying
Designer: Arthur Gredington
Height: 3", 7.6 cm
Colours: Deep red brown - gloss
Issued: 1946-1973

Description	U.K. £	U.S. $	Can. $
Gloss	60.00	135.00	175.00

Model No. 1061
TERRIER - Lying

Designer:	Arthur Gredington
Height:	2", 5.0 cm
Colours:	White with light tan patches - gloss
Issued:	1946-1973

Description	U.K. £	U.S. $	Can. $
Gloss	95.00	165.00	225.00

Model No. 1062
TERRIER- Walking

Designer:	Arthur Gredington
Height:	4", 10.1 cm
Colours:	White with light tan and black patches - gloss
Issued:	1946-1973

Description	U.K. £	U.S. $	Can. $
Gloss	60.00	135.00	175.00

Model No. 1088
COMICAL DACHSHUND

Designer:	Miss Jones
Height:	3 ½", 8.9 cm
Colours:	White and brown - gloss
Issued:	1947-1973
Series:	Fun Models

Description	U.K. £	U.S. $	Can. $
Gloss	55.00	95.00	150.00

Model No. 1202
BOXER "BLUE MOUNTAIN GRETA" - Large

Designer:	Arthur Gredington
Height:	5 ½", 14.0 cm
Colours:	1. Brindle - gloss; matt
	2. Tan - gloss
Issued:	1a. Gloss - 1950-1989
	1b. Matt - 1987-1989
	2. Gloss - 1973-1975

Colourway	U.K. £	U.S. $	Can. $
1a. Brindle - gloss	85.00	150.00	200.00
1b. Brindle - matt	50.00	85.00	135.00
2. Tan - gloss	75.00	125.00	175.00

Model No. 1220
ENGLISH SETTER

Designer:	Arthur Gredington
Height:	8", 20.3 cm
Colours:	Speckled grey - gloss
Issued:	1951-1973

Description	U.K. £	U.S. $	Can. $
Gloss	300.00	600.00	700.00

Model No. 1239
DOG WITH RUFF - Begging

Designer:	Arthur Gredington
Height:	2 ½", 6.4 cm
Colours:	White and light tan - gloss
Issued:	1952-1967

Description	U.K. £	U.S. $	Can. $
Gloss	45.00	85.00	125.00

Note: Originally issued in combination as model no. 1086 "Clown and Dog."

Model No. 1240
DOG - Seated

Designer:	Arthur Gredington
Height:	2", 5.0 cm
Colours:	White and light tan - gloss
Issued:	1952-1952

Description	U.K. £	U.S. $	Can. $
Gloss	45.00	85.00	125.00

Note: Originally produced in combination as model no. 1096 "Sportsman."

Model No. 1241
DOG - Howling

Designer:	Arthur Gredington
Height:	1 ¼", 3.2 cm
Colours:	White and light tan - gloss
Issued:	1952-1952

Description	U.K. £	U.S. $	Can. $
Gloss	35.00	70.00	100.00

Note: Originally produced in combination as model no. 909 "Puppy Love" (Hummel 1).

Model No. 1242
DOG - Barking

Designer:	Arthur Gredington
Height:	1 ¼", 3.2 cm
Colours:	White and light tan - gloss
Issued:	1952-1952

Description	U.K. £	U.S. $	Can. $
Gloss	35.00	75.00	100.00

Note: Originally issued in combination as model no. 906 "Strolling Along" (Hummel 5).

Model No. 1294
POODLE "EBONIT AV BARBETT"

Designer:	Arthur Gredington	
Height:	5 ¾", 14.0 cm	
Colours:	1.	Black - gloss; matt
	2.	White - gloss
Issued:	1.	1953-1967
	2.	1953-1967

Colourway	U.K. £	U.S. $	Can. $
1a. Black - gloss	250.00	400.00	600.00
1b. Black - matt	200.00	350.00	500.00
2. White- gloss	275.00	450.00	675.00

Model No. 1299A
CORGI "BLACK PRINCE" - Large

Designer:	Arthur Gredington
Height:	5 ½", 14.0 cm
Colours:	Black, tan and white - gloss
Issued:	1953-1982
Varieties:	1299B

Description	U.K. £	U.S. $	Can. $
Gloss	65.00	125.00	175.00

Note: For small size see no. 1736.

Model No. 1299B
CORGI - Large

Designer:	Arthur Gredington	
Height:	5 ½", 14.0 cm	
Colours:	1.	Golden brown - gloss
	2.	Golden brown - matt
Issued:	1.	1953-1994
	2.	1987-1994
Varieties:	1299A	

Description	U.K. £	U.S. $	Can. $
1. Gloss	35.00	80.00	125.00
2. Matt	30.00	75.00	100.00

Note: For small size see no. 1736.

Model No. 1378/1/2/3/4/5/6
OLD ENGLISH DOGS - Left and right facing pairs

Designer: Unknown   Series: Mantelpiece Dogs

Colourway	Height	Issued	U.K. £	Price U.S. $	Can. $
1. Red and gold - gloss	13 ¼", 33.6 cm	1955-1973	100.00	175.00	275.00
2. White and gold - gloss	13 ¼", 33.6 cm	1955-1976	75.00	125.00	175.00
3. Red and gold - gloss	11 ½", 29.2 cm	1955-1972	90.00	150.00	225.00
4. White and gold - gloss	11 ½", 29.2 cm	1955-1972	65.00	100.00	140.00
5. Red and gold - gloss	10", 25.4 cm	1955-1973	85.00	135.00	200.00
6. White and gold - gloss	10", 25.4 cm	1955-1989	55.00	85.00	115.00
7. Red and gold - gloss	9", 22.9 cm	1955-1973	80.00	125.00	175.00
8. White and gold - gloss					
a. Original issue	9", 22.9 cm	1955-1989	48.00	75.00	105.00
b. Reissued	9", 22.9 cm	1999-Current	48.00	N/A	N/A
9. Red and gold - gloss	7 ½", 19.1 cm	1955-1973	75.00	125.00	175.00
10. White and gold - gloss	7 ½", 19.1 cm	1955-1989	37.00	55.00	75.00
11. Red and gold - gloss	5 ½", 14.0 cm	1955-1973	65.00	100.00	160.00
12. White and gold - gloss					
a. Original issue	5 ½", 14.0 cm	1955-1989	31.00	45.00	65.00
b. Reissued	5 ½", 14.0 cm	1999-Current	31.00	N/A	N/A
13. Red and gold - gloss	3 ½", 8.9 cm	1955-1973	55.00	90.00	130.00
14. White and gold - gloss					
a. Original issue	3 ½", 8.9 cm	1955-1989	21.00	30.00	40.00
b. Reissued	3 ½", 8.9 cm	1999-Current	21.00	N/A	N/A

Note: Transferred to the Royal Doulton backstamp (DA89-98) in 1989. Three sizes (1378/4/6/7, in the white and gold - gloss colourway) reverted to the Beswick backstamp in September 1999.
Note: Also seen in Opaque white glaze.

Model No. 1386

POODLE

Designer: Arthur Gredington
Height: 3 ½", 8.9 cm

Colourway	Issued	U.K. £	Price U.S. $	Can. $
1. Black - gloss	1955-1990	25.00	45.00	60.00
2. Black - matt	1988-1989	25.00	45.00	60.00
3. Brown - gloss	1953-1973	50.00	85.00	115.00
4. White - gloss	1955-1990	25.00	45.00	60.00
5. White - matt	1984-1989	25.00	45.00	60.00

Model No. 1460
DACHSHUND - Seated

Designer: Arthur Gredington
Height: 2 ¾", 7.0 cm
Colours: 1.   Black and tan - gloss or matt
           2.   Tan - gloss or matt
Issued: 1a. Gloss - 1956 to the present
          1b. Matt - 1984-1989
          2a. Gloss - 1956-1990
          2b. Matt - 1984-1990

Colourway	U.K. £	U.S. $	Can. $
1a. Black/tan - gloss	15.00	N/A	N/A
1b. Black/tan - matt	20.00	40.00	50.00
2a. Tan - gloss	25.00	40.00	50.00
2b. Tan - matt	20.00	40.00	50.00

Model No. 1461
DACHSHUND - Begging

Designer: Arthur Gredington
Height: 4", 10.1 cm
Colours: 1.   Tan - gloss
           2.   Black and tan - gloss
Issued: 1.   1957-1975
          2.   1957-1980

Colourway	U.K. £	U.S. $	Can. $
1. Tan	50.00	85.00	125.00
2. Black and tan	50.00	85.00	125.00

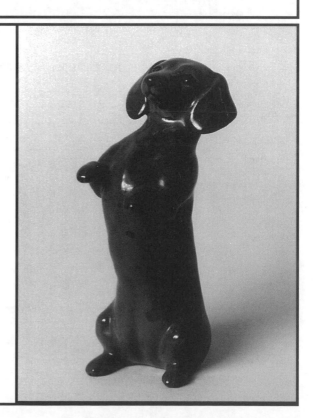

Model No. 1548

LABRADOR "SOLOMON OF WENDOVER"- Large

Designer: Arthur Gredington
Height: 5 ½", 14.0 cm

| | | | Price | |
Colourway	Issued	U.K. £	U.S. $	Can. $
1. Black - gloss	1958-1994	40.00	70.00	95.00
2. Black - matt	1987-1994	35.00	65.00	90.00
3. Golden yellow - gloss	1958-1994	40.00	70.00	95.00
4. Golden yellow - matt	1970-1994	35.00	65.00	90.00

Note: For small size see no. 1956.

Model No. 1731
BULLDOG "BOSUN" - Small

Designer:	Unknown
Height:	2 ½", 6.4 cm
Colours:	Tan and white - gloss; matt
Issued:	1. Gloss - 1960-1997
	2. Matt - 1984-1989

Description	U.K. £	U.S. $	Can. $
1. Gloss	15.00	30.00	45.00
2. Matt	20.00	40.00	60.00

Note: For large size see no. 965.

Model No. 1736
CORGI - Small

Designer:	Unknown
Height:	2 ¾", 7.0 cm
Colours:	Golden brown - gloss; matt
Issued:	1. Gloss - 1961-1996
	2. Matt - 1984-1989

Description	U.K. £	U.S. $	Can. $
1. Gloss	20.00	30.00	45.00
2. Matt	20.00	30.00	45.00

Note: For large size see no. 1299.

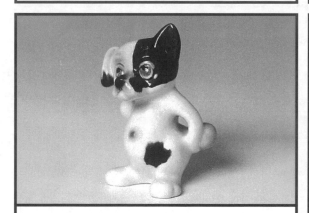

Model No. 1738
PUP WITH BONE

Designer:	Harry Sales
Height:	3 ¾", 9.5 cm
Colours:	White - gloss
Issued:	1961-1967
Series:	Fun Models

Description	U.K. £	U.S. $	Can. $
Gloss	65.00	125.00	175.00

Model No. 1753
BULL TERRIER - Small

Designer:	Arthur Gredington
Height:	3 ½", 8.9 cm
Colours:	White with bright tan patches - gloss
Issued:	1961-1971

Description	U.K. £	U.S. $	Can. $
Gloss	125.00	250.00	350.00

Note: For large size see no. 970.

Model No. 1754

COCKER SPANIEL

Designer: Arthur Gredington
Height: 3", 7.6 cm

Colourway	Issued	U.K. £	Price U.S. $	Can. $
1. Black and white - gloss	1961-1996	15.00	30.00	45.00
2. Black and white - matt	1984-1989	15.00	30.00	45.00
3. Liver and white - gloss	1961-1997	15.00	30.00	45.00
4. Liver and white - matt	1984-1989	15.00	30.00	45.00

Model No. 1762A
ALSATIAN - Small
First Version - 'Wolf-like,' tail not fully attached to leg

Designer: Mr. Garbet
Height: 3 ¼", 8.3 cm
Colours: Black and cream - gloss
Issued: 1961-1963

Description	U.K. £	U.S. $	Can. $
Gloss	45.00	75.00	115.00

Model No. 1762B
ALSATIAN - Small
Second Version - 'Fine head,' tail attached to leg

Designer: Arthur Gredington
Height: 3 ¼", 8.3 cm
Colours: Black and cream - gloss
Issued: 1963-1966

Description	U.K. £	U.S. $	Can. $
Gloss	40.00	65.00	90.00

Note: For large size see no. 969.

Model No. 1763
DALMATION - Small

Designer: Mr. Garbet
Height: 3 ½", 8.9 cm
Colours: White with black spots - gloss; matt
Issued: 1. Gloss - 1961 to the present
            2. Matt - 1984-1989

Description	U.K. £	U.S. $	Can. $
1. Gloss	15.00	N/A	N/A
2. Matt	15.00	30.00	45.00

Note: For large size see no. 961.

Model No. 1786A
WHIPPET "WINGED FOOT MARKSMAN OF ALLWAYS"
First Version - Tail curls between legs

Designer: Arthur Gredington
Height: 4 ½", 11.9 cm
Colours: Light sandy brown - gloss
Issued: 1961-Unknown

Description	U.K. £	U.S. $	Can. $
Gloss	125.00	225.00	350.00

Model No. 1786B
WHIPPET "WINGED FOOT MARKSMAN
OF ALLWAYS"
Second Version - Tail attached to leg

Designer: Arthur Gredington
Height: 4 ½", 11.9 cm
Colours: Light sandy brown - gloss; matt
Issued: 1. Gloss - Unknown-1989
             2. Matt - 1987-1989

Description	U.K. £	U.S. $	Can. $
1. Gloss	65.00	100.00	165.00
2. Matt	65.00	100.00	165.00

Model No. 1791
COLLIE "LOCHINVAR OF LADYPARK" - Large

Designer: Arthur Gredington
Height: 5 ¾", 14.6 cm
Colours: Golden brown and white - gloss; matt
Issued: 1. Gloss - 1961-1994
             2. Matt - 1970-1994

Description	U.K. £	U.S. $	Can. $
1. Gloss	45.00	85.00	125.00
2. Matt	40.00	75.00	100.00

Note: For small size see no. 1814.

Model No. 1792
SHEEPDOG - Large

Designer: Arthur Gredington
Height: 5 ½", 14.0 cm
Colours: Black and white - gloss; matt
Issued: 1. Gloss - 1961-1994
             2. Matt - 1987-1994

Description	U.K. £	U.S. $	Can. $
1. Gloss	50.00	85.00	125.00
2. Matt	45.00	75.00	100.00

Note: For small size see no. 1854.

Model No. 1814
COLLIE - Small

Designer: Arthur Gredington
Height: 3 ¼", 8.3 cm
Colours: Golden brown and white - gloss
Issued: 1962-1975

Description	U.K. £	U.S. $	Can. $
Gloss	65.00	100.00	150.00

Note: For large size see no. 1791.

Model No. 1824
DOG - Singing

Designer:	Albert Hallam
Height:	1 ½", 3.8 cm
Colours:	Tan - gloss
Issued:	1962-1971
Series:	Bedtime Chorus

Description	U.K. £	U.S. $	Can. $
Gloss	65.00	100.00	150.00

Model No. 1852
BOXER - Small

Designer:	Arthur Gredington
Height:	3", 7.6 cm
Colours:	Tan - gloss
Issued:	1962-1975

Description	U.K. £	U.S. $	Can. $
Gloss	45.00	75.00	100.00

Note: For large size see no. 1202.

Model No. 1854
SHEEPDOG - Small

Designer:	Arthur Gredington
Height:	3", 7.6 cm
Colours:	Black and white - gloss; matt
Issued:	1. Gloss - 1962 to the present
	2. Matt - 1987-1989

Description	U.K. £	U.S. $	Can. $
1. Gloss	16.50	N/A	N/A
2. Matt	15.00	25.00	40.00

Note: For large size see no. 1792.

Model No. 1855
RETRIEVER

Designer:	Arthur Gredington
Height:	3 ¼", 8.3 cm
Colours:	1. Black - gloss
	2. Light golden brown - gloss
Issued:	1962-1975

Colourway	U.K. £	U.S. $	Can. $
1. Black	75.00	125.00	175.00
2. Light brown	50.00	85.00	125.00

Model No. 1871
POODLE

Designer:	Arthur Gredington
Height:	4 ¼", 10.8 cm
Colours:	White, red bow - gloss
Issued:	1963-1967
Series:	Advertising ware "Dubonnet"

Description	U.K. £	U.S. $	Can. $
Gloss	75.00	125.00	185.00

Model No. 1872
BULLDOG

Designer:	Arthur Gredington
Height:	3 ¾", 9.5 cm
Colours:	White, pale tan ear and around eyes - gloss
Issued:	1963-1967
Series:	Advertising ware "Dubonnet"

Description	U.K. £	U.S. $	Can. $
Gloss	75.00	125.00	185.00

Model No. 1918
ASHTRAY WITH DOG

Designer:	Albert Hallam
Height:	11" x 8", 27.9 x 20.3 cm
Colours:	1. Pale blue bowl with animal - gloss
	2. Pale brown bowl with animal - gloss
Issued:	1963-1971

Colourway	U.K. £	U.S. $	Can. $
1. Pale blue	100.00	165.00	225.00
2. Pale brown	65.00	100.00	150.00

Note: This ashtray was available with any small dog attached to it. Model shown is no. 1762.

Model No. 1932
DACHSHUND - Ashtray

Designer:	Albert Hallam
Height:	8" x 3", 20.3 x 7.6 cm
Colours:	1. Black and tan dog on charcoal base - gloss
	2. Tan dog on charcoal base - gloss
Issued:	1962-1969

Colourway	U.K. £	U.S. $	Can. $
1. Black/tan	65.00	100.00	150.00
2. Tan	65.00	100.00	150.00

Model No. 1933A
BEAGLE "WENDOVER BILLY" - Large

Designer: Arthur Gredington
Height: 5 ½", 14.0 cm
Colours: Black, tan and white - gloss or matt
Issued: 1. 1964-1989
2. 1987-1989
Varieties: 1933B

Description	U.K. £	U.S. $	Can. $
1. Gloss	50.00	85.00	125.00
2. Matt	40.00	70.00	100.00

Note: For small size see no. 1939.

Model No. 1933B
BEAGLE "WENDOVER BILLY" - on wooden plinth

Designer: Arthur Gredington
Height: 6", 15.0 cm
Colours: Black, tan and white - matt
Issued: 1970-1989
Series: Connoisseur Dogs
Varieties: 1933A

Description	U.K. £	U.S. $	Can. $
Matt	55.00	100.00	135.00

Model No. 1939
BEAGLE "WENDOVER BILLY" - Small

Designer: Arthur Gredington
Height: 3", 7.6 cm
Colours: Black, tan and white - gloss or matt
Issued: 1. Gloss - 1964 to the present
2. Matt - 1984-1989

Description	U.K. £	U.S. $	Can. $
1. Gloss	15.00	N/A	N/A
2. Matt	15.00	25.00	40.00

Note: For large size see no. 1933A.

Model No. 1944
YORKSHIRE TERRIER - Lying

Designer: Arthur Gredington
Height: 3 ½", 8.9 cm
Colours: Grey and tan - gloss
Issued: 1964-1976

Description	U.K. £	U.S. $	Can. $
Gloss	50.00	85.00	135.00

Model No. 1956

LABRADOR - Small

Designer: Arthur Gredington
Height: 3 ¼″, 8.3 cm

			Price	
Colourway	Issued	U.K. £	U.S. $	Can. $
1. Black - gloss	1964 to the present	14.50	N/A	N/A
2. Black - matt	1984-1989	15.00	25.00	35.00
3. Golden brown - gloss	1964 to the present	14.50	N/A	N/A
4. Golden brown - matt	1984-1989	15.00	25.00	35.00

Note: For large size see no. 1548.

Model No. 1982A
STAFFORDSHIRE BULL TERRIER
"BANDITS BRINTIGA"

Designer: Arthur Gredington
Height: 4 ¾", 12.1 cm
Colours: Dark brindle - gloss
Issued: 1964-1969

Description	U.K. £	U.S. $	Can. $
Gloss	250.00	400.00	600.00

Model No. 1982B
STAFFORDSHIRE BULL TERRIER

Designer: Arthur Gredington
Height: 4 ¾", 12.1 cm
Colours: Tan and white - gloss
Issued: 1964-1969

Description	U.K. £	U.S. $	Can. $
Gloss	250.00	400.00	600.00

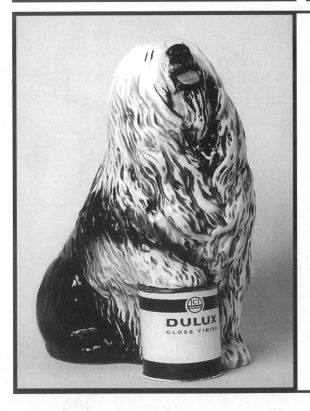

Model No. 1990
OLD ENGLISH SHEEPDOG

Designer: Mr. Mortimer
Height: 12 ½", 31.7 cm
Colours: Black, grey and white - gloss
Issued: 1964-1970
Series: Advertising ware "Dulux"

Description	U.K. £	U.S. $	Can. $
Gloss	400.00	700.00	1,000.00

Model No. 1997
PUG "CUTMIL CUTIE" - Large

Designer: Arthur Gredington
Height: 4 ½", 11.9 cm
Colours: Light sandy brown - gloss or matt
Issued: 1. Gloss - 1965-1982
2. Matt - 1970-1982

Description	U.K. £	U.S. $	Can. $
1. Gloss	60.00	150.00	225.00
2. Matt	50.00	125.00	200.00

Model No. 1998
PUG - Small

Designer: Arthur Gredington
Height: 2 ½", 6.4 cm
Colours: Light sandy brown - gloss or matt
Issued: 1. Gloss - 1966-1990
2. Mattt - 1984-1989

Description	U.K. £	U.S. $	Can. $
1. Gloss	25.00	35.00	60.00
2. Matt	25.00	35.00	60.00

Note: This model has also been seen with head forward.

Model No. 2023
JACK RUSSELL TERRIER - Large

Designer: Arthur Gredington
Height: 5", 12.7 cm
Colours: White body, tan/black head - gloss or matt
Issued: 1. Gloss - 1965-1994
2. Matt - 1987-1994

Description	U.K. £	U.S. $	Can. $
1. Gloss	45.00	85.00	125.00
2. Matt	40.00	75.00	100.00

Note: For small size see no. 2109.

Model No. 2037
SCOTTIE

Designer: Arthur Gredington
Height: 4 ½", 11.9 cm
Colours: Black - gloss or matt
Issued: 1. Gloss - 1965-1990
2. Matt - 1987-1989

Description	U.K. £	U.S. $	Can. $
1. Gloss	45.00	85.00	125.00
2. Matt	40.00	75.00	100.00

Model No. 2038
WEST HIGHLAND TERRIER

Designer:	Arthur Gredington
Height:	4 ¾", 12.1 cm
Colours:	White - gloss or matt
Issued:	1. Gloss - 1965-1994
	2. Matt - 1987-1989

Description	U.K. £	U.S. $	Can. $
1. Gloss	50.00	85.00	125.00
2. Matt	45.00	75.00	100.00

Model No. 2045A
BASSET HOUND "FOCHNO TRINKET"

Designer:	Arthur Gredington
Height:	5", 12.7 cm
Colours:	Black, white and tan - gloss or matt
Issued:	1. Gloss - 1965-1994
	2. Matt - 1987-1994

Description	U.K. £	U.S. $	Can. $
1. Gloss	50.00	85.00	125.00
2. Matt	45.00	75.00	100.00

Model No. 2045B
BASSET HOUND "FOCHNO TRINKET"
- on wooden plinth

Designer:	Arthur Gredington
Height:	6", 15.0 cm
Colours:	Black, white and tan - matt
Issued:	1970-1989
Series:	Connoisseur Dogs

Description	U.K. £	U.S. $	Can. $
Matt	65.00	100.00	150.00

Model No. 2102
YORKSHIRE TERRIER LAUGHING

Designer:	Albert Hallam
Height:	3", 7.6 cm
Colours:	Tan - gloss
Issued:	1967-1972
Series:	Fun Models

Description	U.K. £	U.S. $	Can. $
Gloss	65.00	100.00	150.00

Model No. 2107A
KING CHARLES SPANIEL "BLENHEIM"

Designer:	Arthur Gredington
Height:	5 ¼", 13.3 cm
Colours:	Tan and white - gloss or matt
Issued:	1. Gloss - 1967-1994
	2. Matt - 1987-1994

Description	U.K. £	U.S. $	Can. $
1. Gloss	50.00	85.00	125.00
2. Matt	45.00	75.00	100.00

Model No. 2107B
KING CHARLES SPANIEL
"JOSEPHINE OF BLAGREAVES"

Designer:	Arthur Gredington
Height:	5 ¼", 13.3 cm
Colours:	Black, tan and white - gloss or matt
Issued:	1. Gloss - 1967-1994
	2. Matt - 1987-1994

Description	U.K. £	U.S. $	Can. $
1. Gloss	50.00	85.00	125.00
2. Matt	45.00	75.00	100.00

Model No. 2108
POODLE "IVANOLA GOLD DIGGER"

Designer:	Arthur Gredington
Height:	5 ¾", 14.6 cm
Colours:	White, blue bow - gloss
Issued:	1967-1971

Description	U.K. £	U.S. $	Can. $
Gloss	225.00	375.00	525.00

Model No. 2109
JACK RUSSELL TERRIER - Small

Designer:	Arthur Gredington and
	Albert Hallam
Height:	2 ½", 6.4 cm
Colours:	White with tan head - gloss or matt
Issued:	1. Gloss - 1967 to the present
	2. Matt - 1984-1989

Description	U.K. £	U.S. $	Can. $
1. Gloss	15.00	N/A	N/A
2. Matt	15.00	25.00	40.00

Note: For large size see no. 2023.

Model No. 2112
CAIRN TERRIER

Designer:	Arthur Gredington and Albert Hallam
Height:	2 ¾", 7.0 cm
Colours:	Dark cream - gloss or matt
Issued:	1. Gloss - 1967-1995
	2. Matt - 1984-1989

Description	U.K. £	U.S. $	Can. $
1. Gloss	20.00	35.00	50.00
2. Matt	15.00	30.00	45.00

Model No. 2130
DOG PRAYING

Designer:	Albert Hallam
Height:	3", 7.6 cm
Colours:	Blue - gloss
Issued:	1967-1972
Series:	Fun Models

Description	U.K. £	U.S. $	Can. $
Gloss	50.00	85.00	125.00

Model No. 2221
ST. BERNARD "CORNA GARTH STROLLER"

Designer:	Albert Hallam
Height:	5 ½", 14.0 cm
Colours:	Dark brown, tan and white - gloss or matt
Issued:	1. Gloss - 1968-1989
	2. Matt - 1970-1989

Description	U.K. £	U.S. $	Can. $
1. Gloss	60.00	100.00	150.00
2. Matt	60.00	100.00	150.00

Model No. 2232
OLD ENGLISH SHEEPDOG

Designer:	Albert Hallam
Height:	11 ½", 29.2 cm
Colours:	Grey and white - gloss
Issued:	1968-1989
Series:	Fireside Models

Description	U.K. £	U.S. $	Can. $
Gloss	100.00	175.00	250.00

Note: Transferred to the R.D. backstamp (DA84) 08/89.

Model No. 2235
BASSETHOUND - Wall Plaque

Designer:	Graham Tongue
Height:	6 ¼" x 4 ½", 15.9 x 11.9 cm (concave)
Colours:	Tan and white head
	black satin surround - gloss
Issued:	1968-Unknown
Series:	Wall Plaques

Description	U.K. £	U.S. $	Can. $
Gloss	75.00	125.00	175.00

Model No. 2262
FOXHOUND
Second Version - Thin legs and tail

Designer:	Graham Tongue
Height:	2 ½", 6.4 cm
Colours:	White, tan and black - gloss or matt
Issued:	1. Gloss - 1969-1997
	2. Matt - 1984-1989
Varieties:	941

Description	U.K. £	U.S. $	Can. $
1. Gloss	15.00	25.00	40.00
2. Matt	15.00	25.00	40.00

Model No. 2263
FOXHOUND
Second Version - Thin legs and tail

Designer:	Graham Tongue
Height:	3", 7.6 cm
Colours:	White, tan and black - gloss or matt
Issued:	1. Gloss - 1969-1997
	2. Matt - 1984-1989
Varieties:	942

Description	U.K. £	U.S. $	Can. $
1. Gloss	15.00	25.00	40.00
2. Matt	15.00	25.00	40.00

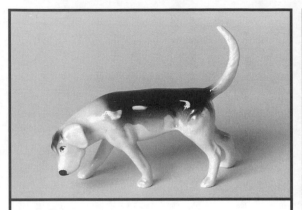

Model No. 2264
FOXHOUND
Second Version - Thin legs and tail

Designer:	Graham Tongue
Height:	3", 7.6 cm
Colours:	White, tan and black - gloss or matt
Issued:	1. Gloss - 1969-1997
	2. Matt - 1984-1989
Varieties:	944

Description	U.K. £	U.S. $	Can. $
1. Gloss	15.00	25.00	40.00
2. Matt	15.00	25.00	40.00

Model No. 2265
FOXHOUND
Second Version - Thin legs and tail

Designer:	Graham Tongue
Height:	2 ¾", 7.0 cm
Colours:	White, tan and black - gloss or matt
Issued:	1. Gloss - 1969-1997
	2. Matt - 1984-1989
Varieties:	943

Description	U.K. £	U.S. $	Can. $
1. Gloss	15.00	25.00	40.00
2. Matt	15.00	25.00	40.00

Model No. 2268
POODLE - Wall Plaque

Designer:	Graham Tongue
Height:	6" x 4 ½", 15.9 x 11.9 cm (Concave)
Colours:	Unknown - gloss
Issued:	1968-Unknown
Series:	Wall Plaques

Description	U.K. £	U.S. $	Can. $
Gloss	95.00	175.00	250.00

Model No. 2271
DALMATIAN

Designer:	Graham Tongue
Height:	13 ¾", 34.9 cm
Colours:	White with black spots - gloss
Issued:	1969-1989
Series:	Fireside Models

Description	U.K. £	U.S. $	Can. $
Gloss	175.00	300.00	450.00

Note: Transferred to R.D.backstamp (DA85) 08/89.

Model No. 2285
AFGHAN HOUND "HAJUBAH OF DAVIEN"

Designer: Graham Tongue
Height: 5 ½", 14.0 cm
Colours: Golden and dark brown - gloss or matt
Issued: 1. Gloss - 1969-1994
2. Matt - 1987-1989

Description	U.K. £	U.S. $	Can. $
1. Gloss	40.00	75.00	100.00
2. Matt	35.00	60.00	90.00

Model No. 2286
DACHSHUND

Designer: Albert Hallam
Height: 10 ½", 26.7 cm
Colours: 1. Black and tan - gloss
2. Tan - gloss
Issued: 1. 1969-1981
2. 1969-1981
Series: Fireside Models

Colourway	U.K. £	U.S. $	Can. $
1. Black/tan	100.00	175.00	250.00
2. Tan	100.00	175.00	250.00

Model No. 2287
GOLDEN RETRIEVER "CABUS CADET"

Designer: Graham Tongue
Height: 5 ½", 14.0 cm
Colours: Light golden brown - gloss or matt
Issued: 1. Gloss - 1969-1994
2. Matt - 1987-1994

Description	U.K. £	U.S. $	Can. $
1. Gloss	45.00	85.00	125.00
2. Matt	40.00	75.00	100.00

Model No. 2299
DOBERMAN PINSCHER "ANNASTOCK LANCE"

Designer: Graham Tongue
Height: 5 ¾", 14.6 cm
Colours: Black and tan - gloss or matt
Issued: 1. Gloss - 1970-1994
2. Matt - 1987-1994

Description	U.K. £	U.S. $	Can. $
1. Gloss	45.00	85.00	125.00
2. Matt	40.00	75.00	100.00

Model No. 2300
BEAGLE

Designer:	Albert Hallam
Height:	12 ¾", 32.4 cm
Colours:	Black, tan and white - gloss
Issued:	1969-1983
Series:	Fireside Models

Description	U.K. £	U.S. $	Can. $
Gloss	150.00	250.00	350.00

Model No. 2314
LABRADOR

Designer:	Graham Tongue
Height:	13 ½", 34.3 cm
Colours:	1. Black - gloss
	2. Golden brown - gloss
Issued:	1970-1989
Series:	Fireside Models

Colourway	U.K. £	U.S. $	Can. $
1. Black	95.00	150.00	225.00
2. Golden brown	110.00	175.00	250.00

Note: Transferred to R.D. backstamp (DA 86) 08/89.

Model No. 2339
POODLE

Designer:	Graham Tongue
Height:	5 ¾", 14.6 cm
Colours:	1. Black - gloss
	2. White - gloss
Issued:	1971-1983

Colourway	U.K. £	U.S. $	Can. $
1. Black	50.00	85.00	125.00
2. White	50.00	85.00	125.00

Model No. 2377
YORKSHIRE TERRIER

Designer:	Graham Tongue
Height:	10 ¼", 26.0 cm
Colours:	Grey and tan - gloss
Issued:	1971-1989
Series:	Fireside Models

Description	U.K. £	U.S. $	Can. $
Gloss	125.00	225.00	325.00

Note: Transferred to R.D. backstamp (DA87) 08/89.

Model No. 2410
ALSATIAN

Designer:	Graham Tongue
Height:	14", 35.5 cm
Colours:	Dark and sandy brown - gloss
Issued:	1972-1989
Series:	Fireside Models

Description	U.K. £	U.S. $	Can. $
Gloss	125.00	225.00	325.00

Note: Transferred to R.D. backstamp (DA88) 08/89.

Model No. 2448
LAKELAND TERRIER

Designer:	Albert Hallam	
Height:	3 ¼", 8.3 cm	
Colours:	Pale tan and black - gloss or matt	
Issued:	1.	Gloss - 1973-1998
	2.	Matt - 1984-1989

Description	U.K. £	U.S. $	Can. $
1. Gloss	15.00	25.00	40.00
2. Matt	15.00	25.00	40.00

Model No. 2454
CHIHUAHUA - Lying on cushion

Designer:	Albert Hallam	
Height:	2 ¾", 7.0 cm	
Colours:	Cream dog, maroon cushion - gloss or matt	
Issued:	1.	Gloss - 1973-1996
	2.	Matt - 1984-1989

Description	U.K. £	U.S. $	Can. $
1. Gloss	17.50	30.00	45.00
2. Matt	17.50	30.00	45.00

Model No. 2581			
COLLIE - on wooden plinth			
Designer:	Graham Tongue		
Height:	8", 20.3 cm		
Colours:	Golden brown and white - matt		
Issued:	1979-1989		
Series:	Connoisseur Dogs		

Description	U.K. £	U.S. $	Can. $
Matt	50.00	85.00	125.00

Note: Transferred to R.D. backstamp (DA24) 08/89.

Model No. 2587			
ALSATIAN - on wooden plinth			
Designer:	Graham Tongue		
Height:	9", 22.9 cm		
Colours:	Dark and sandy brown - matt		
Issued:	1979-1989		
Series:	Connoisseur Dogs		

Description	U.K. £	U.S. $	Can. $
Matt	50.00	85.00	125.00

Note: Transferred to R.D. backstamp (DA26) 08/89.

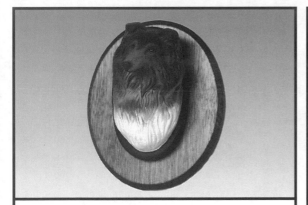

Model No. 2929			
COLLIE - Wall Plaque			
Designer:	Unknown		
Height:	Unknown		
Colours:	Golden brown and white - matt		
Issued:	1986-1989		
Series:	Best of Breed		

Description	U.K. £	U.S. $	Can. $
Matt	95.00	150.00	250.00

Note: Head from model no. 2581 mounted on wood.

Model No. 2932			
ALSATIAN - Wall Plaque			
Designer:	Unknown		
Height:	Unknown		
Colours:	Black and cream - matt		
Issued:	1986-1989		
Series:	Best of Breed		

Description	U.K. £	U.S. $	Can. $
Matt	95.00	150.00	250.00

Note: Head from model no. 2587 mounted on wood.

Model No. 2946
MEAL TIME

Designer:	Unknown
Height:	3 ½", 8.9 cm
Colours:	White and tan - gloss
Issued:	1986-1989
Series:	Playful Puppies

Description	U.K. £	U.S. $	Can. $
Gloss	60.00	100.00	135.00

Note: Taken from Royal Doulton HN 1158.

Model No. 2947
GNAWING

Designer:	Unknown
Height:	4 ¼", 10.8 cm
Colours:	White and tan - gloss
Issued:	1986-1989
Series:	Playful Puppies

Description	U.K. £	U.S. $	Can. $
Gloss	60.00	100.00	135.00

Note: Taken from Royal Doulton HN 1159.

Model No. 2948
PLAY TIME

Designer:	Unknown
Height:	3 ¾", 9.5 cm
Colours:	White and tan - gloss
Issued:	1986-1989
Series:	Playful Puppies

Description	U.K. £	U.S. $	Can. $
Gloss	60.00	100.00	135.00

Note: Taken from Royal Doulton HN 2664.

Model No. 2949
JUGGLING

Designer:	Unknown
Height:	3", 7.6 cm
Colours:	White and tan - gloss
Issued:	1986-1989
Series:	Playful Puppies

Description	U.K. £	U.S. $	Can. $
Gloss	60.00	100.00	135.00

Note: Taken from Royal Doulton HN 1103.

Model No. 2950
NAP TIME

Designer:	Unknown
Height:	4 ½", 11.9 cm
Colours:	White and tan - gloss
Issued:	1986-1989
Series:	Playful Puppies

Description	U.K. £	U.S. $	Can. $
Gloss	60.00	100.00	135.00

Note: Taken from Royal Doulton HN 1099.

Model No. 2951
CAUGHT IT

Designer:	Unknown
Height:	2 ¾", 7.0 cm
Colours:	White and tan - gloss
Issued:	1986-1989
Series:	Playful Puppies

Description	U.K. £	U.S. $	Can. $
Gloss	60.00	100.00	135.00

Note: Taken from Royal Doulton HN 1097.

Model No. 2980
SPANIEL - on plinth

Designer:	Alan Maslankowski
Height:	8 ¼", 21.0 cm
Colours:	See below - matte
Issued:	1987-1989
Series:	Spirited Dogs

Colourway	U.K. £	U.S. $	Can. $
1. Black	60.00	100.00	150.00
2. Black/white	75.00	125.00	175.00
3. Golden	75.00	125.00	175.00
4. Liver/white	75.00	125.00	175.00
5. White	60.00	100.00	150.00

Model No. 2982
PEKINESE - Begging

Designer:	Alan Maslankowski
Height:	5 ½", 14.0 cm
Colours:	Cream - gloss or matt
Issued:	1987-1989
Series:	Good Companions

Description	U.K. £	U.S. $	Can. $
1. Gloss	55.00	100.00	150.00
2. Matt	50.00	100.00	150.00

Note: Transferred to R.D. backstamp (DA113) gloss.

Model No. 2984
NORFOLK TERRIER

Designer:	Alan Maslankowski
Height:	4", 10.1 cm
Colours:	Brown - gloss or matt
Issued:	1987-1989
Series:	Good Companions

Description	U.K. £	U.S. $	Can. $
1. Gloss	60.00	100.00	150.00
2. Matt	60.00	100.00	150.00

Note: Transferred to R.D. backstamp (DA114) gloss.

Model No. 2985
POODLE - on cushion

Designer:	Alan Maslankowski
Height:	5 ½", 14.0 cm
Colours:	White poodle, turquoise cushion - gloss or matt
Issued:	1987-1989
Series:	Good Companions

Description	U.K. £	U.S. $	Can. $
1. Gloss	65.00	100.00	150.00
2. Matt	60.00	100.00	150.00

Note: Transferred to R.D. backstamp (DA115) in gloss.

Model No. 2986

SETTER - on ceramic plinth

Designer: Graham Tongue
Height: 8 ½", 21.6 cm
Series: See below

				Price	
Colourway	Issued	Series	U.K. £	U.S. $	Can. $
1. Black - matt	1987-1989	Spirited Dogs	100.00	175.00	250.00
2. Bronze	1989-1993	Britannia	100.00	175.00	250.00
3. English Setter, white and liver - matt	1987-1989	Spirited Dogs	100.00	175.00	250.00
4. Gordon Setter, black and tan - matt	1988-1989	Spirited Dogs	125.00	200.00	300.00
5. Red Setter, deep red brown - matt	1987-1989	Spirited Dogs	100.00	175.00	250.00
6. White	1987-1989	Spirited Dogs	90.00	150.00	200.00

Model No. 3011
POINTER

Designer:	Graham Tongue	
Height:	8 ½", 21.6 cm	
Colour:	1. Black - matt	
	2. Bronze finish	
	3. White - matt	
	4. White/brown - matt	
Issued:	1. 1987-1989	
	2. 1989-1993	
	3. 1987-1989	
	4. 1987-1989	
Series:	1. Spirited Dogs	2. Britannia
	3. Spirited Dogs	4. Spirited Dogs

Colourway	U.K. £	U.S. $	Can. $
1. Black	75.00	125.00	200.00
2. Bronze finish	75.00	125.00	200.00
3. White	60.00	100.00	150.00
4. White/brown	75.00	125.00	200.00

Note: Transferred to R.D. backstamp (DA110) 08/89 - white/brown in matt.

Model No. 3056
ROTTWEILER

Designer:	Alan Maslankowski	
Height:	5 ¼", 13.3 cm	
Colours:	Black and tan - gloss or matt	
Issued:	1. Gloss - 1988-1989	
	2. Matt - 1988-1989	

Description	U.K. £	U.S. $	Can. $
1. Gloss	60.00	100.00	150.00
2. Matt	60.00	100.00	150.00

Note: Transferred to R.D. backstamp (DA99) in gloss.

Model No. 3058
OLD ENGLISH SHEEP DOG - Walking

Designer:	Warren Platt	
Height:	5 ½", 14.0 cm	
Colours:	Grey and white - gloss or matt	
Issued:	1. 1988-1989 - gloss or matt	
Reissued:	2. 1999 to the present - gloss	

Colourway	U.K. £	U.S. $	Can. $
1. Gloss - Original	37.00	60.00	90.00
2. Gloss - Reissued	37.00	N/A	N/A
3. Matt	60.00	100.00	150.00

Note: Transferred to R.D. backstamp (DA100) in gloss. Reverted to Beswick backstamp 09/99.

Model No. 3060
STAFFORDSHIRE BULL TERRIER

Designer:	Alan Maslankowski
Height:	4", 10.1 cm
Colours:	1. White and tan - gloss or matt
	2. Brindle - gloss or matt
Issued:	1988-1989

Colourway	U.K. £	U.S. $	Can. $
1a. White/tan - gloss	60.00	100.00	150.00
1b. White/tan - matt	60.00	100.00	150.00
2a. Brindle - gloss	60.00	100.00	150.00
2b. Brindle - matt	60.00	100.00	150.00

Note: Transferred to R.D. backstamp (DA101) in gloss.

Model No. 3062A
LABRADOR - on ceramic plinth

Designer:	Alan Maslankowski
Height:	6 ½", 16.5 cm
Colours:	1. Black - matt
	2. Golden - matt
Issued:	1988-1989
Series:	Spirited Dogs
Varieties:	3062B

Colourway	U.K. £	U.S. $	Can. $
1. Black	95.00	150.00	225.00
2. Golden	95.00	150.00	225.00

Note: Transferred to R.D. backstamp (DA111) in golden.

Model No. 3062B
LABRADOR - Standing

Designer:	Alan Maslankowski
Height:	5", 12.7 cm
Colours:	Chocolate brown - gloss
Issued:	1993 in a limited edition of 93
Varieties:	3062A

Description	U.K. £	U.S. $	Can. $
Gloss	135.00	225.00	325.00

Note: Produced for the B.C.C. with a special BCC backstamp.

Model No. 3066
RETRIEVER - on ceramic plinth

Designer:	Graham Tongue	
Height:	7 ½", 19.1 cm	
Colours:	1. Golden - matt	2. Bronze finish
Issued:	1. 1988-1989	2. 1989-1989
Series:	1. Spirited Dogs	2. Britannia

Colourway	U.K. £	U.S. $	Can. $
1. Golden	100.00	175.00	250.00
2. Bronze	100.00	175.00	250.00

Note: Transferred to R.D. backstamp (DA112) in golden.

Model No. 3070
AFGHAN HOUND - Running

Designer:	Alan Maslankowski
Height:	5 ½", 14.0 cm
Colours:	Light brown and cream - gloss or matt
Issued:	1988-1989

Description	U.K. £	U.S. $	Can. $
1. Gloss	75.00	125.00	200.00
2. Matt	75.00	125.00	200.00

Note: Transferred to R.D. backstamp (DA102) in gloss.

Model No. 3073
ALSATIAN - Standing

Designer:	Alan Maslankowski
Height:	5 ¾", 14.6 cm
Colours:	Black and light brown - gloss or matt
Issued:	1. 1988-1989 - gloss or matt
Reissued:	2. 1999 to the present - gloss

Description	U.K. £	U.S. $	Can. $
1 Gloss - Original	38.00	60.00	90.00
2. Gloss - Reissued	38.00	N/A	N/A
3. Matt	60.00	100.00	150.00

Note: Transferred to the R.D. backstamp (DA103) in 1989; reverted to Beswick backstamp 09/99.

Model No. 3080
SHETLAND SHEEPDOG - Seated

Designer:	Alan Maslankowski
Height:	5 ½", 14.0 cm
Colours:	Golden brown and white - gloss or matt
Issued:	1988-1989
Series:	Good Companions

Description	U.K. £	U.S. $	Can. $
1. Gloss	100.00	175.00	235.00
2. Matt	100.00	175.00	235.00

Note: Transferred to R.D. backstamp (DA117) in gloss.

Model No. 3081
BOXER - Standing

Designer:	Alan Maslankowski
Height:	5 ½", 14.0 cm
Colours:	Golden brown and white - gloss or matt
Issued:	1. 1988-1989 - gloss or matt
Reissued:	2. 1999 to the present - gloss

Description	U.K. £	U.S. $	Can. $
1. Gloss - Original	36.00	60.00	90.00
2. Gloss - Reissued	36.00	N/A	N/A
3. Matt	50.00	85.00	135.00

Note: Transferred to the R.D. backstamp (DA104) in 1989; reverted to Beswick backstamp 09/99.

Model No. 3082
CAIRN TERRIER - Standing

Designer: Warren Platt
Height: 4 ¾", 12.1 cm
Colours: Light brown - gloss or matt
Issued: 1988-1989
Series: Good Companions

Description	U.K. £	U.S. $	Can. $
1. Gloss	60.00	100.00	150.00
2. Matt	60.00	100.00	150.00

Note: Transferred to R.D. backstamp (DA118) in gloss.

Model No. 3083
YORKSHIRE TERRIER - Seated

Designer: Warren Platt
Height: 5 ½", 14.0 cm
Colours: Grey and light brown - gloss and matt
Issued: 1988-1989
Series: Good Companions

Description	U.K. £	U.S. $	Can. $
1. Gloss	60.00	100.00	150.00
2. Matt	60.00	100.00	150.00

Note: Transferred to R.D. backstamp (DA119) in gloss.

Model No. 3103
DACHSHUND - Standing

Designer: Alan Maslankowski
Height: 4 ¼", 10.8 cm
Colours: 1. Black and tan - gloss or matt
2. Tan - gloss or matt
Issued: 1987-1989
Series: Good Companions

Colourway	U.K. £	U.S. $	Can. $
1. Black/tan	45.00	75.00	100.00
2. Tan	45.00	75.00	100.00

Note: Transferred to R.D. backstamp (DA116) in gloss.

Model No. 3121
DOBERMAN

Designer: Alan Maslankowski
Height: 5 ¼", 13.3 cm
Colours: Black and tan - gloss or matt
Issued: 1988-1989

Description	U.K. £	U.S. $	Can. $
1. Gloss	55.00	85.00	135.00
2. Matt	55.00	85.00	135.00

Note: Transferred to R.D. backstamp (DA105) in gloss.

Model No. 3129
ROUGH COLLIE

Designer: Warren Platt
Height: 5 ½", 14.0 cm
Colours: Golden brown and white - gloss or matt
Issued: 1988-1989

Description	U.K. £	U.S. $	Can. $
1. Gloss	60.00	100.00	145.00
2. Matt	60.00	100.00	145.00

Note: Transferred to R.D. backstamp (DA106) in gloss.

Model No. 3135
SPRINGER SPANIEL

Designer: Amanda Hughes-Lubeck
Height: 5", 12.7 cm
Colours: Dark brown and white - gloss or matt
Issued: 1. 1988-1989 - gloss or matt
Reissued: 2. 1999 to the present - gloss

Description	U.K. £	U.S. $	Can. $
1. Gloss - Original	37.00	60.00	90.00
2. Gloss - Reissued	37.00	N/A	N/A
3. Matt	60.00	100.00	145.00

Note: Transferred to the R.D. backstamp (DA107) in 1989; reverted to Bewsick backstamp 09/99.

Model No. 3149
WEST HIGHLAND TERRIER - Seated

Designer: Martyn Alcock
Height: 5", 12.7 cm
Colours: White - gloss or matt
Issued: 1989-1989
Series: Good Companions

Description	U.K. £	U.S. $	Can. $
1. Gloss	60.00	95.00	135.00
2. Matt	60.00	95.00	135.00

Note: Transferred to R.D. backstamp (DA120) in gloss.

Model No. 3155
CAVALIER KING CHARLES SPANIEL - Standing

Designer: Warren Platt
Height: 5 ½", 14.0 cm
Colours: 1. Black, tan and white - gloss or matt
2. Tan and white - gloss or matt
Issued: 1989-1989, transferred to DA121 - gloss
Series: Good Companions

Description		U.K. £	U.S. $	Can. $
1a.	Gloss	75.00	125.00	175.00
1b.	Matt	65.00	100.00	150.00
2a.	Gloss	75.00	125.00	175.00
2b.	Matt	65.00	100.00	150.00

Model No. 3258
ALSATIAN - Standing

Designer:	Unknown	
Height:	3 ¼″, 8.3 cm	
Colours:	Black and cream - gloss	
Issued:	1991-1997	

Description	U.K. £	U.S. $	Can. $
Gloss	15.00	25.00	40.00

Model No. 3260
ROTTWEILER - Standing

Designer:	Unknown	
Height:	3 ½″, 8.9 cm	
Colours:	Black and tan - gloss	
Issued:	1991-1998	

Description	U.K. £	U.S. $	Can. $
Gloss	15.00	25.00	40.00

Model No. 3262
YORKSHIRE TERRIER - Standing

Designer:	Unknown	
Height:	3 ½″, 8.9 cm	
Colours:	Grey and sandy brown - gloss	
Issued:	1991-1997	

Description	U.K. £	U.S. $	Can. $
Gloss	15.00	25.00	40.00

Model No. 3270
GOLDEN RETRIEVER - Standing

Designer:	Unknown	
Height:	2 ¾″, 7.0 cm	
Colours:	Pale golden brown - gloss	
Issued:	1991 to the present	

Description	U.K. £	U.S. $	Can. $
Gloss	15.00	N/A	N/A

Model No. 3375
HOUNDS - Seated

Designer:	Martyn Alcock
Height:	2 ¼", 5.7 cm
Colours:	Black, tan and white - gloss
Issued:	1993-1997

Description	U.K. £	U.S. $	Can. $
Gloss	15.00	25.00	40.00

Model No. 3376
GOLDEN RETRIEVERS - Seated

Designer:	Martyn Alcock
Height:	2", 5.0 cm
Colours:	Golden brown - gloss
Issued:	1993-1997

Description	U.K. £	U.S. $	Can. $
Gloss	15.00	25.00	40.00

Model No. 3377
COCKER SPANIEL - Standing

Designer:	Amanda Hughes-Lubeck
Height:	3", 7.6 cm
Colours:	Golden brown - gloss
Issued:	1993-1997

Description	U.K. £	U.S. $	Can. $
Gloss	15.00	25.00	40.00

Model No. 3378
ALSATIAN - Lying

Designer:	Amanda Hughes-Lubeck
Height:	2 ½", 6.4 cm
Colours:	Black and cream - gloss
Issued:	1993 to the present

Description	U.K. £	U.S. $	Can. $
Gloss	15.00	N/A	N/A

Model No. 3379
BULLDOG - Seated

Designer:	Warren Platt
Height:	2 ½", 6.4 cm
Colours:	White with pale tan patch - gloss
Issued:	1993 to the present

Description	U.K. £	U.S. $	Can. $
Gloss	12.00	N/A	N/A

Model No. 3380
JACK RUSSELL TERRIER - Standing

Designer:	Warren Platt
Height:	2 ½", 6.4 cm
Colours:	White with pale brown ears and patches on head - gloss
Issued:	1993-1997

Description	U.K. £	U.S. $	Can. $
Gloss	15.00	25.00	40.00

Model No. 3381
RETRIEVER - Standing

Designer:	Warren Platt
Height:	2", 5.0 cm
Colours:	Golden brown - gloss
Issued:	1993-1997

Description	U.K. £	U.S. $	Can. $
Gloss	15.00	25.00	40.00

Model No. 3382
SCOTTISH TERRIER - Standing

Designer:	Martyn Alcock
Height:	3", 7.6 cm
Colours:	Black - gloss
Issued:	1993 to the present

Description	U.K. £	U.S. $	Can. $
Gloss	12.00	N/A	N/A

Model No. 3383
COCKER SPANIELS - Seated

Designer: Martyn Alcock
Height: 2", 5.0 cm
Colours: Golden brown - gloss
Issued: 1993-1997

Description	U.K. £	U.S. $	Can. $
Gloss	15.00	25.00	40.00

Model No. 3384
BULLDOGS - Seated

Designer: Martyn Alcock
Height: 2 ¼", 5.7 cm
Colours: White with pale tan patches - gloss
Issued: 1994 to the present

Description	U.K. £	U.S. $	Can. $
Gloss	15.00	N/A	N/A

Model No. 3385
DALMATIAN - Standing

Designer: Amanda Hughes-Lubeck
Height: 3", 7.6 cm
Colours: White with black spots - gloss
Issued: 1994-1997

Description	U.K. £	U.S. $	Can. $
Gloss	15.00	25.00	40.00

Model No. 3436
CAVALIER KING CHARLES SPANIEL - Seated

Designer: Amanda Hughes-Lubeck
Height: 2 ½", 6.4 cm
Colours: White with golden brown patches - gloss
Issued: 1994 to the present

Description	U.K. £	U.S. $	Can. $
Gloss	12.00	N/A	N/A

Model No. 3467
WEST HIGHLAND WHITE TERRIERS - Seated
Designer: Amanda Hughes-Lubeck
Height: 2", 5.0 cm
Colours: White - gloss
Issued: 1994 to the present

Description	U.K. £	U.S. $	Can. $
Gloss	15.00	N/A	N/A

Model No. 3468
OLD ENGLISH SHEEPDOGS - Seated
Designer: Warren Platt
Height: 2", 5.0 cm
Colours: Grey and white - gloss
Issued: 1995 to the present

Description	U.K. £	U.S. $	Can. $
Gloss	15.00	N/A	N/A

Model No. 3475
BOXERS - One seated, one lying
Designer: Amanda Hughes-Lubeck
Height: 2 ¼", 5.7 cm
Colours: Tan - gloss
Issued: 1995-1998

Description	U.K. £	U.S. $	Can. $
Gloss	15.00	25.00	40.00

Model No. 3490
ROTTWEILERS - One seated, one lying
Designer: Warren Platt
Height: 2", 5.0 cm
Colours: Black and tan - gloss
Issued: 1995-1997

Description	U.K. £	U.S. $	Can. $
Gloss	15.00	25.00	40.00

Model No. D142
GOLDEN RETRIEVER

Designer: Amanda Hughes-Lubeck
Height: 5", 12.7 cm
Colours: Golden brown - gloss
Issued: 1999 to the present

Description	U.K. £	U.S. $	Can. $
Gloss	37.00	N/A	N/A

Note: Transferred from the Royal Doulton backstamp (DA142) in September 1999.

Model No. D145
LABRADOR - standing

Designer: Warren Platt
Height: 5", 12.7 cm
Colours: 1. Black
2. Golden
Issued: 1999 to the present

Colourway	U.K. £	U.S. $	Can. $
1. Black	37.00	N/A	N/A
2. Golden	37.00	N/A	N/A

Note: Transferred from the Royal Doulton backstamp (DA145) in September 1999.

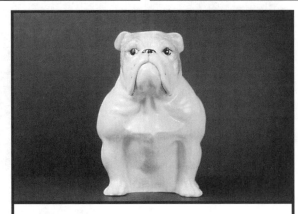

Model No. D222
BULLDOG

Designer: Warren Platt
Height: 5", 12.7 cm
Colours: White with tan patches
Issued: 1999 to the present

Colourway	U.K. £	U.S. $	Can. $
White/tan	27.00	N/A	N/A

Note: Transferred from the Royal Doulton backstamp (DA222) in September 1999.

Chapter Five

FARM ANIMALS - CATTLE

As the number of Beswick collectors grows dramatically, this particular section of Beswick animals has become more popular. This is mainly due to the accurate reproduction of champion-stock animals, where meticulous attention to detail by the designers and modellers at the Beswick factory, and now the Beswick Studio of Royal Doulton, has produced some superb models over the years.

This is very noticeable with the Hereford Cattle, since as the breed standard has changed, the models have been updated. Just compare the models of the early Herefords with the ones that followed; they are very different in shape.

It is also interesting to note that when the calves were discontinued in the mid 1970s, with the exception of the Friesian, public pressure brought about their reintroduction ten years later. Although the later models were altered from the originals, they can all live together as one happy family. Thus, for example, Aberdeen Angus Cattle becomes a set of four rather than just three.

The models of the best-known breeds have survived to the present, but the lesser-known breeds, such as the Galloways, sadly had a short production run and now, as a result, are highly sought after by collectors.

The Connoisseur Range of cattle on polished wooden bases is truly impressive. With a satin matt finish, more detail can generally be achieved than on the gloss models—this, of course, was reflected in the retail price.

INDEX BY MODEL NUMBER

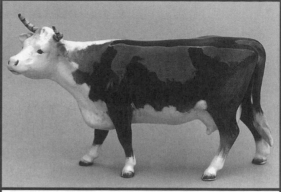

Model No. 854
HEREFORD CALF

Designer:	Arthur Gredington
Height:	4 ½", 11.9 cm
Colour:	1. Brown and white - gloss
	2. Roan - gloss
	3. Blue
Issued:	1940-c.1957

Colourway	U.K. £	U.S. $	Can. $
1. Brown/white	100.00	175.00	250.00
2. Roan	600.00	950.00	1,350.00
3. Blue	300.00	500.00	750.00

Model No. 899
HEREFORD COW
First Version - Horns are upright

Designer:	Arthur Gredington
Height:	5", 12.7 cm
Colour:	Brown and white - gloss
Issued:	1941-1941
Varieties:	948 (Horns point forward)

Colourway	U.K. £	U.S. $	Can. $
Brown/white	275.00	450.00	650.00

Note: Model no. 899 was remodelled in 1941 and became model no. 948.

Model No. 901A
HEREFORD CALF
First Version - Mouth open

Designer:	Arthur Gredington
Height:	4", 10.1 cm
Colour:	1. Roan and white - gloss
	2. Tan and white - gloss
Issued:	1940-Unknown
Varieties:	901B (mouth closed)

Colourway	U.K. £	U.S. $	Can. $
1. Roan/white	600.00	950.00	1,350.00
2. Tan/white	200.00	350.00	525.00

Model No. 901B
HEREFORD CALF
Second Version - Mouth closed

Designer:	Arthur Gredington
Height:	3 ¾", 9.5 cm
Colour:	1. Brown and white - gloss
	2. Roan and white - gloss
Issued:	Unknown-c.1957
Varieties:	901A (mouth open)

Colourway	U.K. £	U.S. $	Can. $
1. Brown/white	100.00	165.00	250.00
2. Roan/white	500.00	800.00	1,200.00

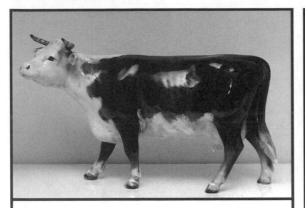

Model No. 948
HEREFORD COW
Second Version - Horns point forward

Designer:	Arthur Gredington
Height:	5", 12.7 cm
Colour:	1. Brown and white - gloss
	2. Roan and white - gloss
Issued:	1941-c.1957
Varieties:	899 (horns are upright)

Colourway	U.K. £	U.S. $	Can. $
1. Brown/white	200.00	350.00	475.00
2. Roan/white		Extremely Rare	

Model No. 949
HEREFORD BULL

Designer:	Arthur Gredington
Height:	5 ¾", 14.6 cm
Colour:	Brown and white - gloss
Issued:	1941-c.1957

Colourway	U.K. £	U.S. $	Can. $
Brown/white	150.00	250.00	375.00

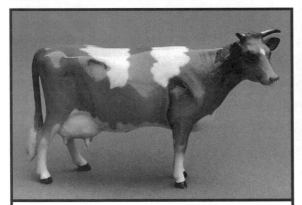

Model No. 1248A
GUERNSEY COW
First Version - Horns and ears separate

Designer:	Arthur Gredington
Height:	4 ¼", 10.8 cm
Colour:	Golden brown and white - gloss
Issued:	1952-1953
Varieties:	1248B (Horns and ears moulded together)

Colourway	U.K. £	U.S. $	Can. $
Golden Brown	200.00	325.00	500.00

Note: Modelled from the Standard of the Guernsey Cattle Society.

Model No. 1248B
GUERNSEY COW
Second Version - Horns and ears are moulded together

Designer:	Arthur Gredington
Height:	4 ¼", 10.8 cm
Colour:	Golden brown and white - gloss or matt
Issued:	1. Gloss - 1953-1989
	2. Matt - 1985-1989
Varieties:	1248A (Horns and ears separate)

Description	U.K. £	U.S. $	Can. $
1. Gloss	80.00	150.00	250.00
2. Matt	70.00	125.00	200.00

Model No. 1248B/1249A
GUERNSEY COW AND CALF - on wooden plinth

Designer:	Arthur Gredington	
Height:	4 ¼", 10.8 cm	
Colour:	Golden brown and white - matt	
Issued:	c.1988	

Description	U.K. £	U.S. $	Can. $
Matt	175.00	275.00	375.00

Note: Cow is no. 1248B; Calf is no. 1249A. Issued as a special commission for the Guernsey Cattle Society c.1988

Model No. 1249A
GUERNSEY CALF

Designer:	Arthur Gredington	
Height:	2 ¾", 7.0 cm	
Colour:	Golden brown and white - gloss or matt	
Issued:	1. Gloss - 1952-1975	
	2. Matt - 1987-1989	
Reissued:	3. Gloss - 1985-1989	

Description	U.K. £	U.S. $	Can. $
1. Gloss	40.00	65.00	90.00
2. Matt	25.00	50.00	75.00
3. Gloss reissued	30.00	55.00	75.00

Model No. 1249B
AYRSHIRE CALF

Designer:	Arthur Gredington	
Height:	2 ¾", 7.0 cm	
Colour:	Brown and white - gloss or matt	
Modelled:	1952	
Issued:	1. Gloss - 1956-1975	
	2. Matt - 1987-1989	
Reissued:	3. Gloss - 1985-1990	

Description	U.K. £	U.S. $	Can. $
1. Gloss	40.00	65.00	90.00
2. Matt	25.00	50.00	75.00
3. Gloss reissued	30.00	55.00	75.00

Model No. 1249C
FRIESIAN CALF

Designer:	Arthur Gredington	
Height:	2 ¾", 7.0 cm	
Colour:	Black and white - gloss or matt	
Modelled:	1952	
Issued:	1. Gloss - 1956-1997	
	2. Matt - 1987-1989	

Description	U.K. £	U.S. $	Can. $
1. Gloss	17.00	30.00	50.00
2. Matt	25.00	45.00	60.00

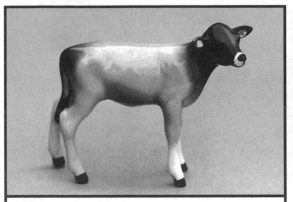

Model No. 1249D
JERSEY CALF

Designer:	Arthur Gredington
Height:	2 ¾", 6.4 cm
Colour:	Light brown with shading darker around the head - gloss or matt
Issued:	1. 1956-1975
	2. 1987-1989
Reissued:	3. 1985-1997

Description	U.K. £	U.S. $	Can. $
1. Gloss	40.00	65.00	90.00
2. Matt	25.00	45.00	60.00
3. Gloss reissued	20.00	35.00	45.00

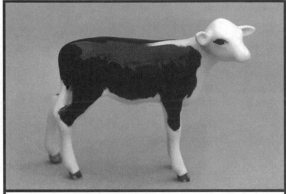

Model No. 1249E
HEREFORD CALF

Designer:	Arthur Gredington
Height:	2 ¾", 7.0 cm
Colour:	Brown and white - gloss
Modelled:	1952
Issued:	This model was especially commissioned, sometime between 1975 and 1985, when the only calf in production was the Friesian.

Description	U.K. £	U.S. $	Can. $
Brown/white	100.00	165.00	250.00

Model No. 1345
JERSEY COW CH. "NEWTON TINKLE"

Designer:	Arthur Gredington
Height:	4 ¼", 10.8 cm
Colour:	Light brown with shading darker around the head - gloss or matt
Issued:	1. Gloss - 1954-1997
	2. Matt - 1985-1989

Description	U.K. £	U.S. $	Can. $
1. Gloss	50.00	75.00	115.00
2. Matt	60.00	100.00	150.00

Model No. 1345/1249D
JERSEY COW AND CALF - on wooden plinth

Designer:	Arthur Gredington
Height:	5 ¼", 13.3 cm
Colour:	Light brown with shading especially around the head - gloss
Issued:	1993-1996
Series:	Plinthed Animals

Description	U.K. £	U.S. $	Can. $
Light Brown	60.00	100.00	130.00

Note: Cow is no. 1345; Calf is no. 1249D.

Model No. 1350
AYRSHIRE COW CH. "ICKHAM BESSIE"

Designer:	Arthur Gredington
Height:	5", 12.7 cm
Colour:	Brown and white - gloss or matt
Issued:	1. Gloss - 1954-1990
	2. Matt - 1985-1989

Description	U.K. £	U.S. $	Can. $
1. Gloss	125.00	200.00	300.00
2. Matt	100.00	150.00	225.00

Model No. 1360
HEREFORD COW

Designer:	Arthur Gredington
Height:	4 ¼", 10.8 cm
Colour:	Brown and white - gloss or matt
Issued:	1. Gloss - 1954-1997
	2. Matt - 1985-1989

Description	U.K. £	U.S. $	Can. $
1. Gloss	30.00	50.00	75.00
2. Matt	60.00	100.00	150.00

Note: Modelled from the standard of the Hereford Cattle Society.

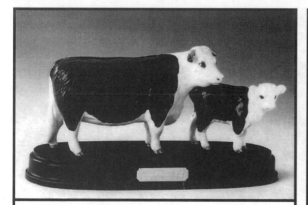

Model No. 1360/1827C
HEREFORD COW AND CALF - on wooden plinth

Designer:	Graham Tongue
Height:	7", 17.8 cm
Colour:	Brown and white - gloss
Issued:	1993-1996
Series:	Plinthed Animals

Description	U.K. £	U.S. $	Can. $
Gloss	55.00	95.00	135.00

Note: Cow is no. 1360; Calf is no. 1827C.

Model No. 1362A
FRIESIAN COW
CH. "CLAYBURY LEEGWATER"

Designer:	Arthur Gredington
Height:	4 ½", 11.9 cm
Colour:	Black and white - gloss or matt
Issued:	1. Gloss - 1954-1997
	2. Matt - 1985-1989
Varieties:	1362B

Description	U.K. £	U.S. $	Can. $
1. Gloss	30.00	50.00	75.00
2. Matt	60.00	100.00	150.00

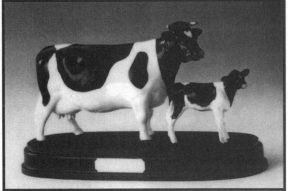

Model No. 1362B
RED FRIESIAN COW

Designer:	Arthur Gredington
Height:	4 ½″, 11.9 cm
Colour:	Brown and white - gloss
Modelled:	1954
Issued:	1992 in an edition of 130
Varieties:	1362A

Colourway	U.K. £	U.S. $	Can. $
Brown/white	600.00	1,000.00	1,500.00

Note: Produced for the Beswick Collectors Circle with special B.C.C. and Beswick backstamps.

Model No. 1362/1249C
FRIESIAN COW AND CALF - on wooden plinth

Designer:	Graham Tongue
Height:	5 ½″, 14.0 cm
Colour:	Black and white - gloss
Issued:	1993-1996
Series:	Plinthed Animals

Colourway	U.K. £	U.S. $	Can. $
Black/white	60.00	100.00	150.00

Note: Cow is no. 1362; Calf is no. 1249C.

Model No. 1363A
HEREFORD BULL
First Version - Horns pertrude from ears

Designer:	Arthur Gredington
Height:	4 ½″, 10.8 cm
Colour:	Brown and white - gloss or matt
Issued:	1. Gloss - 1955-unknown
	2. Matt - 1985-unknown

Description	U.K. £	U.S. $	Can. $
1. Gloss	100.00	175.00	250.00
2. Matt	100.00	175.00	250.00

Model No. 1363B
HEREFORD BULL
Second Version - Horns flush to ears

Designer:	Arthur Gredinton
Height:	4 ½″, 10.8 cm
Colour:	Brown and white - gloss or matt
Issued:	1. Gloss - Unknown-1997
	2. Matt - 1985-1989

Description	U.K. £	U.S. $	Can. $
1. Gloss	30.00	50.00	70.00
2. Matt	55.00	90.00	125.00

Note: Modelled from the standard of the Hereford Cattle Society. This model has also appeared as a money-box.

Model No. 1363C
HEREFORD BULL - on wooden plinth

Designer:	Arthur Gredington
Height:	5 ½", 14.0 cm
Colour:	Brown and white - satin matt
Modelled:	1955
Issued:	1968-1975
Series:	Connoisseur

Colourway	U.K. £	U.S. $	Can. $
Brown/white	175.00	300.00	400.00

Note: Issued on a teak stand. The base was changed to polished wood in 1974.

Model No. 1406A
ABERDEEN ANGUS CALF

Designer:	Arthur Gredington
Height:	3", 7.6 cm
Colour:	Black - gloss
Issued:	1956-1975

Colourway	U.K. £	U.S. $	Can. $
Black	225.00	375.00	550.00

Model No. 1406B
HEREFORD CALF

Designer:	Arthur Gredington
Height:	3", 7.6 cm
Colour:	Brown and white - gloss
Issued:	1956-1975

Colourway	U.K. £	U.S. $	Can. $
Brown/white	125.00	225.00	300.00

Model No. 1406C
DAIRY SHORTHORN CALF

Designer:	Arthur Gredington
Height:	3", 7.6 cm
Colour:	Brown and white with shading - gloss
Issued:	1956-1973

Colourway	U.K. £	U.S. $	Can. $
Brown/white	400.00	650.00	950.00

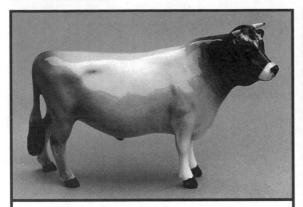

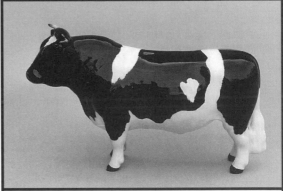

Model No. 1422
JERSEY BULL CH. "DUNSLEY COY BOY"

Designer:	Arthur Gredington
Height:	4 ½", 11.9 cm
Colour:	Light brown with shading and darker head - gloss or matt
Issued	1. Gloss - 1956-1997
	2. Matt - 1985-1989

Description	U.K. £	U.S. $	Can. $
1. Gloss	45.00	75.00	125.00
2. Matt	50.00	90.00	140.00

Model No. 1439A
FRIESIAN BULL
CH. "CODDINGTON HILT BAR"

Designer:	Arthur Gredington
Height:	4 ¾", 12.1 cm
Colour:	Black and white - gloss or matt
Issued:	1. Gloss - 1956-1997
	2. Matt - 1985-1989

Description	U.K. £	U.S. $	Can. $
1. Gloss	30.00	50.00	75.00
2. Matt	50.00	85.00	125.00

Model No. 1439B
FRIESIAN BULL - on teak plinth

Designer:	Arthur Gredington
Height:	5 ½", 14.0 cm
Colour:	Black and white - satin matt
Modelled:	1956
Issued:	1968-1973
Varieties:	1439A
Series:	Connoisseur Cattle

Description	U.K. £	U.S. $	Can. $
Satin matt	150.00	250.00	375.00

Model No. 1439C
RED FRIESIAN BULL

Designer:	Arthur Gredington
Height:	4 ¾", 12.1 cm
Colour:	Brown and white - gloss
Modelled:	1956
Issued:	1992 in an edition of 129

Description	U.K. £	U.S. $	Can. $
Gloss	600.00	950.00	1,500.00

Note: Produced for the Beswick Collectors Circle with special B.C.C. and Beswick backstamps.

Model No. 1451
GUERNSEY BULL
CH. "SABRINA'S SIR RICHMOND 14th"

Designer:	Colin Melbourne
Height:	4 ¾", 11.9 cm
Colour:	Tan/brown and white - gloss or matt
Issued:	1. Gloss - 1956-1989
	2. Matt - 1985-1989

Description	U.K. £	U.S. $	Can. $
1. Gloss	150.00	250.00	375.00
2. Matt	150.00	250.00	375.00

Photograph not
available at press time

Model No. 1454A
AYRSHIRE BULL CH. "WHITEHILL MANDATE"
First Version

Designer:	Colin Melbourne
Height:	5 ¼", 13.3 cm
Colour:	Brown and white with shading - gloss
Issued:	1956-1957

Colourway	U.K. £	U.S. $	Can. $
Brown/white		Extremely Rare	

Model No. 1454B
AYRSHIRE BULL CH. "WHITEHILL MANDATE"
Second Version

Designer:	Colin Melbourne
Height:	5 ¼", 13.3 cm
Colour:	Brown, white and shaded - gloss or matt
Issued:	1. Gloss - 1957-1990
	2. Matt - 1985-1989

Description	U.K. £	U.S. $	Can. $
1. Gloss	250.00	400.00	600.00
2. Matt	250.00	400.00	600.00

Model No. 1504
DAIRY SHORTHORN BULL
CH. "GWERSYLT LORD OXFORD 74th"

Designer:	Arthur Gredington
Height:	5", 12.7 cm
Colour:	Brown and white with shading - gloss
Issued:	1957-1973

Colourway	U.K. £	U.S. $	Can. $
Brown/white	600.00	950.00	1,500.00

Model No. 1510
DAIRY SHORTHORN COW
CH. "EATON WILD EYES 91 ST"

Designer: Arthur Gredington
Height: 4 ¾", 12.1 cm
Colour: Brown and white with shading - gloss
Issued: 1957-1973

Description	U.K. £	U.S. $	Can. $
Gloss	700.00	1,250.00	1,500.00

Model No. 1562
ABERDEEN ANGUS BULL

Designer: Arthur Gredington
Height: 4 ½", 11.9 cm
Colour: Black - gloss or matt
Issued: 1. Gloss - 1958-1989
  2. Matt - 1985-1989

Description	U.K. £	U.S. $	Can. $
1. Gloss	150.00	250.00	350.00
2. Matt	175.00	275.00	400.00

Note: This model was approved by a panel of judges of the Breed Society.

Model No. 1563
ABERDEEN ANGUS COW

Designer: Arthur Gredington
Height: 4 ¼", 10.8 cm
Colour: Black - gloss or matt
Issued: 1. Gloss - 1959-1989
  2. Matt - 1985-1989

Description	U.K. £	U.S. $	Can. $
1. Gloss	150.00	250.00	350.00
2. Matt	200.00	325.00	500.00

Note: This model was approved by a panel of judges of the Breed Society.

Model No. 1740
HIGHLAND COW

Designer: Arthur Gredington
Height: 5 ¼", 3.3 cm
Colour: Tan and brown - gloss or matt
Issued: 1. Gloss - 1961-1990
  2. Matt - 1985-1989

Description	U.K. £	U.S. $	Can. $
1. Gloss	150.00	250.00	375.00
2. Matt	150.00	250.00	375.00

Model No. 1746A
GALLOWAY BULL

Designer:	Arthur Gredington		
Height:	4 ½", 11.9 cm		
Colour:	Black - gloss		
Modelled:	1961		
Issued:	1962-1969		
Varieties:	1746B, 1746C		

Colourway	U.K. £	U.S. $	Can. $
Black	2,000.00	3,000.00	4,000.00

Model No. 1746B
GALLOWAY BULL - BELTED

Designer:	Arthur Gredington		
Height:	4 ½", 11.9 cm		
Colour:	Black and white - gloss		
Modelled:	1961		
Issued:	1963-1969		
Varieties:	1746A, 1746C		

Colourway	U.K. £	U.S. $	Can. $
Black/white	1,375.00	2,250.00	3,000.00

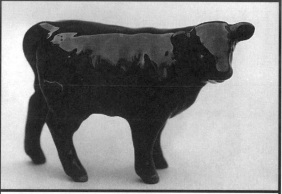

Model No. 1746C
GALLOWAY BULL - SILVER DUNN

Designer:	Arthur Gredington		
Height:	4 ½", 11.9 cm		
Colour:	Fawn and brown - gloss		
Modelled:	1961		
Issued:	1962-1969		
Varieties:	1746A, 1746B		

Colourway	U.K. £	U.S. $	Can. $
Fawn/brown	1,200.00	1,950.00	2,800.00

Model No. 1827A
ABERDEEN ANGUS CALF

Designer:	Arthur Gredington		
Height:	3", 7.6 cm		
Colour:	Black - gloss or matt		
Issued:	1. Gloss - 1985-1989		
	2. Matt - 1987-1989		

Description	U.K. £	U.S. $	Can. $
1. Gloss	175.00	275.00	400.00
2. Matt	175.00	275.00	400.00

Model No. 1827B
CHAROLAIS CALF

Designer:	Arthur Gredington
Height:	3", 7.6 cm
Colour:	Cream - gloss or matt
Issued:	1. Gloss - 1985-1997
	2. Matt - 1987-1989

Description	U.K. £	U.S. $	Can. $
1. Gloss	20.00	30.00	50.00
2. Matt	30.00	50.00	75.00

Model No. 1827C
HEREFORD CALF

Designer:	Arthur Gredington
Height:	3", 7.6 cm
Colour:	Brown and white - gloss or matt
Issued:	1. Gloss - 1985-1997
	2. Matt - 1987-1989

Description	U.K. £	U.S. $	Can. $
1. Gloss	20.00	30.00	50.00
2. Matt	30.00	50.00	75.00

Model No. 1827D
HIGHLAND CALF

Designer:	Arthur Gredington
Height:	3", 7.6 cm
Colour:	Tan and brown - gloss or matt
Issued:	1. Gloss - 1962-1990
	2. Matt - 1987-1989

Description	U.K. £	U.S. $	Can. $
1. Gloss	40.00	65.00	95.00
2. Matt	35.00	60.00	85.00

Model No. 1827E
LIMOUSIN CALF

Designer:	Arthur Gredington
Height:	3", 7.6 cm
Colour:	Brown and white - gloss
Issued:	1998 in a limited edition of 711

Colourway	U.K. £	U.S. $	Can. $
Brown/white	60.00	95.00	135.00

Note: Special colourway produced for The Beswick Collectors Club. The B.C.C. backstamp appears in addition to the normal Beswick backstamp.

Model No. 2008
HIGHLAND BULL

Designer: Arthur Gredington
Height: 5", 12.7 cm
Colour: Tan/brown - gloss or matt
Issued: 1. Gloss - 1965-1990
2. Matt - 1985-1989

Description	U.K. £	U.S. $	Can. $
1. Gloss	150.00	250.00	350.00
2. Matt	135.00	250.00	350.00

Model No. 2463A
CHAROLAIS BULL

Designer: Alan Maslankowski
Height: 5", 12.7 cm
Colour: Cream - gloss or matt
Modelled: 1973
Issued: 1. Gloss - 1979-1997
2. Matt - 1985-1989

Description	U.K. £	U.S. $	Can. $
1. Gloss	35.00	55.00	80.00
2. Matt	50.00	100.00	150.00

Model No. 2463B
LIMOUSIN BULL

Designer: Alan Maslankowski
Height: 5", 12.7 cm
Colour: Brown and white - gloss
Issued: 1998 in a limited edition of 653

Description	U.K. £	U.S. $	Can. $
Gloss	35.00	60.00	85.00

Note: Special colourway produced for The Beswick Collectors Club. The B.C.C. backstamp appears in addition to the normal Beswick backstamp.

Model No. A2463A
CHAROLAIS BULL - on wooden plinth

Designer: Alan Maslankowski
Height: 5 ½", 14.0 cm
Colour: Cream - satin matt
Modelled: 1973
Issued: 1975-1979
Series: Connoisseur Cattle

Description	U.K. £	U.S. $	Can. $
Satin matt	175.00	275.00	400.00

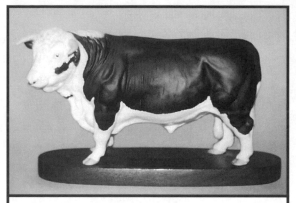

Model No. A2542A
HEREFORD BULL - on wooden plinth

Designer:	Graham Tongue
Height:	7 ½", 19.1 cm
Colour:	Brown and white - satin matt
Modelled:	1975
Issued:	1976-1989
Series:	Connoisseur Cattle

Colourway	U.K. £	U.S. $	Can. $
Brown/white	125.00	200.00	300.00

Note: Transferred to R.D. backstamp (DA19) 08/89.

Model No. A2542B
HEREFORD BULL - on ceramic base

Designer:	Graham Tongue
Height:	7 ½", 19.1 cm
Colour:	Bronze, black shading - satin
Modelled:	1975
Issued:	1989-1992
Series:	Britannia Collection

Colourway	U.K.£	U.S.$	Can.$
Bronze/black	150.00	250.00	350.00

Photograph not
available at press time

Model No. 2549A
POLLED HEREFORD BULL

Designer:	Graham Tongue
Height:	5", 12.7 cm
Colour:	Brown, white ringed nose - gloss or matt
Modelled:	1975
Issued:	1. Gloss - 1977-1997
	2. Matt - 1985-1989

Description	U.K. £	U.S. $	Can. $
1. Gloss	60.00	100.00	125.00
2. Matt	70.00	115.00	150.00

Model 2549B
POLLED HEREFORD BULL- on wooden plinth

Designer:	Graham Tongue
Height:	5", 12.7 cm
Colour:	Bronze, black shading - satin
Modelled:	1975
Issued:	1989-1992
Series:	Britannia Collection

Colourway	U.K.£	U.S.$	Can.$
Bronze/black	100.00	175.00	245.00

Model No. A2574
POLLED HEREFORD BULL - on wooden plinth

Designer:	Graham Tongue
Height:	7 ½", 19.1 cm
Colour:	Brown and white - satin matt
Modelled:	1976
Issued:	1977-1989
Series:	Connoisseur Cattle

Colourway	U.K. £	U.S. $	Can. $
Brown/white	100.00	175.00	245.00

Note: Transferred to R.D. backstamp (DA21) 08/89.

Model No. A2580
FRIESIAN BULL - on wooden plinth

Designer:	Graham Tongue
Height:	7 ½", 19.1 cm
Colour:	Black and white - satin matt
Modelled:	1976
Issued:	1978-1989
Series:	Connoisseur Cattle

Colourway	U.K. £	U.S. $	Can. $
Black	100.00	175.00	245.00

Note: Transferred to R.D. backstamp (DA23) 08/89.

Model No. A2600
CHAROLAIS BULL - on wooden plinth

Designer:	Graham Tongue
Height:	7 ½", 19.1 cm
Colour:	Cream - satin matt
Issued:	1971-1979
Series:	Connoisseur Cattle

Colourway	U.K. £	U.S. $	Can. $
Cream	125.00	200.00	350.00

Note: Transferred R.D. to backstamp (DA27) 08/89.

Model No. A2607
FRIESIAN COW - on wooden plinth

Designer:	Graham Tongue
Height:	7 ½", 19.1 cm
Colour:	Black and white - satin matt
Modelled:	1977
Issued:	1979-1989
Series:	Connoisseur Cattle

Colourway	U.K. £	U.S. $	Can. $
Black/white	125.00	200.00	300.00

Note: Transferred to R.D. backstamp (DA29) 08/89.

Model No. A2607/2690
FRIESIAN COW AND CALF - on wooden plinth

Designer:	Graham Tongue
Height:	6 ½", 16.5 cm
Colour:	Black and white - satin matt
Modelled:	Cow - 1977; Calf - 1982
Issued:	1982-1989
Series:	Connoisseur Cattle

Colourway	U.K. £	U.S. $	Can. $
Black/white	175.00	300.00	375.00

Note: Cow is no. A2607; Calf is no. 2690. Transferred to R.D. backstamp (DA3) 08/89.

Model No. A2648/2652
CHAROLAIS COW AND CALF - on wooden plinth

Designer:	Graham Tongue
Height:	7 ¼", 18.4 cm
Colour:	Cream - satin matt
Modelled:	1979
Issued:	1981-1989
Series:	Connoisseur

Colourway	U.K. £	U.S. $	Can. $
Cream	175.00	300.00	400.00

Note: Cow is no. A2648; Calf is no. 2652 which was never issued individually. Transferred to R.D. backstamp (DA33) 08/89.

Model No. A2667/2669
HEREFORD COW AND CALF - on wooden plinth

Designer:	Graham Tongue
Height:	7", 17.8 cm
Colour:	Brown and white - satin matt
Modelled:	1980
Issued:	1981-1989
Series:	Connoisseur

Colourway	U.K. £	U.S. $	Can. $
Brown/white	175.00	275.00	400.00

Note: Cow is no. A2667; Calf is no. 2669, which was never issued individually. Transferred to R.D. backstamp (DA34) 08/89.

Model No. 2690
RED FRIESIAN CALF

Designer:	Graham Tongue
Height:	2 ¼", 5.7 cm
Colour:	Brown and white - gloss
Modelled:	1980
Issued:	1992 in a special edition of 132

Colourway	U.K. £	U.S. $	Can. $
Brown/white	350.00	575.00	800.00

Note: Produced as a free standing model, in this special colourway for The Beswick Collectors Circle. The B.C.C. backstamp appears in addition to the normal Beswick Backstamp.

Model No. 2792
DAISY THE COW CREAMER

Designer:	Graham Tongue
Height:	5 ¾", 14.6 cm
Colour:	A variety of floral decorations, blue flowers or yellow being the most common, but all on a white background
Issued:	1982-1989
Series:	Fun models

Colourway	U.K. £	U.S. $	Can. $
1. Blue	75.00	125.00	150.00
2. Yellow	75.00	125.00	150.00

Model No. 3075A
CHAROLAIS COW

Designer:	Unknown
Height:	5", 12.7 cm
Colour:	Cream - gloss or matt
Modelled:	1987
Issued:	1. Gloss - 1988-1997
	2. Matt - 1988-1989

Description	U.K. £	U.S. $	Can. $
1. Gloss	30.00	50.00	80.00
2. Matt	45.00	95.00	125.00

Model No. 3075B
LIMOUSIN COW

Designer:	Unknown
Height:	5", 12.7 cm
Colour:	Brown and white - gloss
Issued:	1998 in a limited edition of 656

Description	U.K. £	U.S. $	Can. $
Brown/white	30.00	50.00	75.00

Note: Special colourway produced for The Beswick Collectors Club. The B.C.C. backstamp appears in in addition to the normal Beswick backstamp.

Model No. 3075/1827B
CHAROLAIS COW AND CALF - on wooden plinth

Designer:	3075 - Unknown
	1827B - Arthur Gredington
Height:	6", 15.0 cm
Colour:	Cream - gloss
Issued:	1993-1996

Description	U.K. £	U.S. $	Can. $
Cream	60.00	95.00	125.00

Note: Cow is no. 3075; Calf is no. 1827B.

Model 1363A Version One (left) and Model 1363B Version Two (right)

FARM ANIMALS
OTHERS

It is surprising that this section was never expanded to include rare breeds, but it does include most of the animals one expects to find on a farm, besides cattle.

With the exception of the earlier models, the majority of the animals in this group are realistically portrayed. Examples of this are the goat and kid, which make a delightful pair, and the donkeys, as popular now as they ever were.

INDEX BY MODEL NUMBER

Model No. 323
LAMB ON BASE

Designer:	Miss Greaves
Height:	7 ½", 19.1 cm
Colour:	1. Blue - gloss
	2. Cream - satin matt
	3. Natural - satin matt
Issued:	c.1935-by 1954

Colourway	U.K. £	U.S. $	Can. $
1. Blue	150.00	250.00	350.00
2. Cream	100.00	175.00	245.00
3. Natural	150.00	250.00	350.00

Note: Modelled in Deco style.

Model No. 369
DONKEY

Designer:	Miss Greaves
Height:	8", 20.3 cm
Colour:	1. Blue - gloss
	2. Cream - satin matt
	3. Natural - satin matt
Issued:	1936-by 1954

Colourway	U.K. £	U.S. $	Can. $
1. Blue	150.00	250.00	350.00
2. Cream	100.00	175.00	245.00
3. Natural	150.00	250.00	350.00

Note: Modelled in Deco style.

Model No. 398
GOAT

Designer:	Mr. Owen
Height:	4 ½", 11.9 cm
Colour:	1. Blue - gloss
	2. Green - satin matt
	3. White - satin matt
Issued:	1936-by 1954

Colourway	U.K. £	U.S. $	Can. $
1. Blue	40.00	65.00	95.00
2. Green	30.00	50.00	70.00
3. White	30.00	50.00	70.00

Model No. 832
PIG

Designer:	Arthur Gredington
Height:	3 ¾", 9.5 cm
Colour:	White and pink with grey patches - gloss
Issued:	1940-1971
Set:	833, 834

Colourway	U.K. £	U.S. $	Can. $
White	35.00	55.00	80.00

Model No. 833
PIGLET - Running

Designer:	Arthur Gredington
Height:	1 ¾", 4.5 cm
Colour:	White and pink with grey patches - gloss
Issued:	1940-1971
Set:	832, 834

Colourway	U.K. £	U.S. $	Can. $
White	25.00	40.00	60.00

Model No. 834
PIGLET - Trotting

Designer:	Arthur Gredington
Height:	1 ½", 3.8 cm
Colour:	White and pink with grey patches - gloss
Issued:	1940-1971
Set:	832, 833

Colourway	U.K. £	U.S. $	Can. $
White	25.00	40.00	60.00

Photograph not
available at press time

Model No. 897
DONKEY FOAL

Designer:	Arthur Gredington
Height:	Unknown
Colour:	Natural - gloss
Issued:	1941-Unknown

Description	U.K. £	U.S. $	Can. $
Gloss		Extremely Rare	

Note: Probably not put into production under this
number, see no. 950.

Model No. 935
SHEEP

Designer:	Arthur Gredington
Height:	3 ½", 8.9 cm
Colour:	White - gloss
Issued:	1941-1971
Set:	936, 937, 938

Colourway	U.K. £	U.S. $	Can. $
White	30.00	50.00	70.00

Model No. 936
LAMB

Designer:	Arthur Gredington
Height:	3 ¼", 8.3 cm
Colour:	White - gloss
Issued:	1941-1971
Set:	935, 937, 938

Colourway	U.K. £	U.S. $	Can. $
White	16.00	25.00	35.00

Model No. 937
LAMB

Designer:	Arthur Gredington
Height:	2", 5.0 cm
Colour:	White - gloss
Issued:	1941-1971
Set:	935, 936, 938

Colourway	U.K. £	U.S. $	Can. $
White	16.00	25.00	35.00

Model No. 938
LAMB

Designer:	Arthur Gredington
Height:	2", 5.0 cm
Colour:	White - gloss
Issued:	1941-1971
Set:	935, 936, 937

Colourway	U.K. £	U.S. $	Can. $
White	16.00	25.00	35.00

Model No. 950
DONKEY FOAL

Designer:	Arthur Gredington
Height:	5", 12.7 cm
Colour:	Grey-brown - gloss
Issued:	1941-1962

Colourway	U.K. £	U.S. $	Can. $
Grey-brown	85.00	135.00	200.00

Model No. 1035
GOAT

Designer:	Arthur Gredington
Height:	5 ½", 14.0 cm
Colour:	Tan - gloss
Issued:	1945-1971
Set:	1036

Colourway	U.K. £	U.S. $	Can. $
Tan	125.00	200.00	300.00

Model No. 1036
KID

Designer:	Arthur Gredington
Height:	2 ½", 6.4 cm
Colour:	Tan - gloss
Issued:	1945-1971
Set:	1035

Colourway	U.K. £	U.S. $	Can. $
Tan	85.00	135.00	200.00

Photograph not
available at press time

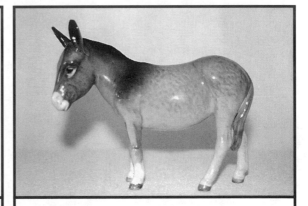

Model No. 1364A
DONKEY
First Version - Tail free from hind leg

Designer:	Mr. Orwell
Height:	4 ½", 11.9 cm
Colour:	Natural brown - gloss
Issued:	1955-1955

Colourway	U.K. £	U.S. $	Can. $
Brown		Extremely Rare	

Note: Probably not put into prodution.

Model No. 1364B
DONKEY
Second Version - Tail attached to hind leg

Designer:	Mr. Orwell	
Height:	4 ½", 11.9 cm	
Colour:	Natural - gloss or matt	
Issued:	1. Gloss - 1955 to the present	
	2. Matt - 1987-1989	

Description	U.K. £	U.S. $	Can. $
1. Gloss	27.50	N/A	N/A
2. Matt	30.00	50.00	70.00

Model No. 1452A
SOW CH "WALL QUEEN 40th"

Designer:	Arthur Gredington
Height:	2 ¾", 7.0 cm
Colour:	White - gloss or matt
Issued:	1. Gloss - 1956-1998
	2. Matt - 1987-1989

Description	U.K. £	U.S. $	Can. $
1. Gloss	20.00	30.00	45.00
2. Matt	25.00	40.00	60.00

Photograph not
available at press time

Model No. 1452B
SOW - on wooden plinth

Designer:	Arthur Gredington
Height:	3 ¾", 9.5 cm
Colour:	White - gloss
Issued:	1993-1995

Colourway	U.K. £	U.S. $	Can. $
White	30.00	50.00	65.00

Model No. 1453A
BOAR Ch. "WALL CHAMPION BOY 53rd"

Designer:	Arthur Gredington
Height:	2 ¾", 7.0 cm
Colour:	White - gloss or matt
Issued:	1. Gloss - 1956-1998
	2. Matt - 1987-1989

Description	U.K. £	U.S. $	Can. $
1. Gloss	20.00	30.00	45.00
2. Matt	25.00	40.00	60.00

Photograph not
available at press time

Model No. 1453B
BOAR - on wooden plinth

Designer:	Arthur Gredington
Height:	3 ¾", 9.5 cm
Colour:	White - gloss
Issued:	1993 -1995

Colourway	U.K. £	U.S. $	Can. $
White	30.00	50.00	65.00

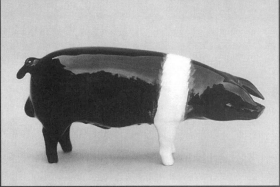

Model No. 1511
WESSEX SADDLEBACK SOW
"MERRYWOOD SILVER WINGS 56th"

Designer:	Colin Melbourne
Height:	2 ¾", 7.0 cm
Colour:	Black and white - gloss
Issued:	1957-1969
Set:	1512

Colourway	U.K. £	U.S. $	Can. $
Black/white	350.00	575.00	775.00

Model No. 1512
WESSEX SADDLEBACK BOAR
"FARACRE VISCOUNT 3rd"

Designer:	Colin Melbourne
Height:	2 ¾", 7.0 cm
Colour:	Black and white - gloss
Issued:	1957-1969
Set:	1511

Colourway	U.K. £	U.S. $	Can. $
Black/white	350.00	575.00	775.00

Model No. 1760
PIGGY BANK

Designer:	Albert Hallam
Height:	8 ½", 21.6 cm
Colour:	White, grey and pink - gloss
Issued:	1961-1967
Series:	Fun Models

Colourway	U.K. £	U.S. $	Can. $
Various	75.00	125.00	175.00

Model No. 1765
BLACK-FACED SHEEP

Designer:	Mr. Garbet
Height:	3 ¼", 8.3 cm
Colour:	Black and white - gloss or matt
Modelled:	1961
Issued:	1. Gloss - 1963 to the present
	2. Matt - 1987-1989
Set:	1828

Description	U.K. £	U.S. $	Can. $
1. Gloss	20.00	N/A	N/A
2. Matt	20.00	30.00	45.00

Model No. 1765/1828
BLACK-FACED SHEEP AND LAMB
- on wooden plinth

Designer:	Mr. Garbet and Arthur Gredington
Height:	3 ¾", 9.5 cm
Colour:	Black and white - gloss
Issued:	1993-1996

Colourway	U.K. £	U.S. $	Can. $
Black/white	30.00	50.00	85.00

Note: Sheep is no. 1765; Lamb is no. 1828.

Model No. 1828
BLACK-FACED LAMB

Designer:	Arthur Gredington
Height:	2 ½", 6.4 cm
Colour:	Black and white - gloss or matt
Modelled:	1962
Issued:	1. Gloss - 1963 to the present
	2. Matt - 1987-1989
Set:	1765

Description	U.K. £	U.S. $	Can. $
1. Gloss	11.50	N/A	N/A
2. Matt	15.00	25.00	35.00

Model No. 1917
MERINO RAM

Designer:	Arthur Gredington
Height:	4 ¼", 10.8 cm
Colour:	Grey with white face - gloss
Modelled:	1963
Issued:	1964-1967

Colourway	U.K. £	U.S. $	Can. $
Grey	325.00	525.00	775.00

Model No. 2103
LAUGHING PIGS

Designer:	Albert Hallam
Height:	2 ¾", 7.0 cm
Colour:	White and pink - gloss
Modelled:	1967
Issued:	1968-1971
Series:	Fun Models

Colourway	U.K. £	U.S. $	Can. $
White/pink	60.00	95.00	135.00

Model No. 2110
DONKEY FOAL

Designer:	Graham Tongue
Height:	4 ½", 11.9 cm
Colour:	Grey-brown - gloss or matt
Modelled:	1967
Issued:	1. Gloss - 1968 to the present
	2. Matt - 1987-1989

Description	U.K. £	U.S. $	Can. $
1. Gloss	20.00	N/A	N/A
2. Matt	20.00	35.00	45.00

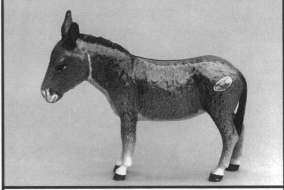

Model No. 2267
DONKEY

Designer:	Albert Hallam and Graham Tongue
Height:	5 ½", 14.0 cm
Colour:	Grey-brown - gloss or matt
Modelled:	1969
Issued:	1. Gloss - 1970 to the present
	2. Matt - 1987-1989

Description	U.K. £	U.S. $	Can. $
1. Gloss	22.50	N/A	N/A
2. Matt	35.00	55.00	80.00

Model No. 2294
PIGLET CANDLEHOLDER

Designer:	Harry Sales
Length:	11" x 3 ½", 27.9 x 8.9 cm
Colour:	1. Blue and white - gloss
	2. Brown - gloss
Modelled:	1969
Issued:	1970-1972
Series:	Fun Models

Colourway	U.K. £	U.S. $	Can. $
1. Blue/white	60.00	95.00	135.00
2. Brown	45.00	70.00	100.00

Note: This candlestick has four candle holders.

Model No. 2746
PIG AND PIGLET "Piggy Back"

Designer:	Graham Tongue
Length:	6 ½", 16.5 cm
Colour:	Pink and white - gloss
Modelled:	1981
Issued:	1983-1994
Series:	Fun Models

Colourway	U.K. £	U.S. $	Can. $
Pink/white	35.00	60.00	85.00

Model No. 3071
BLACK-FACED RAM

Designer:	Mr. Chawner
Height:	3 ¼", 8.3 cm
Colour:	Black and white - gloss or matt
Modelled:	1987
Issued:	1. Gloss - 1988 to the present
	2. Matt - 1988-1989

Description	U.K. £	U.S. $	Can. $
1. Gloss	21.50	N/A	N/A
2. Matt	30.00	50.00	65.00

Model No. 3071/1765
"EWE AND I" - on ceramic plinth

Designer:	Unknown
Height:	4 ½", 11.9 cm
Base:	7 ½", 19.1 cm
Colour:	Black and white - gloss
Issued:	Unknown

Colourway	U.K. £	U.S. $	Can. $
Black/white	65.00	100.00	150.00

Note: Ram is no. 3071; Sheep is no. 1765.
Produced as a special commission.

Model No. G215
TAMWORTH PIG

Designer:	Amanda Hughes-Lubeck
Height:	6", 15.2 cm
Colour:	Brown - gloss
Issued:	1999 to the present

Description	U.K. £	U.S. $	Can. $
Gloss	27.50	N/A	N/A

Note: Transferred from the Royal Doulton backstamp
(DA215) in September 1999.

Model No. G230
GLOUCESTER OLD SPOT PIG

Designer:	Amanda Hughes-Lubeck
Height:	3", 7.6 cm
Colour:	Pink with black markings - gloss
Issued:	1999 to the present

Description	U.K. £	U.S. $	Can. $
Gloss	27.50	N/A	N/A

Note: Transferred from the Royal Doulton backstamp
(DA230) in September 1999.

Chapter Six

FISH

All but two of these fish models are realistically portrayed. The detail on many of them is amazing, for example the Golden Trout. So many colours were used, and the result is simply stunning.

The only stylized version of a fish is one from the Moda series. All the rest are supported on bases, although their fins are still vulnerable to damage. Very few, therefore, have survived intact to the present, and as a result they are particularly hard to find in mint condition, although restored ones do appear.

INDEX BY MODEL NUMBER

Model No. 1032

TROUT

Designer: Arthur Gredington
Height: 6 ¼", 15.9 cm
Colour: Brown and dark green - gloss
Issued: 1945-1975

Model		Price	
No.	U.K. £	U.S. $	Can. $
1032	75.00	150.00	175.00

Model No. 1047

ANGEL FISH

Designer: Arthur Gredington
Height: 7 ¼", 18.4 cm
Colour: Silver, red and green-brown - gloss
Issued: 1946-1967

Model		Price	
No.	U.K. £	U.S. $	Can. $
1047	325.00	500.00	750.00

Model No. 1232

OCEANIC BONITO

Designer:	Arthur Gredington
Height:	7 ¼", 18.4 cm
Colour:	Blue, silver and green - gloss
Issued:	1952-1968

Model		Price	
No.	U.K. £	U.S. $	Can. $
1232	300.00	475.00	700.00

Model No. 1233

ATLANTIC SALMON

Designer:	Arthur Gredington
Height:	6 ½", 16.5 cm
Colour:	Blue, silver and green - gloss
Issued:	1952-1970

Model		Price	
No.	U.K. £	U.S. $	Can. $
1233	175.00	275.00	400.00

Model No. 1235

BARRACUDA

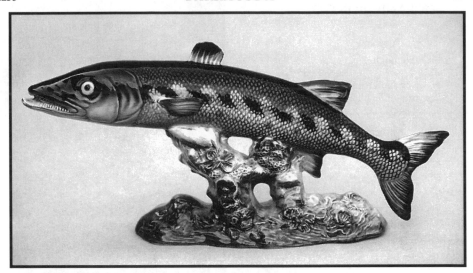

Designer:	Arthur Gredington
Colour:	Blue and silver

Model No.	Finish	Height	Intro.	Disc.	U.K. £	Price U.S. $	Can. $
1235	Gloss	4 ¾", 12.1 cm	1952	1968	300.00	475.00	700.00

Model No. 1243

MARLIN

Designer:	Arthur Gredington
Colour:	Blue, grey and green

Model No.	Finish	Height	Intro.	Disc.	U.K. £	Price U.S. $	Can. $
1243	Gloss	5 ½", 14.0 cm	1952	1970	550.00	875.00	1,300.00

Model No. 1246

GOLDEN TROUT

Designer: Arthur Gredington
Colour: Blue, yellow and green

Model No.	Finish	Height	Intro.	Disc.	U.K. £	Price U.S. $	Can. $
1246	Gloss	6", 15.0 cm	1952	1970	150.00	250.00	350.00

Model No. 1266

LARGE-MOUTHED BLACK BASS

Designer: Arthur Gredington
Colour: Yellow, black, beige and blue

Model No.	Finish	Height	Intro.	Disc.	U.K. £	Price U.S. $	Can. $
1266	Gloss	5", 12.7 cm	1952	1968	300.00	475.00	700.00

Model No. 1304

FISH TRAY/TRINKET DISH

Designer: Arthur Gredington
Colour: Blues, yellow, browns and pink with black - gloss

Model No.	Finish	Length	Intro.	Disc.	U.K.£	Price U.S.$	Can. $
1304	Gloss	5", 12.7 cm	1953	1966	50.00	100.00	150.00

Model No. 1390

TROUT

Designer: Arthur Gredington
Colour: Brown and dark green - gloss
Height: 4", 10.1 cm
Issued: 1955-1975

Model No.	U.K. £	Price U.S. $	Can. $
1390	50.00	85.00	130.00

Model No. 1485

BLACK BASS

Designer: Colin Melbourne
Height: 6", 15.0 cm
Colour: Brown and dark green - gloss
Issued: 1957-1968

| Model | Price | | |
No.	U.K. £	U.S. $	Can. $
1485	650.00	1,000.00	1,500.00

Model No. 1599

TROUT (Ash Bowl)

Designer: Graham Tongue
Height: 5", 12.7 cm
Colour: Brown fish, turquoise-blue bowl - gloss
Issued: 1959-1970

| Model | Price | | |
No.	U.K. £	U.S. $	Can. $
1599	125.00	200.00	300.00

Model No. 1874

ROACH

Designer: Arthur Gredington
Colour: Turquoise and browns

Model No.	Finish	Length	Intro.	Disc.	U.K. £	Price U.S. $	Can. $
1874	Gloss	6 ¼", 15.9 cm	1963	1971	250.00	400.00	600.00

Model No. 1875

PERCH

Designer: Arthur Gredington
Colour: Greens and browns

Model No.	Finish	Length	Intro.	Disc.	U.K. £	Price U.S. $	Can. $
1875	Gloss	6 ¼", 15.9 cm	1963	1971	250.00	400.00	600.00

Model No. 2066

SALMON

Designer:	Graham Tongue
Height:	8", 20.3 cm
Colour:	Browns and silver - gloss
Issued:	1966-1975

Model		Price	
No.	U.K. £	U.S. $	Can. $
2066	225.00	350.00	525.00

Model No. 2087

TROUT

Designer:	Graham Tongue
Height:	6", 15.0 cm
Colour:	Brown with red-brown spots - gloss
Issued:	1967-1975

Model		Price	
No.	U.K. £	U.S. $	Can. $
2087	200.00	325.00	475.00

Model No 2254   **FISH (Stylized Model)**

Designer: Harry Sales
Colour: Dark and light blue
Series: Moda

Model No.	Finish	Height	Intro.	Disc.	U.K. £	Price U.S. $	Can. $
2254	Gloss	4 ½", 11.9 cm	1968	1971	125.00	200.00	295.00

Chapter Seven
HORSES

Beswick is most readily associated with the production of accurately modelled horses. Indeed horses form the largest section by far of all the Beswick range. From 1939 to 1989, Beswick produced over 150 different horse models, the vast majority available in several colourways and in gloss or matt finishes. Although each model had a shape number, many were only listed in price lists and catalogues as horse, mare or foal, which left less knowledgeable collectors and dealers with a considerable identification problem! Some horses do have their names incorporated into their backstamp (for example, the Mountain and Moorland ponies) or numbers imprinted into their base (such as the lying down foal, 915), and of course those with riders are easy to sort out. But those that remain need careful examination to determine exactly which models they are.

A further consideration is colour. Initially Beswick produced horses in dark chestnut, light brown, dark brown, rocking horse grey and even in blue gloss. Later brown, painted white, opaque, palomino, chestnut and light grey glosses were added to the range, and most of the initial colourways were dropped. Special colours were also used for specific models, such as on the 2282 Fjord. From 1970 onwards, matt finishes were introduced in various colours: brown, grey, palomino, white and black. Within each colour there can be considerable variations, from a light tone with shading to an all-over, solid, one-tone version of the same colour. Avid collectors will value the former, which usually indicates an earlier example, painted when more attention was paid to details like well-painted eyes and pink mouths.

The Beswick stable comprises the full spectrum of the equine world, from children's ponies, specific breeds, famous racehorses, to the giant Shires, whilst the *Colin Melbourne* series adds a contemporary touch to the collection.

Arthur Gredington modelled Beswick's first realistic horse in 1939 when he produced the first version of the 1938 Derby winner, *Bois Roussel*. Although a handful of other modellers made contributions to the horse models it was Arthur Gredington who was responsible for the vast majority until he retired in 1968. Graham Tongue then took over, adding many more horses to the range, including a new bronze finish for the Britannia Series. In August 1989 all except three Beswick horses became Doulton Animals and so from that date, although they continued to be produced in the Beswick factory, they were backstamped with the name of the parent company, Royal Doulton. In 1994 to mark the Beswick Centenary it was a horse model that was chosen as a special piece to represent Beswick. This was the large rearing model of *Downland Cancara*. Graham Tongue modelled this magnificent horse. In 1995 Cancara was issued with a Royal Doulton backstamp and the three remaining Beswick horses were completely withdrawn.

1996 saw the revival of the Beswick backstamp on horses when the 1642 Dartmoor pony stallion was commissioned by Doug Middleweek in bright bay gloss as "Warlord." Warlord was followed at the end of 1997 with a brand new model of a Dartmoor Mare "Another Bunch." The set was completed in 1998 with the "birth" of their foal.

Since the publication of the 3rd Edition examples of 855's First version have been discovered. So at the time of writing there is only now ONE horse shape known to have been in general production which has not come to light. This is the action foal 766. Why this remains elusive is something of a mystery. It was illustrated in the 1940 Overseas brochure/price list which stated it as being available on or off a ceramic base in Dark Chestnut and Light Brown colourways. The model was priced at 14 shillings *per dozen* in "Dark Chestnut off stand" and 13 shillings per dozen in "Light Brown off stand!" Surely out of these "dozens" some have survived?

There remains a handful of horse models which reached various stages of production and it is a possibility that there are the odd examples *somewhere*. These include 2451, a mounted piece given the title of "The Outlaw" which was to be part of a "Riders of the World" collection. Unfortunately this was not pursued further than a prototype. "The Outlaw" was modelled by Graham Tongue in March 1973.

At least five other horse models are recorded in the shape book which did not get as far as being generally released. All were designed during the late 1970s, and include: 2468 *Icelandic Pony* and 2626 *Haflinger Pony*, both by Graham Tongue; 2548 *Small Shire* and 2577 *Racehorse* by David Littleton; and 2671 *Classic Horse and Stand*, whose modeller is unknown. The Small Shire, also referrerd to as the "Whitbread" Shire (as it was intended as a souvenir for visitors to the Whitbread Shire Horse Farm in Kent to purchase), does exist as there were a small number actually produced. Examples in grey gloss and matt are now in the hands of a few extremely lucky collectors. Although no examples of the Haflinger have come to my attention, I do know that they exist as I saw them in Graham Tongue's studio several years ago. This was at least ten years following the Haflinger's original modelling and suggests that Doulton were perhaps reconsidering issuing it. They were obviously trial pieces, being in various colourways and were attractive action models. It is a great pity that once more the model was rejected. There could be an Icelandic Pony model in existence, but the racehorse was not illustrated in the shape book and so probably did not get to the stage where models could exist. The same applies to the "Classic Horse and Stand."

Prices for the horses seem to have "levelled off" somewhat. Rarer shapes and colourways will obviously still command a premium, but several models which were considered "rare" in the past have now been found in sufficient numbers to satisfy the more ardent collectors. Hence fewer spectacular auction prices have been realized recently. The 818 Shire continues to be the most commonly seen Beswick equine at Collectors Fairs, invariably in brown gloss. However, a painted white one has surfaced and giving the 818 the distinction of not only being Beswick's longest produced unaltered horse shape, but also the one found in the greatest range of production colours (fourteen colourways have now been located, including blue gloss, and there could be a few more!)

As for the future in terms of Beswick equines, Doug Middleweek's commission of the Darmoor foal "Another Star" (completing the Dartmoor family) was the only equine model produced with a Beswick backstamp in 1998. In 1999 the Dartmoor stallion, mare and foal were made exclusively for Doug Middleweek and Company in a limited edition of 150 as a tableau on a ceramic "moorland" base. Also in 1999 the Beswick Collector's Club commissioned a limited number of the Welsh Champion Pony in black gloss with a Beswick backstamp, of which 580 will be produced. Royal Doulton continued to "trim" the range of horses available and 1998/99 saw the retirement of several equine models which were formerly issued under the Beswick name. However, in September 1999 Royal Doulton announced that — horses would revert to the Beswick backstamp, and — horses previously manufactured under the Royal Doulton backstamp would move to Beswick, an exciting development for collectors!

Note: DA numbers are given for easy cross-reference with *The Charlton Standard Catalogue of Royal Doulton Animals.*

INDEX BY MODEL NUMBER

Model No. 701

BOIS ROUSSEL
RACEHORSE

There are two varieties of Bois Roussell. The first version was introduced in 1939.

FIRST VERSION : The tail is attached to the hind legs all the way down and the legs are long and thick.

Designer: Arthur Gredington
Height: 8", 20.3 cm

Colourway	Finish	Intro.	Disc.	U.K. £	U.S. $	Can. $
Blue	Gloss	1939	1947		Extremely Rare	
Light brown	Gloss	1940	1947	250.00	400.00	575.00
Dark brown	Gloss	1940	1947	275.00	450.00	650.00
Dark chestnut	Gloss	1939	1947	350.00	550.00	800.00
Rocking horse grey	Gloss	c.1940	1947	475.00	750.00	1,100.00

SECOND VERSION: **In 1947 Bois Roussel was remodelled with only the tail-end attached to the leg.**

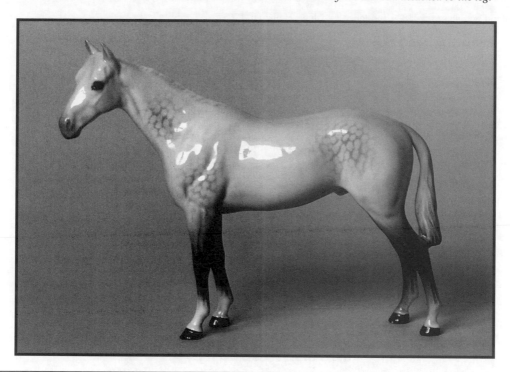

Colourway	Finish	DA #	Intro.	Disc.	U.K. £	U.S. $	Can. $
Brown							
a. Original issue	Gloss	42	1947	1989	48.00	80.00	115.00
b. Reissued	Gloss	42	1999	Current	48.00	N/A	N/A
Brown							
a. Original issue	Matt	42	1979	1989	48.00	80.00	115.00
b. Reissued	Matt	42	1999	Curent	48.00	N/A	N/A
Chestnut	Gloss	—	1958	1967	350.00	575.00	825.00
Grey	Gloss	42	1960	1989	75.00	125.00	175.00
Grey	Matt	—	1970	1989	75.00	125.00	175.00
Opaque	Gloss	—	1960	1967	225.00	375.00	525.00
Painted white	Gloss	—	1952	1967	250.00	425.00	575.00
Palomino	Gloss	—	1960	1989	75.00	125.00	175.00
Palomino	Matt	—	1970	1983	75.00	125.00	175.00
Rocking horse grey	Gloss	—	1947	1962	400.00	650.00	950.00
White	Matt	—	1970	1982	100.00	150.00	235.00

Note: Model No.701 (Second Version) was transferred to the Royal Doulton backstamp (DA42) in 1989. The brown colourway reverted back to the Beswick backstamp in September 1999.

SERIES: *On ceramic stand or wooden plinths*

The stand was shape no. 1809, modelled by Albert Hallam in 1963.

Colourway/stand/finish	Intro.	Disc.	U.K. £	U.S. $	Can. $
Brown/brown ceramic/gloss	c.1963	Unknown	150.00	250.00	350.00
Brown/copper lustre ceramic/gloss	c.1963	Unknown	125.00	200.00	300.00
Chestnut/ceramic/gloss	c.1963	Unknown	375.00	650.00	875.00
Brown/wooden plinth/matt	c.1989	c.1989	75.00	125.00	175.00

Model No. 728

FOAL
(Comical Type)

Designer: Arthur Gredington
Height: 5", 12.7 cm

Colourway	Finish	Intro.	Disc.	U.K. £	U.S. $	Can. $
Blue	Gloss	1939	1954		Extremely Rare	
Brown	Gloss	1940	1971	30.00	50.00	70.00
Chestnut	Gloss	1958	1966	200.00	325.00	475.00
Dark chestnut	Gloss	1939	1954		Extremely Rare	
Grey	Gloss	1961	1971	95.00	150.00	225.00
Opaque	Gloss	1961	1971	125.00	200.00	295.00
Painted white	Gloss	1961	1966	175.00	275.00	400.00
Palomino	Gloss	1961	1971	95.00	150.00	225.00
Rocking horse grey	Gloss	c.1940	1962	250.00	400.00	575.00
Stone/ivory	Satin	Unknown	1954	95.00	150.00	225.00
White	Matt	1970	1970	65.00	100.00	150.00

Model No. 763/1421

FOAL
(Small, Stretched, Upright)

First Version: Long ears

Second Version: Short ears

Designer: Arthur Gredington
Height: 3 ½", 8.9 cm

FIRST VERSION: Long ears, thick legs. When viewed from the back legs almost touch. Tail is straight.

Colourway	Finish	Intro.	Disc.	U.K. £	U.S. $	Can. $
Blue	Gloss	1940	Unknown		Extremely Rare	
Brown	Gloss	1940	Unknown	25.00	40.00	60.00
Rocking horse grey	Gloss	c.1940	Unknown	225.00	350.00	525.00

SECOND VERSION: Short ears, thick legs, but an overall smaller model. Tail is straight.

Colourway	Finish	Intro.	Disc.	U.K. £	U.S. $	Can. $
Blue	Gloss	Unknown	1956		Extremely Rare	
Brown	Gloss	Unknown	1956	25.00	40.00	60.00
Painted white	Gloss	Unknown	1956	150.00	250.00	350.00
Rocking horse grey	Gloss	Unknown	1956	225.00	350.00	525.00

THIRD VERSION: Very thin legs with off hind stretched out well behind the near hind. Tail is slightly bent.

In 1956 model no. 763 was completely remodelled by Arthur Gredington, but the model no. 763 was retained.

Colourway	Finish	Intro.	Disc.	U.K. £	U.S. $	Can. $
Brown	Gloss	1956	1976	25.00	40.00	55.00
Chestnut	Gloss	1958	1967	175.00	275.00	400.00
Grey	Gloss	1961	1976	60.00	100.00	150.00
Opaque	Gloss	1961	1973	85.00	150.00	200.00
Painted white	Gloss	1962	1967	150.00	250.00	350.00
Palomino	Gloss	1956	1976	55.00	85.00	125.00
Rocking horse grey	Gloss	1956	1961	225.00	350.00	525.00
White	Matt	1970	1976	50.00	80.00	125.00

Model No. 766

FOAL - TROTTING
(With Or Without Base)

Designer: Arthur Gredington
Height: 3 ¾", 9.5 cm

VARIATION No. 1. Free standing

Colourway	Finish	Intro.	Disc.	U.K. £	U.S. $	Can. $
Blue	Gloss	1940	By 1954			
Light brown	Gloss	1940	By 1954			
Dark brown	Gloss	1940	By 1954	All colourways are		
Dark chestnut	Gloss	1940	By 1954	extremely rare		
Rocking horse grey	Gloss	1940	By 1954			

VARIATION No. 2. On ceramic base

Colourway	Finish	Intro.	Disc.	U.K. £	U.S. $	Can. $
Blue	Gloss	1940	By 1954			
Light brown	Gloss	1940	By 1954	All colourways are		
Dark brown	Gloss	1940	By 1954	extremely rare		
Dark chestnut	Gloss	1940	By 1954			

Model No. 815

FOAL
(Small, Stretched, Facing Right)

Designer: Arthur Gredington
Height: 3 ¼", 8.3 cm

Colourway	Finsh	DA #	Intro.	Disc.	U.K. £	U.S. $	Can. $
Blue	Gloss	—	1940	1954		Extremely Rare	
Brown	Gloss	74	1940	1989	20.00	30.00	50.00
Brown	Matt	74	1979	1989	20.00	30.00	50.00
Chestnut	Gloss	—	1958	1967	175.00	275.00	400.00
Dark chestnut	Gloss	—	1940	1954		Extremely Rare	
Grey	Gloss	74	*1961*	1989	30.00	50.00	70.00
Opaque	Gloss	—	*1961*	1973	85.00	135.00	200.00
Painted white	Gloss	—	1962	1967	150.00	250.00	350.00
Palomino	Gloss	—	*1961*	1989	25.00	40.00	60.00
Rocking horse grey	Gloss	—	c.1940	1962	225.00	350.00	525.00
White	Matt	—	1970	1982	40.00	65.00	95.00

Note: Model No.815 was transferred to the Beswick backstamp (DA74) in 1989.

Model No. 818   SHIRE MARE

In recognition of 50 years of production of model number 818 a black gloss shire mare was commissioned by the Beswick Collectors Circle in 1990. Approximately 135 of these were issued with a gold backstamp for Circle Members.

Designer: Arthur Gredington
Height: 8 ½", 21.6 cm

FIRST VERSION: *Without Harness*

Colourway	Finish	DA#	Intro.	Disc.	U.K. £	U.S. $	Can. $
Black	Gloss	—	Unknown	Unknown	625.00	1,000.00	2,250.00
Black (BCC90)	Gloss	—	1990	1990	625.00	1,000.00	2,250.00
Blue	Gloss	—	*c.1940*	*1954*		Extremely Rare	
Brown	Gloss	43	1940	1989	40.00	65.00	95.00
Brown	Matt	43	1979	1989	50.00	75.00	125.00
Chestnut	Gloss	—	1958	1967	550.00	875.00	1,300.00
Grey	Gloss	—	*1961*	1989	65.00	100.00	150.00
Iron Grey	Gloss	—	1952	Unknown		Very Rare	
Opaque	Gloss	—	*1961*	1973	200.00	325.00	475.00
Painted white	Gloss	—	*1961*	1970	500.00	800.00	1,200.00
Palomino	Gloss	—	*1961*	1973	650.00	1,000.00	1,500.00
Piebald	Gloss	—	Unknown	Unknown	1,000.00	1,600.00	2,250.00
Rocking horse grey	Gloss	—	*c.1940*	1962	350.00	550.00	825.00
Skewbald	Gloss	—	Unknown	Unknown	700.00	950.00	1,650.00
White	Matt	—	1970	1982	85.00	135.00	200.00

Note: Other than the BCC Special which has a blue and yellow ribbon, all models of No.818 have yellow ribbons.

SECOND VERSION: *Dressed; Series — Harnessed Horses*

Colourway	Finish	Intro.	Disc.	U.K. £	U.S. $	Can. $
Brown	Gloss	1974	1982	125.00	250.00	375.00
Grey	Gloss	1974	1982	150.00	300.00	425.00

Model No. 836

FOAL
(Large, Stretched)

First Version: Parallel fore legs

Second Version: Splayed fore legs

Designer: Arthur Gredington
Height: 5", 12.7 cm

FIRST VERSION: *Parallel fore legs.*

Colourway	Finish	Intro.	Disc.	U.K. £	U.S. $	Can. $
Blue	Gloss	Unknown	Unknown		Extremely Rare	
Brown	Gloss	1940	Unknown	35.00	55.00	80.00
Light Brown	Gloss	c.1940-50	Unknown	50.00	80.00	125.00
Brown	Matt	1979	Unknown	35.00	55.00	80.00
Chestnut	Gloss	1961	Unknown	225.00	350.00	525.00
Grey	Gloss	1961	Unknown	50.00	80.00	125.00
Opaque	Gloss	1961	Unknown	85.00	135.00	200.00
Painted white	Gloss	1961	Unknown	175.00	275.00	400.00
Palomino	Gloss	1961	Unknown	50.00	80.00	125.00
Pink	Gloss	Unknown	Unknown		Extremely Rare	
Rocking horse grey	Gloss	1961	Unknown	275.00	450.00	650.00
White	Matt	1970	Unknown	40.00	65.00	95.00

SECOND VERSION: *Splayed fore legs.*

Colourway	Finish	Intro.	Disc.	U.K. £	U.S. $	Can. $
Brown	Gloss	Unknown	1984	35.00	55.00	80.00
Brown	Matt	Unknown	1984	35.00	55.00	80.00
Chestnut	Gloss	Unknown	1967	225.00	350.00	525.00
Grey	Gloss	Unknown	1983	50.00	80.00	125.00
Opaque	Gloss	Unknown	1973	95.00	150.00	225.00
Painted white	Gloss	Unknown	1967	175.00	275.00	400.00
Palomino	Gloss	Unknown	1984	50.00	80.00	125.00
White	Matt	Unknown	1982	45.00	75.00	100.00

Model No. 855/1090   **STOCKY JOGGING MARE**

FIRST VERSION: Modelled September 1940. Near fore leg is raised off the ground, near hind leg is under the body. Tail attached to the leg all the way down. Legs rather crudely modelled.

Designer: Arthur Gredington
Height: 6", 5.0 cm

Colourway	Finish	Intro.	Disc.	U.K. £	U.S. $	Can. $
Blue	Gloss	1940	1941			
Dark brown	Gloss	1940	1941	All colourways are		
Light brown	Gloss	1940	1941	extremely rare		
Dark chestnut	Gloss	1940	1941			
Rocking horse grey	Gloss	1940	1941			

SECOND VERSION: Modelled September 1941. Near fore leg is raised off the ground, near hind leg is under the body. Tail arched away from the leg. More shape to the joints of the legs.

Colourway	Finish	Intro.	Disc.	U.K. £	U.S. $	Can. $
Blue	Gloss	1941	1947		Extremely Rare	
Brown	Gloss	1941	1947	300.00	500.00	700.00
Dark chestnut	Gloss	1941	1947		Extremely Rare	
Rocking horse grey	Gloss	1941	1947		Extremely Rare	

THIRD VERSION: Shape no. 1090 was modelled in 1947 but retained the number 855.
Off fore leg raised from the ground, off hind leg under the body.
Tail more arched from the body. Head lowered. A chunkier model.

Colourway	Finish	DA #	Intro.	Disc.	U.K. £	U.S. $	Can. $
Blue	Gloss	1947	Unknown		Extremely Rare		
Brown							
a. Original issue	Gloss	44	1947	1989	45.00	75.00	110.00
b. Reissued	Gloss	44	1999	Current	45.00	N/A	N/A
Chestnut	Gloss	—	1958	1967	300.00	500.00	700.00
Grey	Gloss	—	1961	1989	65.00	100.00	150.00
Opaque	Gloss	—	1961	1973	200.00	325.00	475.00
Painted white	Gloss	—	1961	1967	275.00	450.00	650.00
Palomino	Gloss	—	1961	1989	65.00	100.00	150.00
Rocking horse grey	Gloss	—	c.1947	1962	350.00	550.00	825.00
White	Matt	—	1970	1982	95.00	150.00	225.00

Note: Model No.855 (Third Version) was transferred to the Royal Doulton backstamp (DA44) in 1989. The brown gloss colourway reverted to the Beswick backstamp in September 1999.

Model No. 868

HUNTSMAN
(On Rearing Horse)

STYLE ONE: On rearing horse

*FIRST VERSION: Huntsman is sitting straight up and his lower legs are also vertical.
His coat is cut away at the waist. He is riding a common headed horse.*

Designer: Arthur Gredington
Height: 10", 25.4 cm

COLOURWAY No. 1. Orangey red coat, cream breeches.

Colourway	Finish	Intro.	Disc.	U.K. £	U.S. $	Can. $
Brown	Gloss	1940	1952	325.00	525.00	750.00
Dark chestnut	Gloss	1940	1952		Extremely Rare	
Rocking horse grey	Gloss	c.1940	1952		Extremely Rare	

COLOURWAY No. 2. Scarlet coat and white breeches.

Colourway	Finish	Intro.	Disc.	U.K. £	U.S. $	Can. $
Brown	Gloss	1940	1952	300.00	475.00	700.00
Rocking horse grey	Gloss	c.1948	1952		Extremely Rare	

*SECOND VERSION: Huntsman is leaning back slightly. His coat is not cut away at the waist.
The horse's head has an Arab appearance (dished profile).*

Colourway	Finish	Intro.	Disc.	U.K. £	U.S. $	Can. $
Brown	Gloss	1952	1995	125.00	200.00	275.00
Chestnut	Gloss	1958	1967	775.00	1,300.00	1,750.00
Grey	Gloss	1962	1972	600.00	950.00	1,400.00
Opaque	Gloss	1971	1973	250.00	400.00	600.00
Painted white	Gloss	1965	1971	350.00	600.00	850.00
Palomino	Gloss	*1961*	1972	775.00	1,300.00	1,750.00
Rocking horse grey	Gloss	*1952*	*1962*	900.00	1,500.00	2,000.00
White	Matt	1971	1981	175.00	300.00	400.00

SERIES: Britannia Collection

Colourway	Finish	Intro.	Disc.	U.K. £	U.S. $	Can. $
Bronze	Satin	1989	1993	150.00	275.00	375.00

Model No. 915

FOAL
(Lying)

Designer: Arthur Gredington
Height: 3 ¼", 8.3 cm

Colourway	Finish	DA #	Intro.	Disc.	U.K. £	U.S. $	Can. $
Brown							
a. Original issue	Gloss	75	1941	1989	15.00	25.00	35.00
b. Reissued	Gloss	75	1999	Current	15.00	N/A	N/A
Brown	Matt	75	1979	1989	25.00	45.00	60.00
Chestnut	Gloss	—	1958	1967	195.00	325.00	475.00
Grey	Gloss	75	*1961*	1989	40.00	65.00	90.00
Opaque	Gloss	—	*1961*	1973	80.00	125.00	200.00
Painted white	Gloss	—	1962	1967	175.00	300.00	400.00
Palomino	Gloss	—	*1961*	1989	40.00	65.00	90.00
Rocking horse grey	Gloss	—	c.1942	*1962*	225.00	400.00	525.00
White	Matt	—	1970	1982	45.00	75.00	100.00

Note: Model No.915 was transferred to the Royal Doulton backstamp (DA75) in 1989. The brown gloss colourway reverted back to the Beswick backstamp in September 1999.

Model No. 939   GIRL ON JUMPING HORSE

The horse used for model 939 is also that used for model 982 "Huntswoman."

Designer: Arthur Gredington
Height: 9 ¾", 24.7 cm

Colourway	Finish	Intro.	Disc.	U.K. £	U.S. $	Can. $
Brown	Gloss	1941	1965	275.00	475.00	650.00

Model No. 946

FOAL
(Grazing)

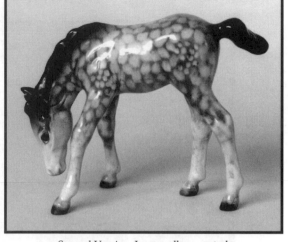

First Version: Off-side hooves almost touch

Second Version: Legs well separated

Designer: Arthur Gredington
Height: 3 ¼", 8.3 cm

FIRST VERSION: *Has common head and the off-side hooves almost touch.*

Colourway	Finish	Intro.	Disc.	U.K. £	U.S. $	Can. $
Brown	Gloss	1941	1955	40.00	65.00	95.00
Rocking horse grey	Gloss	1941	1955	300.00	500.00	700.00

SECOND VERSION: *Much finer head with the legs being well separated.*

Colourway	Finish	DA #	Intro.	Disc.	U.K. £	U.S. $	Can. $
Brown							
a. Original issue	Gloss	76	1955	1989	16.00	25.00	35.00
b. Reissued	Gloss	76	1999	Current	16.00	N/A	N/A
Brown	Matt	76	1979	1989	25.00	45.00	60.00
Chestnut	Gloss	—	1958	1967	195.00	325.00	475.00
Grey	Gloss	76	1961	1989	35.00	60.00	85.00
Opaque	Gloss	—	1961	1967	90.00	150.00	250.00
Painted white	Gloss	—	1961	1967	175.00	275.00	400.00
Palomino	Gloss	76	1961	1989	30.00	50.00	70.00
Rocking horse grey	Gloss	—	1955	1962	300.00	500.00	700.00
White	Matt	—	1970	1982	45.00	75.00	100.00

Note: Model No.946 (Second Version) was transferred to the Royal Doulton backstamp (DA76) in 1989. The brown gloss colourway of this model reverted to the Beswick backstamp in September 1999.

Model No. 947

FOAL
(Large, Head Down)

This model in the dun colourway, along with the Mare (976), was the 1997 Beswick Collectors Club Special. They show both the "Beswick" and BCC97 backstamps. The Foal (in the dun colourway) was issued in a limited edition of 730.

Designer: Arthur Gredington
Height: 4 ½", 11.9 cm

Colourway	Finish	DA #	Intro.	Disc.	U.K. £	U.S. $	Can. $
Brown							
a. Original issue	Gloss	77	1941	1989	22.00	35.00	50.00
b. Reissued	Gloss	77	1999	Current	22.00	N/A	N/A
Brown	Matt	77	1979	1989	25.00	45.00	60.00
Chestnut	Gloss	—	1958	1967	200.00	325.00	500.00
Dun (BCC97)	Gloss	—	1997	1997	60.00	95.00	225.00
Grey	Gloss	—	*1961*	1983	40.00	75.00	95.00
Opaque	Gloss	—	*1961*	1973	75.00	125.00	175.00
Painted white	Gloss	—	1962	1967	195.00	325.00	450.00
Palomino	Gloss	—	*1961*	1983	35.00	60.00	80.00
Rocking horse grey	Gloss	—	c.1942	1962	275.00	450.00	625.00
White	Matt	—	1970	1982	50.00	80.00	110.00

Note: Model No.947 was transferred to the Royal Doulton backstamp (DA77) in 1989. The brown gloss colourway reverted to the Beswick backstamp in September 1999.

Model No. 951   **SHIRE FOAL**
(Large)

Designer: Arthur Gredington
Height: 6 ¼", 15.9 cm

Colourway	Finish	Intro.	Disc.	U.K. £	U.S. $	Can. $
Blue	Gloss	1941	Unknown		Extremely Rare	
Brown	Gloss	1941	1971	50.00	80.00	125.00
Chestnut	Gloss	1958	1967	350.00	550.00	800.00
Grey	Gloss	*1961*	1971	150.00	250.00	350.00
Opaque	Gloss	*1961*	1971	125.00	200.00	275.00
Painted white	Gloss	1962	1967	250.00	400.00	575.00
Palomino	Gloss	*1961*	1971	150.00	250.00	350.00
Rocking horse grey	Gloss	1941	1962	425.00	675.00	1,000.00
White	Matt	1970	1970	100.00	150.00	225.00

Model No. 953　　　　　　　**MARE AND FOAL ON BASE**

The mare is a modern 976 with the foal and the base varying.

FIRST VERSION: *The foal has its tail and near fore leg slightly raised.*
The base was rectangular.

Designer:　Arthur Gredington
Height:　　7 ¾", 19.7 cm

Colourway	Finish	Intro.	Disc.	U.K. £	U.S. $	Can. $
Brown	Gloss	1941	1949		Extremely Rare	
Rocking horse grey	Gloss	1941	1949		Extremely Rare	

SECOND VERSION: Foal has all four legs attached to an irregularly shaped base and the tail hangs straight down.

Model 953, Second Version   Model 953, Third Version

Colourway	Finish	Intro.	Disc.	U.K. £	U.S. $	Can. $
Brown	Gloss	1949	1983	125.00	200.00	300.00
Chestnut	Gloss	1958	1967	600.00	950.00	1,400.00
Grey	Gloss	1958	1972	500.00	800.00	1,200.00
Opaque	Gloss	1971	1973	250.00	425.00	575.00
Painted white	Gloss	1962	1967	450.00	725.00	1,000.00
Palomino	Gloss	1958	1972	425.00	700.00	975.00
Rocking horse grey	Gloss	1950	1962	750.00	1,200.00	1,800.00
White	Matt	1971	1981	150.00	250.00	350.00

THIRD VERSION: Foal is model no. 1813, second version, on an irregularly shaped base.

Colourway	Finish	Intro.	Disc.	U.K. £	U.S. $	Can. $
Brown mare with an orangey bay foal	Gloss	1981	1983	95.00	175.00	250.00
Brown mare and foal, green matt base	Matt	1981	1983	100.00	175.00	250.00

Model No. 975   **CANTERING SHIRE**

This model in the black colourway was the 1996 Beswick Collectors Club Special.

Designer: Arthur Gredington
Height: 8 ¾", 22.2 cm

Colourway	Finish	DA #	Intro.	Disc.	U.K. £	U.S. $	Can. $
Black (BCC96)	Gloss	—	1996	1996	125.00	200.00	300.00
Brown	Gloss	45	1943	1989	55.00	95.00	125.00
Brown	Matt	—	1980	1989	65.00	100.00	150.00
Chestnut	Gloss	—	1958	1967	550.00	900.00	1,300.00
Grey	Gloss	—	*1961*	1989	95.00	150.00	225.00
Opaque	Gloss	—	1966	1967	200.00	325.00	475.00
Painted white	Gloss	—	1962	1967	350.00	600.00	800.00
Palomino	Gloss	—	*1961*	1970	300.00	500.00	700.00
Rocking horse grey	Gloss	—	*c.1944*	*1962*	425.00	700.00	1,000.00
White	Matt	—	1971	1982	100.00	150.00	225.00

Note: Model No.975 was transferred to the Royal Doulton Backstamp (DA45) in 1989.
This model is also known in flambé.

Model No. 976

MARE
(Facing Left)

This model and the foal (947) in dun gloss were the 1997 Beswick Collectors Club Special. They have both the "Beswick" and BCC97 backstamps. The Mare (in the dun colourway) was issued in a limited edition of 710.

Designer: Arthur Gredington
Height: 6 ¾", 17.2 cm

Colourway	Finish	DA #	Intro.	Disc.	U.K. £	U.S. $	Can. $
Brown	Gloss	46	1941	1989	40.00	65.00	95.00
Brown	Matt	46	1979	1989	50.00	80.00	125.00
Chestnut	Gloss	—	1958	1967	375.00	600.00	875.00
Dun (BCC97)	Gloss	—	1997	1997	125.00	200.00	300.00
Grey	Gloss	46	1962	1989	75.00	125.00	200.00
Opaque	Gloss	—	*1961*	1973	175.00	275.00	400.00
Painted white	Gloss	—	*1961*	1967	325.00	525.00	750.00
Palomino	Gloss	—	*1961*	1983	75.00	125.00	200.00
Rocking horse grey	Gloss	—	*c.1942*	*1962*	400.00	650.00	950.00
White	Matt	—	1970	1982	75.00	125.00	200.00

Model No. 982   HUNTSWOMAN

The horse used for model 982 is the same as that used for model 939 "Girl on Jumping Horse."

STYLE ONE: Rider and Horse Jumping

Designer: Arthur Gredington
Height: 10", 25.4 cm

Colourway	Finish	Intro.	Disc.	U.K. £	U.S. $	Can. $
Brown	Gloss	1942	1967	250.00	450.00	600.00

Model No. 996

FOAL
(Small, Gambolling left)

Designer: Arthur Gredington
Height: 3 ¼", 8.3 cm

Colourway	Finish	Intro.	Disc.	U.K. £	U.S. $	Can. $
Brown	Gloss	1943	1976	30.00	50.00	65.00
Chestnut	Gloss	1958	1967	175.00	275.00	400.00
Grey	Gloss	*1961*	1976	40.00	65.00	95.00
Opaque	Gloss	*1961*	1973	75.00	125.00	175.00
Painted white	Gloss	*1961*	1967	175.00	275.00	400.00
Palomino	Gloss	*1961*	1976	40.00	65.00	95.00
Rocking horse grey	Gloss	*c.1944*	*1962*	225.00	350.00	525.00
White	Matt	1970	1976	40.00	65.00	95.00

Model No. 997

FOAL
(Small, Stretched, Facing Left)

Designer: Arthur Gredington
Height: 3 ¼", 8.3 cm

Colourway	Finish	DA #	Intro.	Disc.	U.K. £	U.S. $	Can. $
Brown							
a. Original issue	Gloss	78	1943	1989	15.00	25.00	35.00
b. Reissued	Gloss	78	1999	Current	15.00	N/A	N/A
Brown	Matt	78	1979	1989	30.00	50.00	65.00
Chestnut	Gloss	—	1958	1967	175.00	275.00	400.00
Grey	Gloss	78	1961	1989	40.00	60.00	95.00
Opaque	Gloss	—	1961	1973	80.00	100.00	150.00
Painted white	Gloss	—	1961	1967	165.00	275.00	375.00
Palomino	Gloss	—	1961	1989	40.00	60.00	95.00
Rocking horse grey	Gloss	—	c.1944	1962	200.00	325.00	500.00
White	Matt	—	1970	1982	40.00	60.00	95.00

Note: Model No.997 was transferred to the Royal Doulton backstamp (DA78) in 1989. The brown gloss colourway reverted to the Beswick backstamp in September 1999.

Model No. 1014

WELSH COB
(Rearing)

FIRST VERSION: The tail is attached to the ceramic base.

Designer: Arthur Gredington
Height: 10 ¼", 26.0 cm

Colourway	Finish	Intro.	Disc.	U.K. £	U.S. $	Can. $
Black	Gloss	Unknown	Unknown	175.00	300.00	400.00
Brown	Gloss	1944	Unknown	75.00	125.00	200.00
Chestnut	Gloss	1958	Unknown	450.00	750.00	1,200.00
Grey	Gloss	*1961*	Unknown	375.00	650.00	1,100.00
Opaque	Gloss	*1961*	Unknown	225.00	375.00	500.00
Painted white	Gloss	*1962*	Unknown	400.00	675.00	900.00
Palomino	Gloss	*1961*	Unknown	250.00	450.00	600.00
Piebald	Gloss	Unknown	Unknown		Extremely Rare	
Rocking horse grey	Gloss	*c.1945*	Unknown	600.00	950.00	1,400.00
White	Matt	1970	Unknown	150.00	250.00	350.00

SECOND VERSION: Tail hangs loose.

Colourway	Finish	DA #	Intro.	Disc.	U.K. £	U.S. $	Can. $
Black	Gloss		*c.1990*	*c.1990*	150.00	250.00	350.00
Brown	Gloss	41	Unknown	1989	75.00	125.00	175.00
Chestnut	Gloss	—	Unknown	1967	450.00	750.00	1,000.00
Grey	Gloss	—	Unknown	1973	375.00	600.00	900.00
Grey	Matt	—	Unknown	1983	175.00	275.00	400.00
Opaque	Gloss	—	Unknown	1973	225.00	375.00	500.00
Painted white	Gloss	—	Unknown	1967	400.00	650.00	900.00
Palomino	Gloss	—	Unknown	1973	325.00	525.00	750.00
White	Matt	—	Unknown	1983	125.00	200.00	300.00

Model No. 1033

SHETLAND PONY
(Woolly Shetland Mare)

Designer: Arthur Gredington
Height: 5 ¾", 14.6 cm

Colourway	Finish	DA#	Intro.	Disc.	U.K. £	U.S. $	Can. $
Brown							
a. Original issue	Gloss	47	1945	1989	27.00	40.00	55.00
b. Reissued	Gloss	47	1999	Current	27.00	N/A	N/A
Brown	Matt	—	Unknown	Unknown		Extremely Rare	
Chestnut	Gloss	—	Unknown	Unknown	500.00	800.00	1,200.00
Dapple grey	Gloss	—	Unknown	Unknown	500.00	800.00	1,200.00
Palomino	Gloss	—	Unknown	Unknown	500.00	800.00	1,200.00
White	Matt	—	1973	1982	60.00	95.00	150.00

Note: Model No.1033 was transferred to the Royal Doulton backstamp (DA47) in 1989. The brown gloss colourway reverted to the Beswick backstamp in September 1999.

Model No. 1034   SHETLAND FOAL

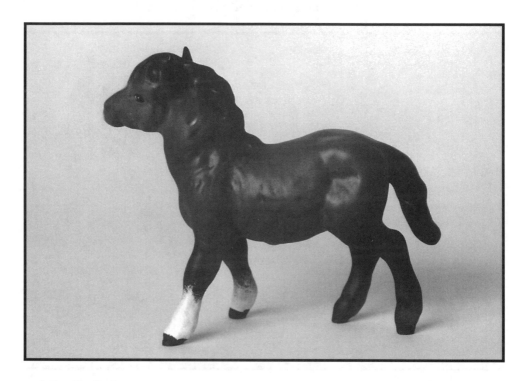

Designer: Arthur Gredington
Height: 3 ¾", 9.5 cm

Colourway	Finish	DA #	Intro.	Disc.	U.K. £	U.S. $	Can. $
Brown							
a. Original issue	Gloss	79	1945	1989	15.00	25.00	35.00
b. Reissued	Gloss	79	1999	Current	15.00	N/A	N/A
Brown	Matt	79	1979	1989	25.00	50.00	75.00
White	Matt	—	1973	1982	40.00	75.00	90.00

Note: Model No.1034 was transferred to the Royal Doulton backstamp (DA79) in 1989. The brown gloss colourway reverted to the Beswick backstamp in September 1999.

Model No. 1037   **RACEHORSE AND JOCKEY**
(Walking Racehorse)

The jockey's silks, for an extra payment, could be decorated as the purchaser wished. A great many colourways and number cloths could exist.

Colourway No. 1 - Stripes on saddlecloth   Colourway No. 2 - Number on saddlecloth

Designer: Arthur Gredington
Height: 8 ½", 21.6 cm

STYLE ONE: Walking Racehorse

Colourway No. 1. Stripes on saddlecloth

Colourway	Finish	Intro.	Disc.	U.K. £	U.S. $	Can. $
Brown	Gloss	1945	Unknown	300.00	475.00	700.00

Colourway No. 2. Number on saddlecloth

Colourway	Finish	Intro.	Disc.	U.K. £	U.S. $	Can. $
Brown	Gloss	Unknown	1976	250.00	400.00	625.00
Chestnut	Gloss	Unknown	Unknown		Extremely Rare	

Model No. 1050   GRAZING SHIRE

Designer: Arthur Gredington
Height: 5 ½", 14.0 cm

Colourway	Finish	Intro.	Disc.	U.K. £	U.S. $	Can. $
Brown	Gloss	1946	1970	75.00	125.00	200.00
Chestnut	Gloss	1958	1967	475.00	750.00	1,100.00
Grey	Gloss	1962	1970	550.00	950.00	1,250.00
Opaque	Gloss	*1961*	1970	225.00	350.00	525.00
Painted white	Gloss	1962	1967	600.00	1,000.00	1,350.00
Palomino	Gloss	*1961*	1970	500.00	850.00	1,150.00
Rocking horse grey	Gloss	*c.1947*	1962	750.00	1,250.00	1,750.00

Model No. 1053

SHIRE FOAL
(Small)

Designer: Arthur Gredington
Height: 5", 12.7 cm

Colourway	Finish	Intro.	Disc.	U.K. £	U.S. $	Can. $
Brown	Gloss	1946	1984	35.00	55.00	80.00
Brown	Matt	1979	1984	30.00	50.00	70.00
Chestnut	Gloss	1958	1967	325.00	550.00	750.00
Grey	Gloss	*1961*	1973	150.00	250.00	350.00
Opaque	Gloss	*1961*	1973	125.00	200.00	300.00
Painted white	Gloss	1962	1967	250.00	425.00	575.00
Palomino	Gloss	*1961*	1973	150.00	250.00	350.00
Rocking horse grey	Gloss	*c.1947*	1962	400.00	675.00	900.00
White	Matt	1970	1982	75.00	125.00	200.00

Model No. 1084

FOAL
(Medium, Almost Stood Square)

Designer: Arthur Gredington
Height: 4 ½", 11.9 cm

Colourway	Finish	Intro.	Disc.	U.K. £	U.S. $	Can. $
Brown	Gloss	1947	1984	30.00	50.00	70.00
Brown	Matt	1979	1983	25.00	50.00	70.00
Chestnut	Gloss	1958	1967	275.00	450.00	625.00
Grey	Gloss	*1961*	1973	85.00	135.00	200.00
Opaque	Gloss	*1961*	1973	80.00	135.00	200.00
Painted white	Gloss	*1961*	1967	185.00	300.00	450.00
Palomino	Gloss	*1961*	1973	70.00	125.00	175.00
Rocking horse grey	Gloss	*c.1948*	1962	325.00	525.00	750.00
White	Matt	1970	1982	60.00	100.00	150.00

Model No. 1085

FOAL
(Medium, Head Down)

Designer: Arthur Gredington
Height: 3 ½", 8.9 cm

Colourway	Finish	Intro.	Disc.	U.K. £	U.S. $	Can. $
Brown	Gloss	1947	1971	40.00	65.00	95.00
Chestnut	Gloss	1958	1967	300.00	500.00	675.00
Grey	Gloss	*1961*	1971	125.00	200.00	275.00
Opaque	Gloss	*1961*	1971	100.00	150.00	250.00
Painted white	Gloss	*1961*	1967	175.00	300.00	400.00
Palomino	Gloss	*1961*	1971	100.00	150.00	225.00
Rocking horse grey	Gloss	*c.1948*	1962	350.00	600.00	800.00
White	Matt	1970	1970	75.00	125.00	175.00

Model No. 1145

KNIGHT IN ARMOUR
(The Earl of Warwick)

Designer: Arthur Gredington
Height: 10 ¾", 27.8 cm

Colourway	Finish	Intro.	Disc.	U.K. £	U.S. $	Can. $
Grey	Gloss	1949	1973	900.00	1,400.00	2,000.00

Model No. 1182   **SWISH TAIL HORSE**

First Version: The tail is attached to the   Second Version: The tail is slightly lower
quarter almost parallel to the ground   down and only to the edge of the quarters

Designer: Arthur Gredington
Height: 8 ¾", 22.2 cm

FIRST VERSION: The tail is attached to the quarters almost parallel to the ground.

Colourway	Finish	Intro.	Disc.	U.K. £	U.S. $	Can. $
Brown	Gloss	1950	c.1982	70.00	115.00	165.00
Brown	Matt	1970	c.1982	60.00	95.00	150.00
Chestnut	Gloss	1958	1967	300.00	500.00	700.00
Grey	Gloss	1961	c.1982	80.00	130.00	175.00
Grey	Matt	1970	c.1982	80.00	130.00	175.00
Opaque	Gloss	*1961*	1973	200.00	300.00	450.00
Painted white	Gloss	*1961*	1967	325.00	525.00	750.00
Palomino	Gloss	*1961*	c.1982	80.00	130.00	175.00
Palomino	Matt	1970	c.1982	80.00	130.00	175.00
Rocking horse grey	Gloss	*c.1951*	1962	400.00	650.00	900.00
White	Matt	1970	c.1982	85.00	135.00	200.00

SECOND VERSION: The tail is attached slightly lower down and only to the edge of the quarters.

Colourway	Finish	DA #	Intro.	Disc.	U.K. £	U.S. $	Can. $
Brown	Gloss	48	c.1982	1989	50.00	80.00	125.00
Brown	Matt	48	c.1982	1989	40.00	65.00	100.00
Grey	Gloss	—	c.1982	1989	60.00	95.00	150.00
Grey	Matt	—	c.1982	1989	60.00	95.00	150.00
Palomino	Gloss	—	c.1982	1983	60.00	95.00	150.00
Palomino	Matt	—	c.1982	1983	60.00	95.00	150.00
White	Matt		c.1982	1982	65.00	100.00	150.00

Note: Model No.1182 (Second Version) was transferred to the Royal Doulton backstamp (DA48) in 1989.

Model No. 1197

PONY
(Head Up)

Designer: Arthur Gredington
Height: 5 ½", 14.0 cm

Colourway	Finish	Intro.	Disc.	U.K. £	U.S. $	Can. $
Brown	Gloss	1950	1975	60.00	95.00	150.00
Chestnut	Gloss	1958	1967	325.00	525.00	750.00
Grey	Gloss	1962	1975	85.00	135.00	200.00
Opaque	Gloss	1961	1973	150.00	250.00	350.00
Painted white	Gloss	1961	1967	275.00	450.00	625.00
Palomino	Gloss	1961	1975	75.00	125.00	175.00
Piebald	Gloss	Unknown	Unknown	Extremely Rare		
Rocking horse grey	Gloss	c.1951	1962	350.00	600.00	800.00
White	Matt	1970	1975	75.00	125.00	175.00

Model No. 1261

PALOMINO
(Prancing Arab Type)

FIRST VERSION: Thicker tail with more definition.

  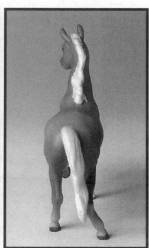

| Model No. 1261 First Version | First Version - Thicker tail | Second Version - Thinner tail |

Designer: Arthur Gredington   Height: 6 ¾", 17.2 cm

Colourway	Finish	Intro.	Disc.	U.K. £	U.S. $	Can. $
Brown	Gloss	*1961*	Unknown	60.00	95.00	140.00
Brown	Matt	1970	Unknown	55.00	90.00	130.00
Chestnut	Gloss	*1958*	1967	325.00	550.00	750 00
Grey	Gloss	*1961*	Unknown	75.00	125.00	175.00
Grey	Matt	1970	Unknown	70.00	120.00	165.00
Opaque	Gloss	*1961*	1973	150.00	250.00	350.00
Painted white	Gloss	*1961*	1967	225.00	375.00	500.00
Palomino	Gloss	1952	Unknown	70.00	120.00	165.00
Palomino	Matt	1970	Unknown	60.00	95.00	140.00
Rocking horse grey	Gloss	*c.1956*	1962	350.00	550.00	800.00
White	Matt	1970	Unknown	75.00	120.00	175.00

SECOND VERSION: Thinner tail with little definition.

Colourway	Finish	DA #	Intro.	Disc.	U.K. £	U.S. $	Can. $
Brown							
a. Original issue	Gloss	49	Unknown	1989	45.00	70.00	100.00
b. Reissued	Gloss	49	1999	Current	45.00	N/A	N/A
Brown	Matt	49	Unknown	1989	40.00	65.00	95.00
Grey							
a. Original issue	Gloss	49	Unknown	1989	45.00	70.00	100.00
b. Reissued	Gloss	49	1999	Current	45.00	N/A	N/A
Grey	Matt	—	Unknown	1989	55.00	90.00	130.00
Palomino							
a. Original issue	Gloss	49	Unknown	1989	45.00	70.00	100.00
b. Reissued	Gloss	49	1999	Current	45.00	N/A	N/A
Palomino	Matt	—	Unknown	1989	45.00	70.00	100.00
White	Matt	—	Unknown	1982	60.00	95.00	140.00

Note: Model No.1261 (Second Version) was transferred to the Royal Doulton backstamp (DA49) in 1989. The brown, grey and palomino gloss colourways reverted to the Beswick backstamp in September 1999.

Model No. 1265   ARAB "XAYAL"

The charcoal grey colourway with four white socks is the authentic colouring for " Xayal. " The charcoal grey colourway
varies from black to charcoal grey.

Arab " Xayal "

Arab " Xayal " Connoisseur Horse

Designer: Arthur Gredington
Height: 6 ¼", 15.9 cm

Colourway	Finish	DA#	Intro.	Disc.	U.K. £	U.S. $	Can. $
Brown	Gloss	50	1952	1989	50.00	80.00	125.00
Charcoal grey	Gloss	—	1952	1984	85.00	135.00	200.00
Chestnut	Gloss	—	1958	1967	250.00	400.00	600.00
Grey	Gloss	50	1961	1989	75.00	125.00	175.00
Opaque	Gloss	—	1961	1973	150.00	250.00	350.00
Painted white	Gloss	—	1961	1967	225.00	375.00	500.00
Palomino	Gloss	50	1961	1989	70.00	120.00	165.00
Rocking horse grey	Gloss	—	c.1953	1962	350.00	550.00	825.00
White	Matt	—	1961	1984	75.00	125.00	175.00

SERIES: Connoisseur Horses

Height: 7 ¼", 18.4 cm

Colourway	Finish	Intro.	Disc.	U.K. £	U.S. $	Can. $
Dark brown	Matt	1970	1989	95.00	150.00	225.00

Note: Model No.1265 was transferred to the Royal Doulton backstamp (DA50) in 1989.

Model No. 1359

SUFFOLK PUNCH
CHAMPION "HASSE DAINTY"

Designer: Mr. Orwell
Height: 8", 20.3 cm

Colourway	Finish	Intro.	Disc.	U.K. £	U.S. $	Can. $
Light chestnut	Gloss	1954	Unknown	300.00	500.00	700.00
Dark chestnut	Gloss	Unknown	1971	300.00	500.00	700.00
Grey	Gloss	1965	1965	550.00	900.00	1,300.00
Palomino	Gloss	Unknown	Unknown	550.00	900.00	1,300.00

COLOURWAY DESCRIPTIONS

Light Chestnut: Light chestnut horse with much lighter chestnut hooves. Blended thin stripe down the front of the head. Mane and tail are cream with yellow ribbon braided through the mane ending with cream and maroon. Two maroon bows on the tail.

Dark Chestnut: Much darker chestnut horse with dark chestnust mane and tail. Definite white blaze extending over muzzle, and four short white socks. The mane ribbon is lemon with pink at the end and the tail bows are lemon and pink and indistinct.

Model No. 1361   **HACKNEY**

The black colourway is the authentic colouring of "Black Magic of Nork" and has white patches on the flanks.

Designer: Mr. Orwell
Height: 7 ¾", 19.7 cm

Colourway	Finish	Intro.	Disc.	U.K. £	U.S. $	Can. $
Black	Gloss	1955	1983	175.00	300.00	400.00
Black	Matt	1980	1983	150.00	250.00	350.00
Brown	Gloss	1955	1982	85.00	150.00	250.00
Chestnut	Gloss	1958	1967	400.00	650.00	900.00
Grey	Gloss	*1961*	1975	350.00	550.00	800.00
Opaque	Gloss	*1961*	1973	200.00	325.00	475.00
Painted white	Gloss	*1961*	1967	350.00	550.00	800.00
Palomino	Gloss	*1961*	1970	275.00	450.00	625.00
Rocking horse grey	Gloss	*c.1956*	1962	425.00	700.00	1,000.00
White	Matt	1970	1982	85.00	175.00	250.00

Model No. 1373   **PINTO PONY**

First Version: Tail attached to hind leg from hock down   Second Version: Tail hangs loose

Designer: Arthur Gredington
Height: 6 ½", 16.5 cm

FIRST VERSION: Tail is attached to the hind leg from the hock down.

Colourway	Finish	Intro.	Disc.	U.K. £	U.S. $	Can. $
Chestnut	Gloss	1958	1967	400.00	650.00	1,000.00
Grey	Gloss	1962	1970	450.00	725.00	1,000.00
Palomino	Gloss	*1961*	1970	450.00	725.00	1,000.00
Piebald (black and white)	Gloss	1972	Unknown	95.00	175.00	275.00
Skewbald (brown and white)	Gloss	1955	Unknown	95.00	175.00	275.00

SECOND VERSION: Tail hangs loose.

Colourway	Finish	DA #	Intro.	Disc.	U.K. £	U.S. $	Can. $
Piebald (black and white)	Gloss	67	Unknown	1989	85.00	150.00	225.00
Piebald (black and white)	Matt	67	Unknown	1989	75.00	125.00	200.00
Skewbald (brown and white)	Gloss	67	Unknown	1989	75.00	125.00	200.00
Skewbald (brown and white)	Matt	67	Unknown	1989	75.00	125.00	200.00

Model No. 1374   # GALLOPING HORSE

Model no. 1374 was the horse used for no. 1377 Canadian Mounted Cowboy. However no. 1374 has only three hooves attached to the base compared to four hooves attached in the ridden variety.

Designer: Mr. Orwell
Height: 7 ½", 19.1 cm

Colourway	Finish	Intro.	Disc.	U.K. £	U.S. $	Can. $
Brown	Gloss	1955	1975	175.00	300.00	425.00
Chestnut	Gloss	1958	1967	400.00	675.00	950.00
Grey	Gloss	1962	1973	225.00	375.00	500.00
Palomino	Gloss	*1961*	1973	150.00	250.00	375.00

Model No. 1375

CANADIAN MOUNTIE

Designer: Arthur Gredington
Height: 8 ¼", 21.0 cm

Colourway	Finish	Intro.	Disc.	U.K. £	U.S. $	Can. $
Black	Gloss	1955	1976	450.00	725.00	1,150.00

Model No. 1377   CANADIAN MOUNTED COWBOY

The horse used for model 1377 was also that used for model 1374.

Designer: Mr. Orwell
Height: 8 ¾", 22.2 cm

Colourway	Finish	Intro.	Disc.	U.K. £	U.S. $	Can. $
Palomino	Gloss	1955	1973	650.00	1,000.00	1,500.00

Model No. 1391   **MOUNTED INDIAN**

Designer: Mr. Orwell
Height: 8 ½", 21.6 cm

Colourway	Finish	Intro.	Disc.	U.K. £	U.S. $	Can. $
Skewbald	Gloss	1955	1990	300.00	500.00	750.00

Model No. 1407   **ARAB FOAL**

Designer: Arthur Gredington
Height: 4 ½", 11.9 cm

Colourway	Finish	DA #	Intro.	Disc.	U.K. £	U.S. $	Can. $
Brown							
a. Original issue	Gloss	80	1956	1989	15.00	25.00	35.00
b. Reissued	Gloss	80	1999	Current	15.00	N/A	N/A
Brown	Matt	80	1979	1989	25.00	40.00	60.00
Chestnut	Gloss	—	1958	1967	250.00	425.00	575.00
Grey	Gloss	80	*1961*	1989	40.00	65.00	95.00
Opaque	Gloss	—	*1961*	1973	65.00	100.00	150.00
Painted white	Gloss	—	*1961*	1967	225.00	350.00	525.00
Palomino	Gloss	80	*1961*	1989	30.00	50.00	75.00
Rocking horse grey	Gloss	—	*c.1957*	1962	300.00	475.00	700.00
White	Matt	—	1970	1982	45.00	75.00	125.00

Note: Model No.1407 was transferred to the Royal Doulton backstamp (DA80) in 1989. The brown gloss colourway reverted to the Beswick backstamp in September 1999.

Model No. 1480

PONY
(Boy's Pony)

Designer: Arthur Gredington
Height: 3 ¾", 9.5 cm

Colourway	Finish	Intro.	Disc.	U.K. £	U.S. $	Can. $
Brown	Gloss	1957	1967	85.00	135.00	200.00
Chestnut	Gloss	1958	1967	450.00	725.00	1,000.00
Grey	Gloss	1957	1967	350.00	575.00	800.00
Opaque	Gloss	1957	1967	135.00	200.00	300.00
Painted white	Gloss	1957	1967	350.00	575.00	800.00
Palomino	Gloss	1957	1967	85.00	135.00	200.00
Rocking horse grey	Gloss	1957	1962	450.00	725.00	1,000.00

Model No. 1483

PONY
(Girl's Pony)

Designer: Arthur Gredington
Height: 5", 12.7 cm

Colourway	Finish	Intro.	Disc.	U.K. £	U.S. $	Can. $
Brown	Gloss	1957	1967	100.00	165.00	235.00
Chestnut	Gloss	1958	1967	450.00	725.00	1,000.00
Grey	Gloss	1957	1967	350.00	550.00	800.00
Opaque	Gloss	1957	1967	125.00	200.00	300.00
Painted white	Gloss	1957	1967	350.00	550.00	800.00
Palomino	Gloss	1957	1967	275.00	450.00	650.00
Rocking horse grey	Gloss	1957	1962	500.00	800.00	1,250.00
Skewbald (brown and white)	Gloss	1957	1967	135.00	200.00	300.00

Model No. 1484   **HUNTSMAN'S HORSE**

This model was used as the horse in model no. 1501 "The Huntsman. "

Designer: Arthur Gredington
Height: 6 ¾", 17.2 cm

Colourway	Finish	Intro.	Disc.	U.K. £	U.S. $	Can. $
Brown	Gloss	1957	1982	50.00	85.00	125.00
Chestnut	Gloss	1958	1967	275.00	450.00	650.00
Grey	Gloss	1957	1982	75.00	125.00	175.00
Opaque	Gloss	1957	1973	150.00	250.00	350.00
Painted white	Gloss	1957	1967	350.00	575.00	800.00
Palomino	Gloss	1957	1982	65.00	100.00	150.00
Rocking horse grey	Gloss	1957	1962	450.00	700.00	1,000.00
White	Matt	1970	1982	65.00	100.00	150.00

Model No. 1499   **GIRL ON PONY**

The pony used for model no. 1499 was also available separately as model no. 1483 "Girl's Pony." The Girl on Pony is available in two variations, one with the girl looking straight ahead and the other has the girl looking down at the pony's neck. There is no price difference between the two variations. Examples have been found with a red jacket.

Designer: Arthur Gredington
Height: 5 ½", 14.0 cm

Colourway	Finish	Intro.	Disc.	U.K. £	U.S. $	Can. $
Brown	Gloss	1957	1965	600.00	950.00	1,400.00
Light dapple grey	Gloss	c.1961	1965	650.00	1,050.00	1,500.00
Palomino	Gloss	c.1957	1965	650.00	1,050.00	1,500.00
Rocking horse grey	Gloss	c.1961	1962	750.00	1,200.00	1,750.00
Skewbald	Gloss	1957	1965	150.00	250.00	350.00

Model No. 1500   **BOY ON PONY**

The pony used for model number 1500 was also available separately as model number 1480 "Boy's Pony."

Designer: Arthur Gredington
Height: 5 ½", 14.0 cm

Colourway	Finish	Intro.	Disc.	U.K. £	U.S. $	Can. $
Brown	Gloss	c.1961	1976	300.00	475.00	700.00
Light dapple grey	Gloss	c.1961	1976	650.00	1,000.00	1,500.00
Palomino	Gloss	1957	1976	125.00	200.00	300.00
Rocking horse grey	Gloss	c.1961	1962	750.00	1,200.00	1,750.00
Skewbald	Gloss	Unknown	Unknown	750.00	1,200.00	1,750.00

Model No. 1501   **HUNTSMAN**

STYLE TWO: Standing

Designer: Arthur Gredington
Height: 8 ¼", 21.0 cm

Colourway	Finish	Intro.	Disc.	U.K. £	U.S. $	Can. $
Brown	Gloss	1957	1995	100.00	165.00	235.00
Chestnut	Gloss	1965	1967	550.00	875.00	1,300.00
Grey	Gloss	1962	1975	225.00	350.00	525.00
Opaque	Gloss	1971	1973	175.00	275.00	400.00
Painted white	Gloss	1958	1971	275.00	450.00	650.00
Palomino	Gloss	1965	1971	500.00	800.00	1,175.00
Rocking horse grey	Gloss	*c.1958*	1962	750.00	1,200.00	1,750.00
White	Matt	1971	1981	125.00	200.00	300.00

Model No. 1516

APPALOOSA
(Spotted Walking Pony)

Designer: Arthur Gredington
Height: 5 ¼", 13.3 cm

Colourway	Finish	Intro.	Disc.	U.K. £	U.S. $	Can. $
Brown	Gloss	*1958*	*1967*	175.00	275.00	400.00
Chestnut	Gloss	*1958*	1967	500.00	800.00	1,175.00
Grey	Gloss	*1958*	1967	350.00	550.00	825.00
Opaque	Gloss	*1958*	1967	175.00	275.00	400.00
Painted white	Gloss	*1958*	1967	400.00	650.00	950.00
Palomino	Gloss	*1958*	1967	325.00	525.00	750.00
Rocking Horse Grey	Gloss	*1958*	1962	550.00	875.00	1,300.00
Spotted (British)	Gloss	1957	1966	250.00	400.00	575.00

Model No. 1546

H.M. QUEEN ELIZABETH II
ON IMPERIAL

The horse "Imperial' was also available separately as model number 1557.

Designer: Mr. Folkard
Height: 10 ½", 26.7 cm

Colourway	Finish	Intro.	Disc.	U.K. £	U.S. $	Can. $
Chestnut	Gloss	1958	1981	300.00	475.00	700.00

Model No. 1549

HORSE
(Head Tucked, Leg Up)

There are two version of model no. 1549, the first has the tail angled towards the off-hind hock, the second has the tail straight down. At the present time the dates cannot be determined as to when the mould was changed.

Model 1549 - First Version

First Version - Tail angled toward off-hind hock

Second Version - Tail straight down

Designer: Pal Zalmen
Height: 7 ½", 19.1 cm

FIRST VERSION: Tail angled towards the off-hind hock

Colourway	Finish	Intro.	Disc.	U.K. £	U.S. $	Can. $
Brown	Gloss	1958	Unknown	65.00	100.00	150.00
Chestnut	Gloss	1958	1967	300.00	475.00	675.00
Grey	Gloss	*1961*	Unknown	85.00	125.00	200.00
Grey	Matt	1981	Unknown	75.00	125.00	200.00
Opaque	Gloss	1964	1973	150.00	250.00	400.00
Painted white	Gloss	*1961*	1967	250.00	450.00	625.00
Palomino	Gloss	*1961*	Unknown	75.00	125.00	175.00
Palomino	Matt	1981	Unknown	65.00	115.00	150.00
Rocking horse grey	Gloss	*c.1959*	*1962*	375.00	625.00	850.00
White	Matt	1970	Unknown	85.00	125.00	200.00

SECOND VERSION: Tail is straight down

Colourway	Finish	DA #	Intro.	Disc.	U.K. £	U.S. $	Can. $
Brown							
a. Original issue	Gloss	51	Unknown	1989	48.00	75.00	115.00
b. Reissued	Gloss	51	1999	Current	48.00	N/A	N/A
Grey	Gloss	—	Unknown	1989	65.00	90.00	140.00
Grey	Matt	—	Unknown	1989	55.00	90.00	140.00
Palomino	Gloss	—	Unknown	1989	55.00	80.00	125.00
Palomino	Matt	—	Unknown	1989	45.00	80.00	125.00
White	Matt	—	Unknown	1982	75.00	100.00	150.00

Note: Model No.1549 (Second Version) was transferred to the Royal Doulton backstamp (DA51) in 1989. The brown gloss colourway reverted to the Beswick backstamp in September 1999.

Model No. 1557 "IMPERIAL"

This horse was used in model no. 1546 with Queen Elizabeth as rider.

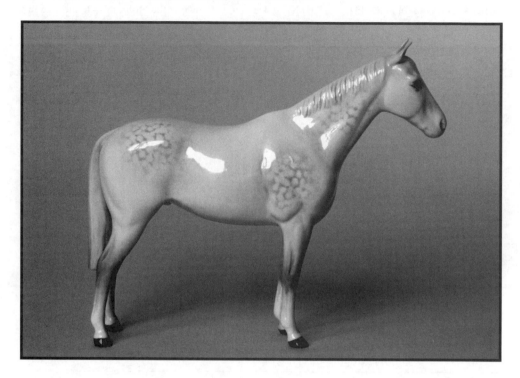

Designer: Albert Hallam and James Hayward
Height: 8 ¼", 21.0 cm

Colourway	Finish	Intro.	Disc.	U.K. £	U.S. $	Can. $
Brown	Gloss	1958	1982	65.00	100.00	150.00
Chestnut	Gloss	1958	1967	225.00	400.00	600.00
Grey	Gloss	1958	1982	85.00	150.00	225.00
Opaque	Gloss	1958	1973	175.00	300.00	400.00
Painted white	Gloss	1958	1967	350.00	475.00	625.00
Palomino	Gloss	1958	1982	75.00	150.00	225.00
Rocking horse grey	Gloss	1958	1962	425.00	625.00	850.00
White	Matt	1970	1982	95.00	150.00	225.00

Model No. 1564   **LARGE RACEHORSE**

This is the underlying model for the Connoisseur horse 1564 and the Harnessed version 1564.

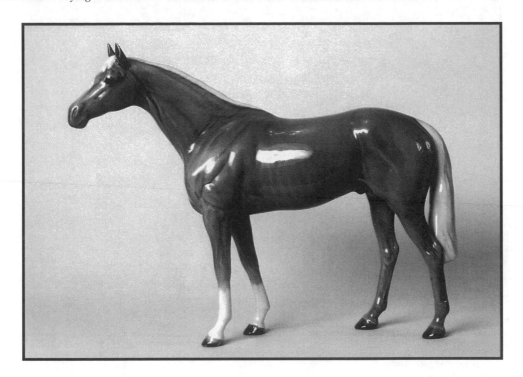

Designer: Arthur Gredington
Height: 11 ¼", 28.5 cm

Colourway	Finish	Intro.	Disc.	U.K. £	U.S. $	Can. $
Brown	Gloss	1959	1982	95.00	150.00	225.00
Chestnut	Gloss	1959	1967	450.00	700.00	1,000.00
Grey	Gloss	1959	1982	175.00	275.00	400.00
Opaque	Gloss	1959	1973	200.00	350.00	500.00
Painted white	Gloss	1959	1967	550.00	875.00	1,300.00
Palomino	Gloss	1959	1982	100.00	150.00	250.00
Rocking horse grey	Gloss	1959	1962	750.00	1,200.00	1,750.00
White	Matt	1970	1982	95.00	150.00	225.00

SERIES: Connoisseur Horse

Designer: Arthur Gredington
Height: 12 ¼", 31.1 cm

Colourway	Finish	Intro.	Disc.	U.K. £	U.S. $	Can. $
Brown	Matt	1970	1981	145.00	250.00	375.00

SERIES: Harnessed Horses

Height: 11 ¼", 28.5 cm

Colourway	Finish	Intro.	Disc.	U.K. £	U.S. $	Can. $
Brown	Gloss	1974	By 1981	145.00	250.00	375.00

Model No. 1588

H.R.H. DUKE OF EDINBURGH
ON ALAMEIN

Designer: Mr. Folkard
Height: 10 ½", 26.7 cm

Colourway	Finish	Intro.	Disc.	U.K. £	U.S. $	Can. $
Light dapple grey	Gloss	1958	1981	350.00	550.00	800.00

Model No. 1624   LIFEGUARD

STYLE ONE: With trumpet

Designer: Arthur Gredington
Height: 9 ½" 24.0 cm

Colourway	Finish	Intro.	Disc.	U.K. £	U.S. $	Can. $
Light dapple grey	Gloss	1959	1977	425.00	700.00	1,100.00

Model No. 1641

CONNEMARA PONY
"TERESE OF LEAM"

SERIES: Mountain and Moorland Ponies

Designer: Arthur Gredington
Height: 7", 17.8 cm

Colourway	Finish	Intro.	Disc.	U.K. £	U.S. $	Can. $
Grey	Gloss	1961	1984	125.00	200.00	300.00

Model No. 1642

DARTMOOR PONY
"JENTYL" / "WARLORD"

Warlord was commissioned, in a limited edition of 1,500, by P. R. Middleweek & Co. as the first in a series of Dartmoor Ponies.

SERIES: Mountain and Moorland Ponies

Designer: Arthur Gredington
Height: 6 ¼", 15.9 cm

Name	Colourway/Finish	Intro.	Disc.	U.K. £	U.S. $	Can. $
"Jentyl"	Brown/Gloss	1961	1984	100.00	165.00	250.00
"Warlord"	Bay/Gloss	1996	1996	45.00	70.00	110.00

Note: See also The Dartmoor Family page 348.

Model No. 1643

WELSH MOUNTAIN PONY
"COED COCH MADOG"

SERIES: Mountain and Moorland Ponies

First Version: Tail is attached to off-side hind leg

Second Version: Tail hangs loose

Designer: Arthur Gredington
Height: 6 ¼", 15.9 cm

FIRST VERSION: Tail is attached to off-side hind leg.

Colourway	Finish	Intro.	Disc.	U.K. £	U.S. $	Can. $
Grey	Gloss	1961	Unknown	150.00	250.00	350.00

SECOND VERSION: Tail hangs loose.

Colourway	Finish	Intro.	Disc.	U.K. £	U.S. $	Can. $
Grey	Gloss	Unknown	1989	200.00	325.00	475.00

Model No. 1644

HIGHLAND PONY
"MACKIONNEACH"

SERIES: Mountain and Moorland Ponies

Designer: Arthur Gredington
Height: 7 ¼", 18.4 cm

Colourway	Finish	Intro.	Disc.	U.K. £	U.S. $	Can. $
Dun	Gloss	1961	1989	100.00	165.00	250.00
Dark Dun	Gloss	Unknown	Unknown	150.00	250.00	325.00
Light Grey	Gloss	Unknown	Unknown	500.00	800.00	1,200.00
Opaque	Gloss	Unknown	Unknown		Extremely Rare	

Model No. 1645

EXMOOR PONY
"HEATHERMAN"

SERIES: Mountain and Moorland Ponies

Designer: Arthur Gredington
Height: 6 ½", 16.5 cm

Colourway	Finish	Intro.	Disc.	U.K. £	U.S. $	Can. $
Bay	Gloss	1961	1983	125.00	200.00	300.00

Model No. 1646

NEW FOREST PONY
"JONATHEN 3ʀᴅ"

SERIES: Mountain and Moorland Ponies

First Version: Tail is attached to the near-side hock

Second Version: Tail hangs loose

Designer: Arthur Gredington
Height: 7", 17.8 cm

FIRST VERSION: Tail is attached to the near-side hock.

Colourway	Finish	Intro.	Disc.	U.K. £	U.S. $	Can. $
Bay	Gloss	1961	Unknown	125.00	200.00	300.00

SECOND VERSION: Tail hangs loose.

Colourway	Finish	Intro.	Disc.	U.K. £	U.S. $	Can. $
Bay	Gloss	Unknown	1984	100.00	165.00	250.00

Model No. 1647

FELL PONY
"DENE DAUNTLESS"

SERIES: Mountain and Moorland Ponies

Designer: Arthur Gredington
Height: 6 ¾", 17.2 cm

Colourway	Finish	Intro.	Disc.	U.K. £	U.S. $	Can. $
Black	Gloss	1961	1982	125.00	200.00	300.00

Model No. 1648

SHETLAND PONY
"ESCHONCHAN RONAY"

SERIES: Mountain and Moorland Ponies

Designer: Arthur Gredington
Height: 4 ¾", 12.1 cm

Colourway	Finish	Intro.	Disc.	U.K. £	U.S. $	Can. $
Brown	Gloss	1961	1989	75.00	125.00	175.00

Model No. 1671

DALES PONY
"MAISIE"

SERIES: Mountain and Moorland Ponies

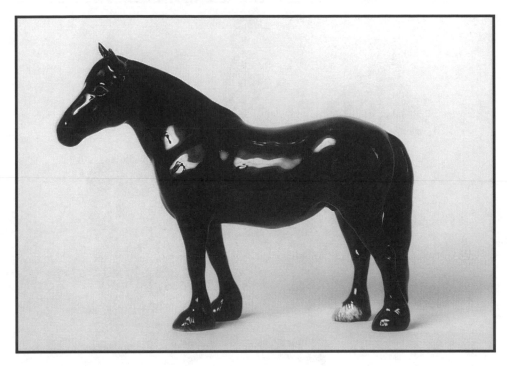

Designer: Arthur Gredington
Height: 6 ½", 16.5 cm

Colourway	Finish	Intro.	Disc.	U.K. £	U.S. $	Can. $
Black	Gloss	1961	1982	125.00	200.00	300.00

Model No. 1730   HUNTSWOMAN

STYLE TWO: *Rider and horse stood still*

Designer: Arthur Gredington
Height: 8 ¼", 21.0 cm

Colourway	Finish	Intro.	Disc.	U.K. £	U.S. $	Can. $
Brown	Gloss	1960	1975	250.00	400.00	600.00
Grey	Gloss	1960	1995	150.00	250.00	375.00
Opaque	Gloss	1971	1973	200.00	325.00	475.00
Painted white	Gloss	1960	1971	425.00	675.00	1,000.00
Rocking horse grey	Gloss	1960	1962	750.00	1,200.00	1,750.00
White	Matt	1971	1981	150.00	250.00	375.00

Model No. 1734   **LARGE HUNTER**

FIRST VERSION: The head looks slightly overlarge and the body too much on the thin size. The tail hangs straight down.

Designer: Arthur Gredington
Height: 11 ¼", 28.5 cm

Colourway	Finish	Intro.	Disc.	U.K. £	U.S. $	Can. $
Brown	Gloss	1961	1963	275.00	450.00	650.00
Chestnut	Gloss	1961	1963	525.00	850.00	1,225.00
Grey	Gloss	1961	1963	450.00	725.00	1,050.00
Opaque	Gloss	1961	1963	275.00	450.00	650.00
Painted white	Gloss	1961	1963	550.00	875.00	1,300.00
Palomino	Gloss	1961	1963	425.00	675.00	1,000.00
Rocking horse grey	Gloss	1961	1962	750.00	1,200.00	1,750.00

Second Version: Head and body in proportion

Large Hunter - Connoisseur Horse

SECOND VERSION: Head and body in proportion. The tail is slightly arched away from the body

Height: 11 ¾", 29.8 cm

Colourway	Finish	Intro.	Disc.	U.K. £	U.S. $	Can. $
Brown	Gloss	1963	1984	90.00	175.00	300.00
Chestnut	Gloss	1963	1967	500.00	800.00	1,200.00
Grey	Gloss	1963	1984	125.00	200.00	300.00
Opaque	Gloss	1963	1973	175.00	250.00	400.00
Painted white	Gloss	1963	1967	500.00	800.00	1,200.00
Palomino	Gloss	1963	1983	115.00	200.00	300.00
White	Matt	1970	1982	90.00	200.00	300.00

SERIES: Connoisseur Horses

Height: 12 ¼", 31.1 cm

Colourway	Finish	Intro.	Disc.	U.K. £	U.S. $	Can. $
Grey	Matt	1970	1982	125.00	200.00	300.00

Model No. 1771   **ARAB "BAHRAM"**

Arab "Bahram"

Arab "Bahram" Connoisseur Horse

Designer: Arthur Gredington
Height: 7 ½", 19.1 cm

Colourway	Finish	DA #	Intro.	Disc.	U.K. £	U.S. $	Can. $
Brown	Gloss	52	1961	1989	60.00	100.00	145.00
Brown	Matt	52	1980	1989	55.00	90.00	125.00
Chestnut	Gloss	—	1961	1967	200.00	325.00	475.00
Grey	Gloss	—	1961	1989	80.00	135.00	185.00
Grey	Matt	—	1980	1989	80.00	135.00	185.00
Opaque	Gloss	—	1961	1973	15000	225.00	350.00
Painted white	Gloss	—	1961	1967	400.00	650.00	950.00
Palomino	Gloss	—	1961	1989	70.00	125.00	165.00
Palomino	Matt	—	1980	1989	60.00	100.00	145.00
Rocking horse grey	Gloss	—	1961	1962		Extremely Rare	
White	Matt	—	1970	1982	60.00	100.00	145.00

SERIES: Connoisseur Horses

Height: 8 ¼", 21.0 cm

Colourway	Finish	Intro.	Disc.	U.K. £	U.S. $	Can. $
Grey	Matt	1970	1989	125.00	200.00	300.00

Model No. 1772

THOROUGHBRED STALLION
(Large)

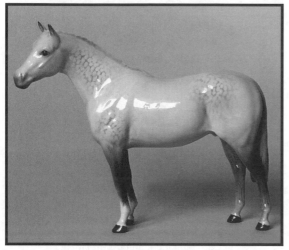

Thoroughbred Stallion

Thoroughbred Stallion - Connoisseur Horse

Designer: Arthur Gredington
Height: 8", 20.3 cm

Colourway	Finish	DA #	Intro.	Disc.	U.K. £	U.S. $	Can. $
Brown							
a. Original issue	Gloss	53	1961	1989	48.00	75.00	115.00
b. Reissued	Gloss	53	1999	Current	48.00	N/A	N/A
Chestnut	Gloss	—	1961	1967	300.00	475.00	700.00
Grey	Gloss	53	1961	1989	80.00	135.00	185.00
Grey	Matt	—	1970	1982	125.00	200.00	300.00
Opaque	Gloss	—	1961	1973	150.00	250.00	350.00
Painted white	Gloss	—	1961	1967	400.00	650.00	950.00
Palomino	Gloss	—	1961	1983	90.00	145.00	200.00
Rocking horse grey	Gloss	—	1961	1962		Extremely Rare	
White	Matt	—	1970	1982	60.00	100.00	145.00

Note: Model No.1772 was transferred to the Royal Doulton backstamp (DA53) in 1989. The brown gloss version reverted to the Beswick backstamp in September 1999.

SERIES: Connoisseur Horses

Height: 8 ¾", 22.2 cm

Colourway	Finish	Intro.	Disc.	U.K. £	U.S. $	Can. $
Bay	Matt	1970	1989	100.00	165.00	250.00

Model No. 1772A

APPALOOSA STALLION

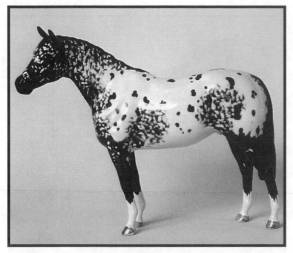

Colourway No. 1, More detailed paintwork, striped hooves

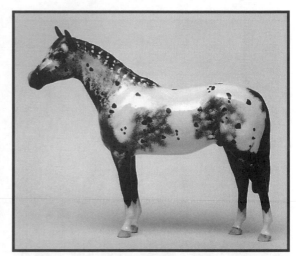

Colourway No. 2, Less distinct roan areas, cream hooves

Designer: Arthur Gredington
Height: 8", 20.3 cm

COLOURWAY No. 1. More detailed paintwork with the head and neck in particular more "mottled." Striped hooves.

Colourway	Finish	Intro.	Disc.	U.K. £	U.S. $	Can. $
Black and white	Gloss	c.1967	Unknown	175.00	275.00	400.00

COLOURWAY No. 2. Less distinct roan areas of black on head and neck and brown on lower body quarters. Cream hooves.

Colourway	Finish	DA#	Intro.	Disc.	U.K. £	U.S. $	Can. $
Black and white							
a. Original issue	Gloss	68	Unknown	1989	60.00	95.00	150.00
b. Reissued	Gloss	68	1999	Current	60.00	N/A	N/A

Note: Model No.1772A was transferred to the Royal Doulton backstamp (DA68) in 1989. Colourway No.2 reverted to the Beswick backstamp in September 1999.

Model No. 1793

WELSH COB
(Standing)

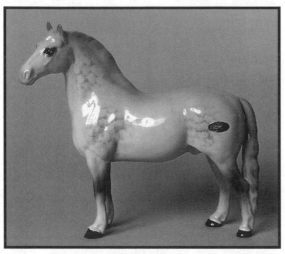

First Version: Tail hangs straight down

Second Version - Top part of tail arched away from body

Designer: Arthur Gredington
Height: 7 ½", 19.1 cm

FIRST VERSION: *Tail hangs straight down.*

Colourway	Finish	Intro.	Disc.	U.K. £	U.S. $	Can. $
Brown	Gloss	1962	c.1975/76	90.00	145.00	200.00
Chestnut	Gloss	1962	c.1975/76	500.00	800.00	1,175.00
Grey	Gloss	1962	c.1975/76	175.00	275.00	400.00
Opaque	Gloss	1962	c.1975/76	200.00	325.00	475.00
Painted white	Gloss	1962	c.1975/76	425.00	675.00	1,000.00
Palomino	Gloss	1962	1970	400.00	650.00	950.00
Piebald	Gloss	Unknown	Unknown		Very Rare	
White	Matt	1970	c.1975/76	90.00	145.00	200.00

SECOND VERSION: *The tail was altered so that the top part (dock) arched away from the body.*

Colourway	Finish	Intro.	Disc.	U.K. £	U.S. $	Can. $
Brown	Gloss	c.1975/76	1982	75.00	125.00	175.00
Grey	Gloss	c.1975/76	1982	145.00	225.00	350.00
White	Matt	c.1975/76	1982	75.00	125.00	175.00

Model No. 1811　　　　　　　　## MARE AND FOAL

The mare and foal are available separately as model nos. 1812 mare and 1813 foal.

Designer:　　Arthur Gredington
Height:　　　6", 15.0 cm

Colourway	Finish	Intro.	Disc.	U.K. £	U.S. $	Can. $
Brown mare and chestnut foal	Gloss	1962	1975	175.00	275.00	400.00
Grey mare and black foal	Gloss	1962	1975	150.00	250.00	350.00

Model No. 1812

MARE
(Facing Right, Head Down)

Model no. 1811 was paired with foal model no. 1813 to make model no. 1811 "Mare and Foal."

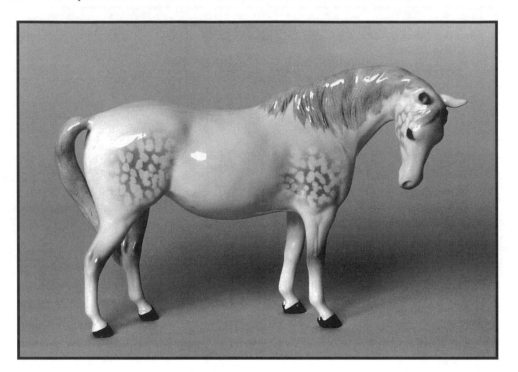

Designer: Arthur Gredington
Height: 5 ¾", 14.6 cm

Colourway	Finish	DA #	Intro.	Disc.	U.K. £	U.S. $	Can. $
Brown	Gloss	54	1962	1989	45.00	70.00	100.00
Brown	Matt	—	1970	1989	40.00	65.00	95.00
Chestnut	Gloss	—	1962	1967	425.00	675.00	1,000.00
Grey	Gloss	—	1962	1989	60.00	95.00	145.00
Grey	Matt	—	1970	1989	55.00	90.00	135.00
Opaque	Gloss	—	1962	1973	150.00	250.00	350.00
Painted white	Gloss	—	1962	1967	300.00	475.00	700.00
Palomino	Gloss	—	1962	1989	55.00	90.00	135.00
Palomino	Matt	—	1970	1983	50.00	80.00	125.00
"Treacle"	Gloss	—	1992	1992	75.00	125.00	175.00
"Treacle"	Matt	—	1992	1992	75.00	125.00	175.00
White	Matt	—	1970	1982	60.00	95.00	145.00

Note: "Treacle" (allover treacle brown gloss or matt finish, no other painted features) seems to have originated from Sinclairs, who offered this piece by mail order in 1992. The figures were supposed to be brown gloss, but a limited number of treacle ones surfaced.

Model No. 1813

FOAL
(Larger Thoroughbred Type)

First Version - Fine head and legs

Second Version - Plain head, thicker, less shapely legs

Designer: Arthur Gredington
Height: 4 ½", 11.9 cm

FIRST VERSION: Fine head and legs, off fore leg is placed well behind the near fore leg.

Colourway	Finish	Intro.	Disc.	U.K. £	U.S. $	Can. $
Brown	Gloss	1962	1982	30.00	50.00	75.00
Brown	Matt	1979	1982	30.00	50.00	75.00
Chestnut	Gloss	1962	1967	250.00	400.00	600.00
Grey	Gloss	1962	1982	45.00	75.00	100.00
Opaque	Gloss	1962	1973	90.00	150.00	200.00
Painted white	Gloss	1963	1967	200.00	325.00	475.00
Palomino	Gloss	1962	1982	35.00	60.00	85.00
White	Matt	1970	c.1982	55.00	90.00	130.00

SECOND VERSION: Plain head, thicker legs with less shape, off fore leg almost parallel to near fore leg.

Colourway	Finish	DA #	Intro.	Disc.	U.K. £	U.S. $	Can. $
Brown	Gloss	81	1982	1982	25.00	45.00	60.00
Brown	Matt	81	1982	1989	25.00	45.00	60.00
Grey	Gloss	—	1982	1989	30.00	50.00	75.00
Palomino	Gloss	—	1982	1989	25.00	45.00	70.00
Orange bay	Gloss	—	1982	c.1984	55.00	90.00	135.00
White	Matt	—	c.1982	1982	40.00	65.00	95.00

Model No. 1816

FOAL
(Smaller Thoroughbred Type, Facing Left)

First Version: Fine head, thin delicate legs

Second Version: Head and legs thicker

Designer: Arthur Gredington
Height: 3 ½", 8.9 cm

FIRST VERSION: Fine head and very thin delicate legs.

Colourway	Finish	Intro.	Disc.	U.K. £	U.S. $	Can. $
Brown	Gloss	1963	1975	30.00	50.00	70.00
Chestnut	Gloss	1963	1967	200.00	325.00	475.00
Grey	Gloss	1963	1975	45.00	70.00	100.00
Opaque	Gloss	1963	1973	75.00	125.00	175.00
Painted white	Gloss	1963	1967	175.00	275.00	400.00
Palomino	Gloss	1963	1975	40.00	65.00	95.00
White	Matt	1970	1975	40.00	65.00	95.00

SECOND VERSION: Head and legs made thicker and less shape to the legs.

Colourway	Finish	DA#	Intro.	Disc.	U.K. £	U.S. $	Can. $
Brown	Gloss	82	1975	1989	20.00	30.00	50.00
Brown	Matt	82	1979	1989	20.00	30.00	50.00
Grey	Gloss		1975	1983	30.00	50.00	70.00
Palomino	Gloss		1975	1989	30.00	50.00	70.00
White	Matt		1975	1982	30.00	50.00	70.00

Model No. 1817

FOAL
(Smaller Thoroughbred Type, Facing Right)

Designer: Arthur Gredington
Height: 3 ¼", 8.3 cm

Colourway	Finish	Intro.	Disc.	U.K. £	U.S. $	Can. $
Brown	Gloss	1963	1975	40.00	65.00	95.00
Chestnut	Gloss	1963	1967	200.00	325.00	475.00
Grey	Gloss	1963	1975	55.00	90.00	135.00
Opaque	Gloss	1963	1973	75.00	125.00	175.00
Painted white	Gloss	1963	1967	200.00	325.00	475.00
Palomino	Gloss	1963	1975	50.00	80.00	125.00
White	Matt	1970	1975	40.00	65.00	95.00

Model No. 1862   **HORSE AND JOCKEY**

STYLE TWO: Standing horse and jockey

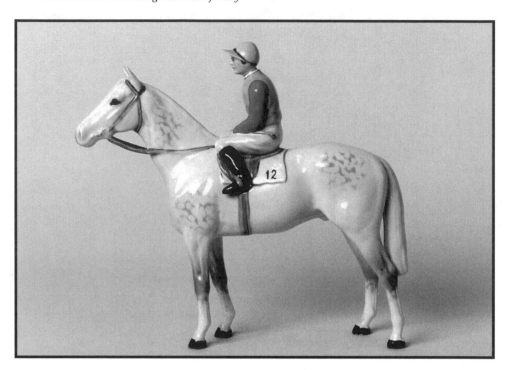

Designer: Arthur Gredington
Height: 8", 20.3 cm

Colourway	Finish	Intro.	Disc.	U.K. £	U.S. $	Can. $
Brown	Gloss	1963	1984	325.00	475.00	775.00
Light dapple grey	Gloss	1963	1983	400.00	600.00	950.00
Painted white	Gloss	Unknown	Unknown		Extremely Rare	

Model No. 1991

MARE
(Facing Right, Head Up)

FIRST VERSION: The end only of the tail is attached to the hock.

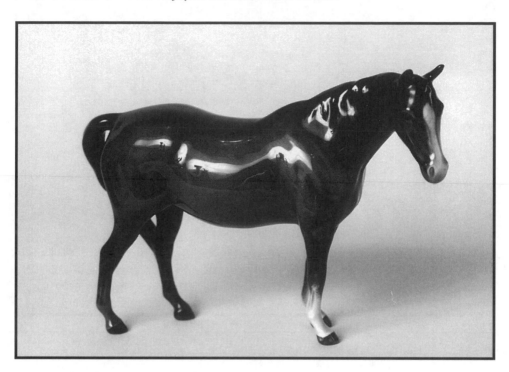

Designer: Arthur Gredington
Height: 5 ½", 14.0 cm

Colourway	Finish	Intro.	Disc.	U.K. £	U.S. $	Can. $
Brown	Gloss	1965	Unknown	45.00	70.00	100.00
Brown	Matt	1970	Unknown	40.00	65.00	95.00
Chestnut	Gloss	1965	Unknown	300.00	475.00	700.00
Grey	Gloss	1965	Unknown	60.00	95.00	140.00
Grey	Matt	1970	Unknown	50.00	80.00	125.00
Opaque	Gloss	1965	Unknown	125.00	200.00	300.00
Painted white	Gloss	1965	Unknown	275.00	450.00	650.00
Palomino	Gloss	1965	Unknown	50.00	80.00	125.00
Palomino	Matt	1970	Unknown	45.00	70.00	100.00
White	Matt	1970	Unknown	60.00	95.00	140.00

SECOND VERSION: The tail is attached to the quarters and the hock.

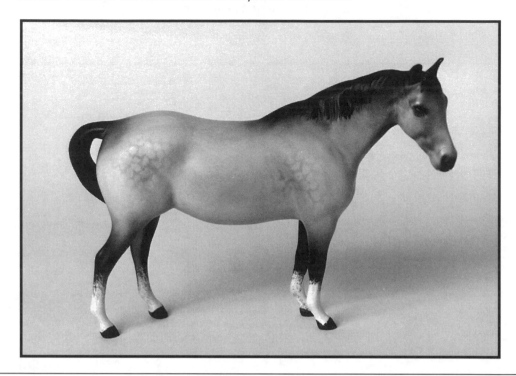

Colourway	Finish	DA #	Intro.	Disc.	U.K. £	U.S. $	Can. $
Brown							
a. Original issue	Gloss	55	Unknown	1989	27.00	45.00	65.00
b. Reissued	Gloss	55	1999	Current	27.00	N/A	N/A
Brown	Matt	55	Unknown	1989	35.00	55.00	80.00
Grey	Gloss	55	Unknown	1989	45.00	70.00	100.00
Grey	Matt	—	Unknown	1989	45.00	70.00	100.00
Palomino	Gloss	55	Unknown	1989	40.00	65.00	95.00
Palomino	Matt	—	Unknown	1989	35.00	55.00	80.00
White	Matt	—	Unknown	1982	45.00	70.00	100.00

Note: Model No.1991 (Second Version) was transferred to the Royal Doulton backstamp (DA55) in 1989. The brown gloss colourway reverted to the Beswick backstamp in September 1999.

Model No. 1992

THOROUGHBRED STALLION
(Small)

Designer: Arthur Gredington
Height: 5 ½", 14.0.cm

Colourway	Finish	DA #	Intro.	Disc.	U.K. £	U.S. $	Can. $
Brown	Gloss	56	1965	1989	35.00	60.00	85.00
Brown							
a. Original issue	Matt	56	1970	1989	27.00	45.00	65.00
b. Reissued	Matt	56	1999	Current	27.00	N/A	N/A
Chestnut	Gloss	—	1965	1967	225.00	350.00	550.00
Grey	Gloss	56	1965	1989	45.00	70.00	100.00
Grey	Matt	—	1970	1989	45.00	70.00	100.00
Opaque	Gloss	—	1965	1973	85.00	135.00	200.00
Painted white	Gloss	—	1965	1967	225.00	350.00	500.00
Palomino	Gloss	—	1965	1989	50.00	80.00	125.00
Palomino	Matt	—	1970	1989	40.00	65.00	95.00
White	Matt	—	1970	1982	50.00	80.00	125.00

Note: Model No.1992 was transferred to the Royal Doulton backstamp (DA56) in 1989. The brown matt colourway reverted to the Beswick backstamp in September 1999.

Model No. 2065   **ARKLE**

SERIES: Connoisseur Horses

Designer:	Arthur Gredington
Height:	11 7/8", 30.1 cm

Colourway	Finish	DA #	Intro.	Disc.	U.K. £	U.S. $	Can. $
Bay							
a. Original issue	Matt	15	1970	1989	167.00	265.00	400.00
b. Reissued	Matt	15	1999	Current	167.00	N/A	N/A

Note: Model No.2065 was transferred to the Royal Doulton backstamp (DA15) in 1989. It reverted to the Beswick backstamp in September 1999.

Model No. 2084

ARKLE
PAT TAAFFE UP

SERIES: Connoisseur Horses

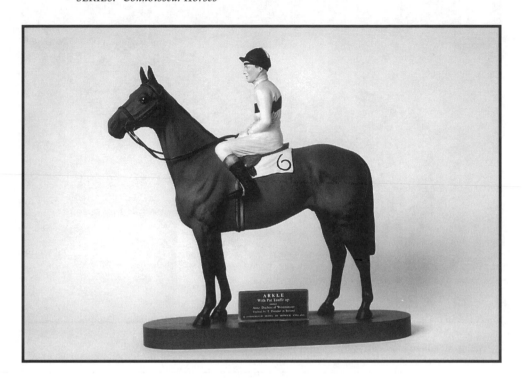

Designer: Arthur Gredington
Height: 12 ½", 21.7 cm

Colourway	Finish	Intro.	Disc.	U.K. £	U.S. $	Can. $
Bay	Matt	1970	1982	300.00	500.00	700.00

Model No. 2186   **QUARTER HORSE**

Designer: Arthur Gredington
Height: 8 ¼", 21.0 cm

Colourway	Finish	Intro.	Disc.	U.K. £	U.S. $	Can. $
Brown	Gloss	1969	1982	100.00	165.00	250.00
Brown	Matt	1970	1982	85.00	135.00	200.00
Opaque	Gloss	1970	1982	275.00	450.00	650.00
White	Matt	1973	1982	80.00	125.00	195.00

Model No. 2210

HIGHWAYMAN

SERIES: Connoisseur Horses

| Designer: | Albert Hallam |
| Height: | 13 ¾", 34.9 cm |

Colourway	Finish	Intro.	Disc.	U.K. £	U.S. $	Can. $
Bay	Matt	1970	1975	850.00	1,350.00	2,000.00

Model No. 2242   **ARAB STALLION**

This is an authentic rendition of an Arab horse. It is on a pottery (base) stand.

Designer: Albert Hallam
Height: 8 ½", 21.6 cm

Colourway	Finish	Intro.	Disc.	U.K. £	U.S. $	Can. $
Brown	Gloss	1970	1975	375.00	650.00	875.00

Model No. 2269   **ARAB STALLION WITH SADDLE**

SERIES: Connoisseur Horses

Designer: Albert Hallam
Height: 9 ½", 24.0 cm

Colourway	Finish	Intro.	Disc.	U.K. £	U.S. $	Can.
Dappled grey	Matt	1970	1975	800.00	1,300.00	1,900.00

Model No. 2275

BEDOUIN ARAB

SERIES: Connoisseur Horses

Designer: Albert Hallam
Height: 11 ½", 29.2 cm

Colourway	Finish	Intro.	Disc.	U.K. £	U.S. $	Can. $
Chestnut	Matt	1970	1975	900.00	1,500.00	2,250.00

Model No. 2282   **NORWEGIAN FJORD HORSE**

Designer: Albert Hallam
Height: 6 ½", 16.5 cm

Colourway	Finish	Intro.	Disc.	U.K. £	U.S. $	Can. $
Dun	Gloss	1970	1975	350.00	600.00	825.00

Model No. 2309   **BURNHAM BEAUTY**

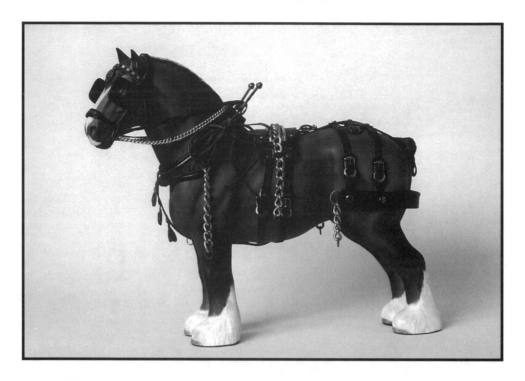

| Designer: | Albert Hallam |
| Height: | 10 ¾", 27.8 cm |

Colourway	Finish	Intro.	Disc.	U.K. £	U.S. $	Can. $
Brown	Gloss	1972	1982	85.00	175.00	250.00
White	Matt	1974	1982	85.00	175.00	250.00

SERIES: Connoisseur Horses

Height: 11 ¼", 28.5 cm

Colourway	Finish	Intro.	Disc.	U.K. £	U.S. $	Can. $
Bay	Matt	1971	1982	100.00	175.00	300.00

SERIES: Harnessed Horses

Height: 10 ¾", 27.8 cm

Colourway	Finish	Intro.	Disc.	U.K. £	U.S. $	Can. $
Brown	Matt	1979	1982	125.00	200.00	300.00

Model No. 2340   **CARDIGAN BAY**

Two versions of model no. 2340 exist. The first version has only two hooves attached to the base making it unstable and prone to breakage. The base was remodelled to better support the model and has three hooves attached to it.

SERIES: *Connoisseur Horses*

FIRST VERSION: Two legs attached to the base - off hind leg is not attached to the base.

Designer: Albert Hallam
Height: 9 ¼", 23.5 cm

Colourway	Finish	Intro.	Disc.	U.K. £	U.S. $	Can. $
Brown	Matt	1971	c.1972	500.00	800.00	1,200.00

SECOND VERSION: Three legs attached to the base - off hind leg is attached to the base.

Colourway	Finish	Intro.	Disc.	U.K. £	U.S. $	Can. $
Brown	Matt	c.1972	1976	375.00	600.00	875.00

Model No. 2345

NIJINSKY

SERIES: Connoisseur Horses

Designer:	Albert Hallam
Height:	11 ¼", 28.5 cm

Colourway	Finish	DA #	Intro.	Disc.	U.K. £	U.S. $	Can. $
Bay							
a. Original issue	Matt	16	1971	1989	167.00	265.00	400.00
b. Reissued	Matt	16	1999	Current	167.00	N/A	N/A

Note: Model No.2345 was transferred to the Royal Doulton backstamp (DA16) in 1989. It reverted to the Beswick backstamp in September 1999.

Model No. 2352

NIJINSKY
LESTER PIGGOTT UP

SERIES: *Connoisseur Horses*

Designer: Albert Hallam
Height: 12 ½", 31.7 cm

Colourway	Finish	Intro.	Disc.	U.K. £	U.S. $	Can. $
Bay	Matt	1971	1982	300.00	475.00	700.00

Model No. 2421 THE WINNER

Designer: Albert Hallam
Height: 9 ½", 24.0 cm

Colourway	Finish	Intro.	Disc.	U.K. £	U.S. $	Can. $
Brown	Gloss	1973	1982	95.00	150.00	350.00
Brown	Matt	1973	1982	85.00	135.00	200.00
White	Matt	1973	1982	85.00	135.00	200.00

Model No. 2422

MILL REEF

The mahogany bay (gloss) variety was sold through Lawleys, Royal Doulton's retail shops, in the mid 1980s. When Mill Reef was withdrawn from the range at the end of 1989 a white matt variety was sold at the Beswick factory shop.

Designer: Albert Hallam
Height: 9", 22.9 cm

Colourway	Finish	Intro.	Disc.	U.K. £	U.S. $	Can. $
Mahogany bay	Gloss	1985	1988	125.00	200.00	300.00
White	Matt	1989	Unknown	95.00	145.00	225.00

SERIES: Connoisseur Horses

Colourway	Finish	Intro.	Disc.	U.K. £	U.S. $	Can. $
Brown/wooden plinth	Matt	1973	1989	100.00	175.00	250.00

Model No. 2431

MOUNTIE STALLION

SERIES: Connoisseur Horses

Designer: Graham Tongue
Height: 10", 25.4 cm

Colourway	Finish	Intro.	Disc.	U.K. £	U.S. $	Can. $
Black	Gloss	1973	1975	600.00	950.00	1,400.00

Model No. 2459

SHIRE MARE
(Lying)

Designer: Unknown
Height: 5", 12.7 cm

Colourways	Finish	Intro.	Disc.	U.K. £	U.S. $	Can. $
Brown	Gloss	1973	Unknown	300.00	475.00	700.00
Grey	Gloss	1973	1976	250.00	400.00	600.00

Model No. 2460

SHIRE FOAL
(Lying)

Designer: Unknown
Height: 3 ½", 8.9 cm

Colourway	Finish	Intro.	Disc.	U.K. £	U.S. $	Can. $
Dark brown	Gloss	1973	1976	135.00	200.00	325.00

Model No. 2464

PERCHERON

SERIES: Harnessed Horses

Designer: Unknown
Height: 9 ¾", 24.7 cm

Colourway	Finish	Intro.	Disc.	U.K. £	U.S. $	Can. $
Dappled grey	Matt	1974	1982	350.00	600.00	825.00

GREY MATT
1182 Swish Tail, 1st version; 2703 Spirit of Youth
2914 Spirit of Earth; 1549 Head tucked, 2nd version

ROCKING HORSE GREY
855 Stocky Jogging Mare, 3rd version; 975 Shire
1483 Girl's Pony; 951 Shire Foal; 915 Lying Foal
836 Foal, 1st version

BROWN MATT
2186 Quarter Horse; 1772 Connoisseur Thoroughbred
818 Shire; 1812 Mare; 1261 Palomino; 2875 Sunlight Foal
1407 Arab Foal

PALOMINO MATT
2688 Spirit of the Wind; 2703 Spirit of Youth
2689 Spirit of Freedom; 2916 Spirit of Peace

EARLY BROWN GLOSS
855 Stocky Jogging Mare, 2nd version
763 Foal, 1st version; 701 "Bois Roussel," 1st version

BROWN GLOSS
1182 Swish Tail, 1st version; 2703 Spirit of Youth
1265 Arab "Xayal;" 728 Comical Foal
946 Grazing Foal, 1st version; 1793 Welsh Cob, 1st version

CHESTNUT GLOSS
1772 Thoroughbred; 976 Mare
1265 Arab "Xayal;" 836 Foal, 1st version
1085 Foal; 763 Foal, 1st version

PALOMINO GLOSS
1516 Walking Pony; 1771 Arab "Bahram"
1197 Head-up Pony; 1817 Foal; 1053 Shire Foal
763 Foal, 3rd version; 1373 Pinto Pony, 1st version

1516 Spotted Walking Pony; 1772A Appaloosa
later colour version, earlier colour version
1483 Girl's Pony, Skewbald
1373 Pinto, Skewbald 1st version, Piebald 2nd version

OPAQUE GLOSS
1484 Hunter; 1050 Grazing Shire
1516 Walking Pony; 815 Foal; 1084 Foal; 1992 Horse

MISCELLANEOUS MODELS
2282 Norwegian Fjord; 1644 Highland Pony
2460 Lying Shire Foal; 2459 Lying Shire Mare

ARAB HORSES
2275 Bedouin Arab
2242 Arab Horse (authentic)
2269 Arab Stallion with Saddle (authentic)

PAINTED WHITE GLOSS
1564 Large Racehorse
1501 Huntsman; 996 Foal; 701 "Bois Roussel," 2nd version
868 Rearing Huntsman, 2nd version

GREY GLOSS
1501 Huntsman; 1730 Huntswoman
1812 Mare; 1085 Foal; 1862 Horse and Jockey
1197 Head-up Pony

MOUNTED MODELS
1877 Canadian Mounted Cowboy; 1145 Knight in Armour
1391 Mounted Indian; 1499 Girl on Pony
1375 Canadian Mountie; 1500 Boy on Pony

WHITE MATT
1501 Huntsman; 898 Rearing Huntsman, 2nd version
1033 Shetland Mare; 1034 Shetland Foal; 1730 Huntswoman

Lamb on base (323)

Mule (369)

Fox Toothbrush Holder (664)

Rabbit Toothbrush Holder (665)

Squirrel (315)

Frog - on pottery base (368)

Monkey - on pottery base (397)

Cheetah - Standing (3009)

Lion Cub - Facing right (1508)

Tiger (2096)

Puma on Rock, Style Two (1823)

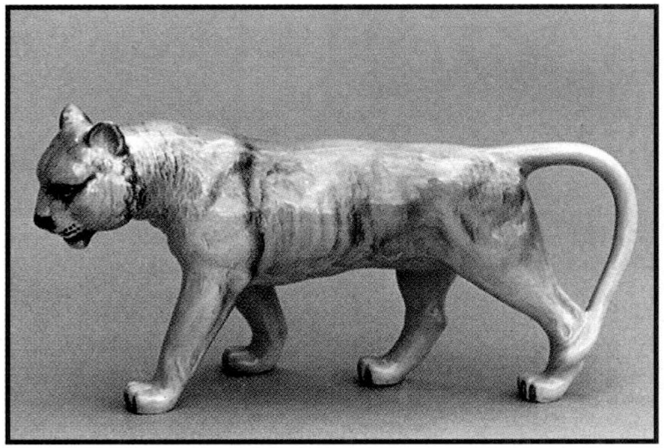

Lioness - Facing left (1507)

Tigeress (1486)

Puma on Rock, Style One (1702)

Lion - Facing right (1506)

Leopard (1082)

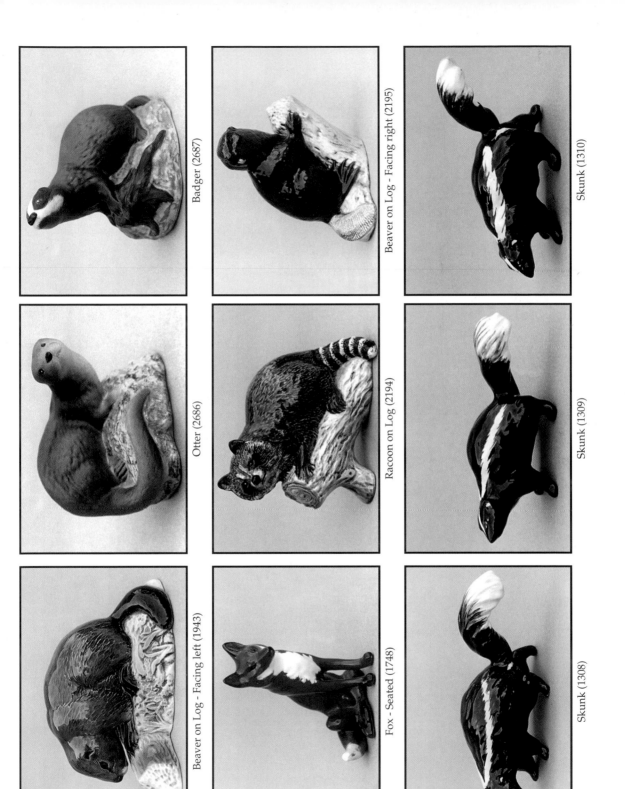

Badger (2687)

Beaver on Log - Facing right (2195)

Skunk (1310)

Otter (2686)

Racoon on Log (2194)

Skunk (1309)

Beaver on Log - Facing left (1943)

Fox - Seated (1748)

Skunk (1308)

Golden Trout (1246)

Perch (1875)

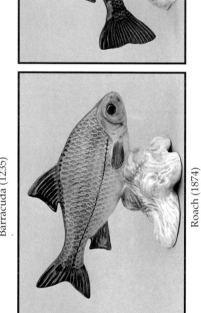

Roach (1874)

Barracuda (1235)

Atlantic Salmon (1233)

Large-Mouthed Black Bass (1266)

Salmon (2066)

Trout (1390)

Oceanic Bonito (1232)

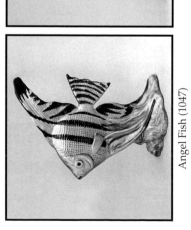

Angel Fish (1047)

Model No. 2465   CLYDESDALE

SERIES: Harnessed Horses

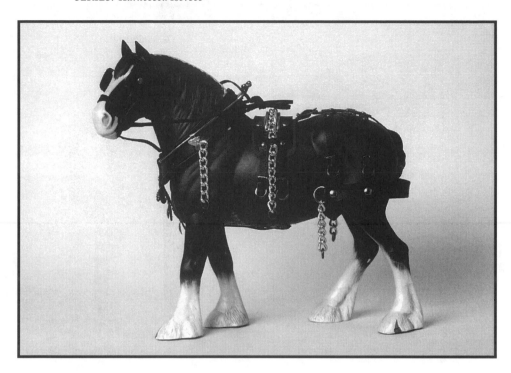

Designer: Unknown
Height: 10 ¾", 27.8 cm

FIRST VERSION: Working Harness

Colourway	Finish	Intro.	Disc.	U.K. £	U.S. $	Can. $
Chocolate Brown	Matt	1974	1982	175.00	275.00	400.00

SECOND VERSION: Show Harness

Colourway	Finish	Intro.	Disc.	U.K. £	U.S. $	Can. $
Chocolate Brown	Matt	1974	1982	225.00	350.00	525.00

Model No. 2466   **BLACK BEAUTY**

This model was used in model no. 2466/2536 Black Beauty and Foal.

Designer: Graham Tongue
Height: 7 ¼", 18.4 cm

Colourway	Finish	DA #	Intro.	Disc.	U.K. £	U.S. $	Can. $
Black							
a. Original issue	Matt	65	1974	1989	40.00	65.00	95.00
b. Reissued	Matt	65	1999	Current	45.00	N/A	N/A

Note: Model No.2466 was transferred to the Royal Doulton backstamp (DA65) in 1989. It reverted to the Beswick backstamp in September 1999.

Model No. 2466/2536   **BLACK BEAUTY AND FOAL**

A special edition of this model was commissioned by Lawleys by Post to celebrate the centenary of Beswick's Gold Street factory.

Centenary Edition (1898 - 1998)

General Issue

Designer: Graham Tongue
Height: 9 ½", 24.0 cm
Length: 13 ½", 34.3 cm

Colourway	Finish	DA #	Intro.	Disc.	U.K. £	U.S. $	Can. $
Black (centenary)	Matt	17	1998	1998	125.00	200.00	300.00
Black	Matt	17	1999	Current	110.00	N/A	N/A

Note: Model No.2466/2536 was transferred from Royal Doulton backstamp (DA17) in September 1999.

Model No. 2467   **LIPIZZANER WITH RIDER**

SERIES: Connoisseur Horses

First Version - Hind legs attached to a circular base   Second Version - Tail and rear legs attached to oval base

Designer: Graham Tongue
Height: 10", 25.4 cm

FIRST VERSION: Hind legs attached to a circular base.

Colourway	Finish	Intro.	Disc.	U.K. £	U.S. $	Can. $
White	Gloss	1974	Unknown	400.00	650.00	950.00

SECOND VERSON: Tail and rear legs attached to an oval base.

Colourway	Finish	Intro.	Disc.	U.K. £	U.S. $	Can. $
White	Gloss	Unknown	1981	325.00	525.00	750.00

Model No. 2505   **STEEPLECHASER**

Designer: Graham Tongue
Height: 8 ¾", 22.2 cm

Colourway	Finish	Intro.	Disc.	U.K. £	U.S. $	Can. $
Dark brown	Gloss	1975	1981	350.00	600.00	875.00

Model No. 2510   **RED RUM**

STYLE ONE: *Large Size - 12"*

SERIES: *Connoisseur Horses*

Designer: Graham Tongue
Height: 12", 30.5 cm

Colourway	Finish	DA #	Intro.	Disc.	U.K. £	U.S. $	Can. $
Bay							
a. Original Issue	Matt	18	1975	1989	167.00	265.00	400.00
b. Reissued	Matt	18	1999	Current	167.00	N/A	N/A

Note: Model No.2510 was transferred to the Royal Doulton backstamp (DA18) in 1989. It reverted to the Beswick backstamp in September 1999.

Model No. 2511

RED RUM
BRIAN FLETCHER UP

SERIES: Connoisseur Horses

Designer: Graham Tongue
Height: 12 ¼", 31.1 cm

Colourway	Finish	Intro.	Disc.	U.K. £	U.S. $	Can. $
Bay	Matt	1975	1982	300.00	475.00	700.00

Model No. 2535

PSALM
ANN MOORE UP

SERIES: Connoisseur Horses

Designer: Graham Tongue
Height: 12 ¾", 32.4 cm

Colourway	Finish	Intro.	Disc.	U.K. £	U.S. $	Can. $
Brown	Matt	1975	1982	300.00	500.00	700.00

Model No. 2536   **BLACK BEAUTY FOAL**

Designer: Graham Tongue
Height: 3 ½", 8.9 cm

Colourway	Finish	DA #	Intro.	Disc.	U.K. £	U.S. $	Can. $
Black							
a. Original issue	Matt	66	1976	1989	27.00	45.00	65.00
b. Reissued	Matt	66	1999	Current	27.00	N/A	N/A
Brown	Matt	—	1984	Unknown	30.00	50.00	70.00
Chocolate brown	Matt	—	1984	Unknown	30.00	50.00	70.00
Palomino	Matt	—	1984	Unknown	35.00	60.00	80.00
White	Matt	—	1984	Unknown	30.00	50.00	70.00

Note: Model No.2536 was transferred to the Royal Doulton backstamp (DA66) in 1989. The black matt colourway reverted to the Beswick backstamp in September 1999.

Model No. 2540   **PSALM**

SERIES: *Connoisseur Horses*

Designer: Graham Tongue
Height: 11 ½", 29.2 cm

Colourway	Finish	Intro.	Disc.	U.K. £	U.S. $	Can. $
Brown	Matt	1975	1982	200.00	325.00	475.00

Model No. 2541A

WELSH MOUNTAIN STALLION
"GREDINGTON SIMWNT"

This model of Gredington Simwnt was greatly adapted to produce "The Spirit of Whitfield."

SERIES: Connoisseur Horses

Designer: Graham Tongue
Height: 9", 22.9 cm

Colourway	Finish	Intro.	Disc.	U.K. £	U.S. $	Can. $
Light grey	Matt	1976	1989	200.00	325.00	475.00

Model No. 2558   **GRUNDY**

SERIES: *Connoisseur Horses*

Designer: Graham Tongue
Height: 11 ¼", 28.5 cm

Colourway	Finish	DA #	Intro.	Disc.	U.K. £	U.S. $	Can. $
Chestnut	Matt	20	1977	1989	125.00	200.00	300.00

Model No. 2562   **LIFEGUARD**

STYLE TWO: With sword

SERIES: Connoisseur Horses

Designer: Graham Tongue
Height: 14 ½", 36.8 cm

Colourway	Finish	DA #	Intro.	Disc.	U.K. £	U.S. $	Can. $
Black	Gloss	22	1977	1989	350.00	550.00	825.00

Note: Model No.2562 was transferred to the Royal Doulton backstamp (DA22) in 1989.

Model No. 2578

SHIRE HORSE
(Large action shire)

Designer: Alan Maslankowski
Height: 8 ¼", 21.0 cm

Colourway	Finish	DA #	Intro.	Disc.	U.K. £	U.S. $	Can. $
Brown	Gloss	—	1980	1982	175.00	275.00	400.00
Brown	Matt	62	1978	1989	150.00	250.00	350.00
Grey	Gloss	—	1978	1982	275.00	450.00	650.00
Grey	Matt	—	1980	1983	250.00	400.00	600.00

SERIES: Harnessed Horses

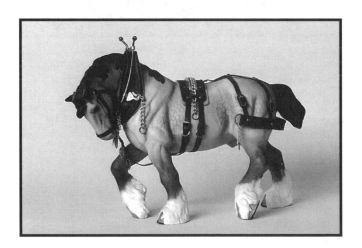

Colourway	Finish	Intro.	Disc.	U.K. £	U.S. $	Can. $
Brown	Matt	1978	1982	175.00	275.00	400.00
Grey	Matt	1978	1982	275.00	450.00	650.00

BLUES AND ROYALS

SERIES: *Connoisseur Horses*

Designer: Graham Tongue
Height: 14 ½", 36.8 cm

Colourway	Finish	DA #	Intro.	Disc.	U.K. £	U.S. $	Can. $
Black	Matt	25	1987	1989	375.00	600.00	900.00

Note: Model No.2582 was transferred to the Royal Doulton backstamp (DA25) in 1989.

Model No. 2605

MORGAN STALLION
" TARRYALL MAESTRO "

SERIES: Connoisseur Horses

Designer: Graham Tongue
Height: 11 ½", 29.2 cm

Colourway	Finish	DA #	Intro.	Disc.	U.K. £	U.S. $	Can. $
Black	Matt	28	1979	1989	175.00	275.00	400.00

Note: Model No.2605 was transferred to the Royal Doulton backstamp (DA28) in 1989.

Model No. 2608

THE MINSTREL

SERIES: Connoisseur Horses

Designer: Graham Tongue
Height: 13 ¼", 33.6 cm

Colourway	Finish	DA #	Intro.	Disc.	U.K. £	U.S. $	Can. $
Chestnut	Matt	31	1980	1989	150.00	250.00	350.00

Note: Model No.2608 was transferred to the Royal Doulton backstamp (DA31) in 1989.

Model No. 2671   # MOONLIGHT

SERIES: Connoisseur Horses

Designer: Graham Tongue
Height: 11 ¼", 28.5 cm

Colourway	Finish	DA #	Intro.	Disc.	U.K. £	U.S. $	Can. $
"Moonlight" - Grey	Matt	35	1982	1989	125.00	200.00	300.00
"Nightshade" - Black	Matt	—	1986	1989	165.00	275.00	400.00
"Sunburst" - Palomino	Matt	36	1986	1989	165.00	275.00	400.00

Note: Model No.2671 was transferred to the Royal Doulton backstamp (DA35 and DA36) in 1989.

Model No. 2674

TROY

SERIES: Connoisseur Horses

Designer: Graham Tongue
Height: 11 ¾", 29.8 cm

Colourway	Finish	DA #	Intro.	Disc.	U.K. £	U.S. $	Can. $
Bay	Matt	37	1981	1989	125.00	200.00	300.00

Note: Model No.2674 was transferred to the Royal Doulton backstamp (DA37) in 1989.

Model No. 2688

SPIRIT OF THE WIND

Designer: Graham Tongue
Height: 8", 20.3 cm

Colourway	Finish	DA #	Intro.	Disc.	U.K. £	U.S. $	Can. $
Brown	Gloss	57	1982	1989	55.00	90.00	130.00
Brown	Matt	57	1982	1989	50.00	80.00	115.00
Grey	Gloss	—	1982	1989	75.00	125.00	175.00
Grey	Matt	—	1982	1989	75.00	125.00	175.00
Palomino	Gloss	—	1982	1989	65.00	100.00	150.00
Palomino	Matt	—	1982	1989	65.00	100.00	150.00

SERIES: On Wooden Plinth

Colourway/Plinth	Finish	DA #	Intro.	Disc.	U.K. £	U.S. $	Can. $
Black/Brown	Matt	57	1986	1989	55.00	90.00	130.00
Brown/Brown							
a. Original Issue	Gloss	57	1986	1989	64.00	100.00	150.00
b. Reissued	Gloss	57	1999	Current	64.00	N/A	N/A
Brown/Brown							
a. Original issue	Matt	57	1986	1989	70.00	120.00	165.00
b. Reissued	Matt	57	1999	Current	70.00	N/A	N/A
White/Black	Matt	57	1982	1989	45.00	70.00	100.00

Note: Transferred to Royal Doulton backstamp (DA57) in 1989, the brown colourway reverted to the Beswick backstamp in September 1999.

Series: On Ceramic Plinth

Colourway	Finish	DA #	Intro.	Disc.	U.K. £	U.S. $	Can. $
Brown	Gloss	—	c.1987	c.1987	75.00	125.00	175.00

SERIES: Britannia Collection

Colourway	Finish	Intro.	Disc.	U.K. £	U.S. $	Can. $
Bronze	Gloss	1989	1993	65.00	100.00	150.00

Model No. 2689

SPIRIT OF FREEDOM

Model number 2689 was used together with model number 2353 to become the Spirit of Affection.

Designer: Graham Tongue
Height: 7", 17.8 cm

Colourway	Finish	DA #	Intro.	Disc.	U.K. £	U.S. $	Can. $
Brown	Gloss	58	1982	1989	60.00	90.00	135.00
Brown	Matt	58	1982	1989	55.00	85.00	135.00
Grey	Gloss	—	1982	1989	80.00	125.00	175.00
Grey	Matt	—	1982	1989	80.00	125.00	175.00
Palomino	Gloss	—	1982	1989	75.00	115.00	165.00
Palomino	Matt	—	1982	1989	75.00	115.00	165.00

SERIES: On Wooden Plinth

The black and brown versions were mounted on brown wooden plinths and the white version was issued on a black wooden plinth.

Colourway/Plinth	Finish	DA #	Intro.	Disc.	U.K. £	U.S. $	Can. $
Black/brown	Matt	58	1987	1989	55.00	85.00	125.00
Brown/brown							
a. Original Issue	Gloss	58	1986	1989	64.00	100.00	150.00
b. Reissued	Gloss	58	1999	Current	64.00	N/A	N/A
Brown/brown							
a. Original issue	Matt	58	1986	1989	64.00	100.00	150.00
b. Reissued	Matt	58	1999	Current	64.00	.00	.00
White/black	Matt	58	1982	1989	50.00	80.00	125.00

Note: Transferred to Royal Doulton backstamp (DA58) in 1989, the brown colourway reverted to the Beswick backstamp in September 1999.

SERIES: On Ceramic Plinth

Colourway	Finish	DA #	Intro.	Disc.	U.K. £	U.S. $	Can. $
Brown	Gloss	—	c.1987	c.1987	75.00	130.00	175.00

Model No. 2689/2536   **SPIRIT OF AFFECTION**

The Spirit of Affection is the Spirit of Freedom with the Black Beauty Foal. In all versions but one, the mare and the foal are the same colour. The brown, grey and palomino versions were mounted on a brown wooden plinth and the white version was mounted on a black wooden plinth.

SERIES: On Wooden Plinth

Designer: Graham Tongue
Height: 8", 20.3 cm

Colourway	Finish	DA #	Intro.	Disc.	U.K. £	U.S. $	Can. $
Brown	Matt	64	1982	1989	95.00	150.00	225.00
Grey mare, chocolate brown foal	Matt	—	1984	1989	115.00	185.00	275.00
Palomino	Matt	—	1984	1989	125.00	200.00	300.00
White							
a. Original issue	Matt	64	1982	1989	80.00	130.00	190.00
b. Reissued	Matt	64	1999	Current	80.00	N/A	N/A

Note: Model No.2689/2536 was transferred to the Royal Doulton backstamp (DA64) in 1989. The white matt version reverted to the Beswick backstamp in September 1999.

Model No. 2703   **SPIRIT OF YOUTH**

The Spirit of Youth is the same model as 2466 "Black Beauty."

Designer: Graham Tongue
Height: 7", 17.8 cm

Colourway	Finish	DA #	Intro.	Disc.	U.K. £	U.S. $	Can. $
Brown	Gloss	59	1982	1989	60.00	100.00	150.00
Brown	Matt	59	1982	1989	55.00	90.00	150.00
Grey	Gloss	—	1982	1989	80.00	150.00	200.00
Grey	Matt	—	1982	1989	80.00	150.00	200.00
Palomino	Gloss	—	1982	1989	70.00	125.00	165.00
Palomino	Matt	—	1982	1989	70.00	125.00	165.00

SERIES: On Wooden Plinth

The black and brown models were issued on a brown wooden plinth and the white model was issued on a black wooden plinth.

Colourway/Plinth	Finish	DA #	Intro.	Disc.	U.K. £	U.S. $	Can. $
Black / Brown	Matt	59	1987	1989	55.00	90.00	130.00
Brown/Brown							
a. Original Issue	Gloss	59	1982	1989	64.00	100.00	150.00
b. Reissued	Gloss	59	1999	Current	64.00	N/A	N/A
Brown/Brown	Matt	59	1986	1989	70.00	125.00	165.00
White/Black	Matt	59	1982	1989	50.00	85.00	120.00

SERIES: On Ceramic Plinth

Colourway	Finish	DA #	Intro.	Disc.	U.K. £	U.S. $	Can. $
Brown	Gloss	—	c.1987	c.1987	70.00	125.00	165.00

Note: Model No.2703 was transferred to the Royal Doulton backstamp (DA59) in 1989. The white colourway was reverted back to the Beswick backstamp in September 1999.

Model No. 2829

SPIRIT OF FIRE

Designer: Graham Tongue
Height: 8", 20.3 cm

Colourway	Finish	DA #	Intro.	Disc.	U.K. £	U.S. $	Can. $
Brown	Gloss	60	1984	1989	55.00	80.00	125.00
Brown	Matt	60	1984	1989	50.00	75.00	125.00
Grey	Gloss	—	1984	1989	75.00	125.00	175.00
Grey	Matt	—	1984	1989	75.00	125.00	175.00
Palomino	Gloss	—	1984	1989	65.00	100.00	150.00
Palomino	Matt	—	1984	1989	65.00	100.00	150.00

SERIES: On Wooden Plinth

The black and brown versions were issued on a brown wooden plinth and the white version was issued on a black wooden plinth.

Colourway/Plinth	Finish	DA #	Intro.	Disc.	U.K. £	U.S. $	Can. $
Black/Brown	Matt	60	1986	1989	55.00	80.00	130.00
Brown/Brown	Matt	60	1986	1989	70.00	125.00	150.00
White/Black	Matt	60	1984	1989	50.00	80.00	125.00

SERIES: On Ceramic Plinth

Colourway	Finish	Intro.	Disc.	U.K. £	U.S. $	Can. $
Brown	Gloss	c.1987	c.1987	70.00	125.00	165.00

Note: Model No.2829 was transferred to the Royal Doulton backstamp (DA60) in 1989.

Model No. 2837　　　　　　　　**SPRINGTIME**

SERIES: *Spirited Foals*

Designer:　　Graham Tongue
Height:　　　4 ½", 11.9 cm

VARIATION No. 1 Free Standing

Colourway	Finish	DA #	Intro.	Disc.	U.K. £	U.S. $	Can. $
Brown							
a. Original issue	Gloss	69	1984	1989	25.00	45.00	60.00
b. Reissued	Gloss	69	1999	1999	25.00	45.00	60.00

VARIATION No. 2 On Wooden Plinth

Colourway/Plinth	Finish	DA #	Intro.	Disc.	U.K. £	U.S. $	Can. $
Black/Brown	Matt	—	1987	1989	30.00	50.00	70.00
Brown/Brown	Matt	69	1986	1989	30.00	50.00	70.00
White/Black							
a. Original issue	Matt	69	1984	1989	26.00	45.00	60.00
b. Reissued	Matt	69	1999	Current	26.00	N/A	N/A

Note:　Model No.2837 was transferred to the Royal Doulton backstamp (DA69) in 1989. The white colourway reverted to the Beswick backstamp in September 1999.

Model No. 2839

YOUNG SPIRIT

Young Spirit was originally illustrated in a catalogue with his ears sticking out slightly. The model was changed to have the ears flat against the foals head, probably due to the potential problem of breakage in shipping. No date has been established for the mould change but it is probably either in the early stages of production, i.e. prototype or shortly after issue.

SERIES: Spirited Foals

Designer:　Graham Tongue
Height:　　4 ½", 11.9 cm

VARIATION No. 1 Free Standing

Colourway	Finish	DA #	Intro.	Disc.	U.K. £	U.S. $	Can. $
Brown	Gloss	70	1984	1989	25.00	45.00	60.00

VARIATION No. 2 On Wooden Plinth

Colourway/Plinth	Finish	DA #	Intro.	Disc.	U.K. £	U.S. $	Can. $
Black/Brown	Matt	70	1987	1989	25.00	45.00	60.00
Brown/Brown	Matt	70	1986	1989	30.00	50.00	55.00
White/Black	Matt	70	1984	1989	25.00	45.00	60.00

Note:　Model No.2839 was transferred to the Royal Doulton backstamp (DA70) in 1989.

Model No. 2875   **SUNLIGHT**

SERIES: Spirited Foals

Designer: Graham Tongue
Height: 4 ½", 11.9 cm

VARIATION No. 1 Free Standing

Colourway	Finish	DA #	Intro.	Disc.	U.K. £	U.S. $	Can. $
Brown	Gloss	71	1987	1989	25.00	45.00	60.00

VARIATION No. 2 On Wooden Plinth

Colourway/Plinth	Finish	DA #	Intro.	Disc.	U.K. £	U.S. $	Can. $
Black/Brown	Matt	71	1987	1989	25.00	40.00	60.00
Brown/Brown	Matt	71	1987	1989	35.00	55.00	80.00
White/Black	Matt	71	1985	1989	20.00	35.00	50.00

Note: Model No.2875 was transferred to the Royal Doulton backstamp (DA71) in 1989.

Model No. 2876

ADVENTURE

SERIES: Spirited Foals

Designer: Graham Tongue
Height: 4 ½", 11.9 cm

VARIATION No. 1 Free Standing

Colourway	Finish	DA #	Intro.	Disc.	U.K. £	U.S. $	Can. $
Brown	Gloss	72	1987	1989	25.00	45.00	60.00

VARIATION No. 2 On Wooden Plinth

Colourway/Plinth	Finish	DA #	Intro.	Disc.	U.K. £	U.S. $	Can. $
Black/Brown	Matt	—	1987	1989	30.00	50.00	65.00
Brown/Brown	Matt	72	1987	1989	30.00	50.00	65.00
White/Black	Matt	72	1985	1989	25.00	45.00	60.00

Note: Model No.2876 was transferred to the Royal Doulton backstamp (DA72) in 1989.

Model No. 2914   **SPIRIT OF EARTH**

Designer: Graham Tongue
Height: 7 ½", 19.1 cm

Colourway	Finish	DA #	Intro.	Disc.	U.K. £	U.S. $	Can. $
Brown	Gloss	61	1987	1989	70.00	125.00	175.00
Brown	Matt	61	1987	1989	65.00	100.00	160.00
Grey	Gloss	—	1987	1989	95.00	175.00	225.00
Grey	Matt	—	1987	1989	85.00	165.00	200.00

SERIES: On Wooden Plinth

Colourway/Plinth	Finish	DA #	Intro.	Disc.	U.K. £	U.S. $	Can. $
Black/Brown	Matt	—	1987	1989	65.00	125.00	150.00
Brown/Brown	Matt	61	1987	1989	75.00	135.00	175.00
White/Black	Matt	61	1986	1989	60.00	100.00	140.00

SERIES: On Ceramic Plinth

Colourway/Plinth	Finish	DA #	Intro.	Disc.	U.K. £	U.S. $	Can. $
Brown/Ceramic	Gloss		c.1987	c.1987	85.00	150.00	200.00

SERIES: Britannia Collection

Colourway	Finish	Intro.	Disc.	U.K. £	U.S. $	Can. $
Brown	Gloss	1989	1993	75.00	125.00	175.00

Note: Model No.2914 was transferred to the Royal Doulton backstamp (DA61) in 1989.

Model No. 2916   SPIRIT OF PEACE

Designer: Graham Tongue
Height: 4 ¾", 12.1 cm

Colourway	Finish	DA #	Intro.	Disc.	U.K. £	U.S. $	Can. $
Brown	Gloss	—	1987	1989	60.00	95.00	140.00
Brown	Matt	63	1987	1989	55.00	90.00	130.00
Grey	Gloss	—	1987	1989	85.00	135.00	200.00
Grey	Matt	—	1987	1989	85.00	135.00	200.00
Palomino	Gloss	—	1987	1989	70.00	115.00	165.00
Palomino	Matt	—	1987	1989	70.00	115.00	165.00

SERIES: On Wooden Plinth

The black and brown versions were issued on a brown wooden plinth and the white version was issued on a black wooden plinth.

Colourway/Plinth	Finish	DA #	Intro.	Disc.	U.K. £	U.S. $	Can. $
Black/Brown	Matt	—	1987	1989	60.00	95.00	140.00
Brown/Brown	Matt	63	1987	1989	70.00	115.00	165.00
White/Black	Matt	63	1986	1989	50.00	80.00	120.00

SERIES: On Ceramic Plinth

Colourway	Finish	Intro.	Disc.	U.K. £	U.S. $	Can. $
Brown	Gloss	c.1987	c.1987	85.00	135.00	200.00

Note: Model No.2916 was transferred to the Royal Doulton backstamp (DA63) in 1989.

Model No. 2935   **SPIRIT OF NATURE**

Designer: Graham Tongue
Height: 5 ½", 14.0 cm

Colourway	Finish	Intro.	Disc.	U.K. £	U.S. $	Can. $
Brown	Gloss	1987	1989	55.00	90.00	130.00
Brown	Matt	1987	1989	50.00	80.00	120.00
Grey	Gloss	1987	1989	75.00	125.00	175.00
Grey	Matt	1987	1989	75.00	125.00	175.00
Palomino	Gloss	1987	1989	65.00	100.00	150.00
Palomino	Matt	1987	1989	65.00	100.00	150.00

SERIES: On Wooden Plinth

    The black and brown versions were mounted on brown wooden plinths and the white version was mounted on a black wooden plinth.

Colourway/Plinth	Finish	DA #	Intro.	Disc.	U.K. £	U.S. $	Can. $
Black/Brown	Matt	—	1987	1989	60.00	95.00	140.00
Brown/Brown	Matt	73	1987	1989	65.00	100.00	150.00
White/Black	Matt	—	1987	1989	50.00	80.00	120.00

SERIES: On Ceramic Plinth

Colourway	Finish	Intro.	Disc.	U.K. £	U.S. $	Can. $
Brown	Gloss	c.1987	c.1987	75.00	100.00	175.00

Note: Model No.2935 was transferred to the Royal Doulton backstamp (DA73) in 1989.

Model No. 3426

CANCARA

Modelled from "Downland Cancara" graded Trakehner stallion famous for advertising Lloyds Bank. Backstamp - "1994 Special Beswick Centenary."

SERIES: On wooden plinth

Designer: Graham Tongue
Height: 16 ½", 41.9 cm

Colourway	Finish	DA #	Intro.	Disc.	U.K. £	U.S. $	Can. $
Black							
a. Original issue	Matt	234	1994	1994	290.00	575.00	700.00
b. Reissued	Matt	234	1999	Current	290.00	N/A	N/A

Note: Model No.3426 was transferred to the Royal Doulton (DA234) backstamp in 1989. It reverted to the Beswick backstamp in September 1999.

Model No. 3464

TALLY HO

This model was made exclusively for the mail order company Grattans. The horse and rider, from the model "Rearing Huntsman," with three hounds are on a natural effect base (all gloss). This model stands on a wooden plinth which is topped with green baise and has a brass plaque on the front. Backstamp - "Beswick Ware Made in England Tally Ho! Beswick Centenary 1894-1994 © 1994 Royal Doulton."

Designer: Unknown
Height: 11" x 14", 27.9 x 35.5 cm

Colourway	Finish	Intro.	Disc.	U.K. £	U.S. $	Can. $
Brown	Gloss	1994	1994	300.00	475.00	700.00

Model No. A182

FIRST BORN

Designer: Amanda Hughes-Lubeck
Height: 7", 17.8 cm

Colourway	Finish	Intro.	Disc.	U.K. £	U.S. $	Can. $
Chestnut mare and foal	Matt	1999	Current	110.00	N/A	N/A

Note: Model DA182 was transferred from the Royal Doulton backstamp in September 1999.

Model No. A183

SPIRIT OF THE WILD

Designer: Warren Platt
Height: 12", 30.5 cm

Colourway	Finish	Intro.	Disc.	U.K. £	U.S. $	Can. $
Brown	Matt	1999	Current	85.00	N/A	N/A
White	Matt	1999	Current	64.00	N/A	N/A

Note: Model DA183 was transferred from the Royal Doulton backstamp in September 1999.

Model No. A184

DESERT ORCHID

Designer: Warren Platt
Height: 7¾", 19.7 cm

Colourway	Finish	Intro.	Disc.	U.K. £	U.S. $	Can. $
Light grey	Matt	1999	Current	110.00	N/A	N/A

Note: Model DA184 was transferred from the Royal Doulton backstamp in September 1999.

Model No. A193   **MY FIRST HORSE**

Designer: Amanda Hughes-Lubeck
Height: 8 ¼", 21.0 cm

Colourway	Finish	Intro.	Disc.	U.K. £	U.S. $	Can. $
Brown	Gloss	1999	Current	56.00	N/A	N/A

Note: Model DA193 was transferred from the Royal Doulton backstamp in September 1999.

Model No. A226   **RED RUM**

STYLE TWO: Small size - 9"

Designer: Amanda Hughes-Lubeck
Height: 9", 22.9 cm

Colourway	Finish	Intro.	Disc.	U.K. £	U.S. $	Can. $
Brown	Matt	1999	Current	110.00	N/A	N/A

Note: Model DA193 was transferred from the Royal Doulton backstamp in September 1999.

Model No. A244   **NEW FOREST PONY**

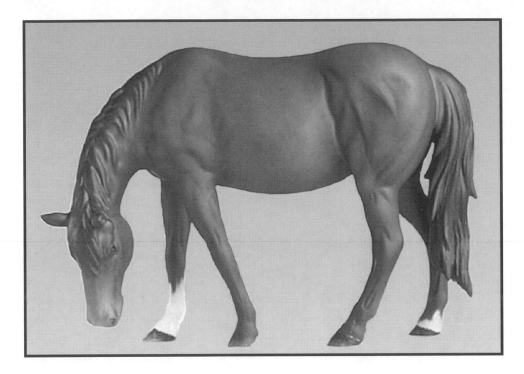

Designer: Shane Ridge
Height: 6", 15.0 cm

Colourway	Finish	Intro.	Disc.	U.K. £	U.S. $	Can. $
Brown	Matt	1999	Current	48.00	N/A	N/A

Note: Model DA244 was transferred from the Royal Doulton backstamp in September 1999.

Model No. A259

PALOMINO

Designer: Shane Ridge
Height: 6 ¾", 17.2 cm

Colourway	Finish	Intro.	Disc.	U.K. £	U.S. $	Can. $
Palomino	Gloss	1999	Current	56.00	N/A	N/A

Note: Model DA259 was transferred from the Royal Doulton backstamp in September 1999.

Model No. A260

HUNTER

Designer: Graham Tongue
Height: 8", 20.3 cm

Colourway	Finish	Intro.	Disc.	U.K. £	U.S. $	Can. $
Grey	Gloss	1999	Current	62.00	N/A	N/A

Note: Model DA260 was transferred from the Royal Doulton backstamp in September 1999.

Model No. A261   **HACKNEY PONY**

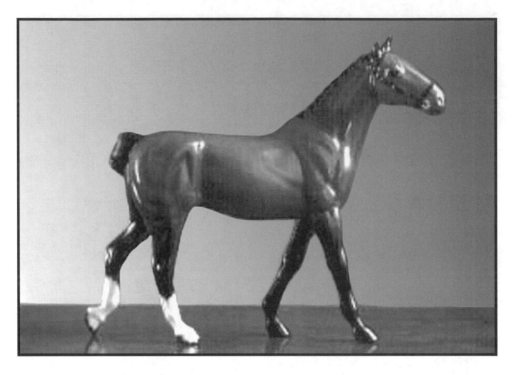

Designer: Martyn C. R. Alcock
Height: 6 ¾", 17.2 cm

Colourway	Finish	Intro.	Disc.	U.K. £	U.S. $	Can. $
Brown	Gloss	1999	Current	45.50	N/A	N/A

Note: Model DA261 was transferred from the Royal Doulton backstamp in September 1999.

ANOTHER STAR

This model was commissioned for P.R. Middleweek and Co. from the John Beswick Studios and was issued in a special edition of 1,500.

Designer: Warren Platt
Height: 2 ½", 6.4 cm

Colourway	Finish	Intro.	Disc.	U.K. £	U.S. $	Can. $
Light Brown	Gloss	1998	Ltd. Ed.	35.00	60.00	85.00

Note: See also "The Dartmoor Family" page 348.

THE DARTMOOR FAMILY

Commissioned by P.R. Middleweek & Co. to commemorate the Millennium, this tableau is composed of *Warlord, Another Bunch* and *Another Star,* and was issued in 1999 in a limited edition of 150.

Modeller: Arthur Gredington, Graham Tongue, Warren Platt
Height: 7 ¼", 18.4 cm

Colourway	Finish	Intro.	Disc.	U.K. £	U.S. $	Can. $
Red bay (Warlord) Red bay (Another Bunch) Light brown (Another Star)	Gloss	1999	Ltd. Ed.	250.00	425.00	600.00

SHETLAND PONY/
"HOLLYDELL DIXIE"

This Shetland Pony was the 1995 Beswick Collectors Circle "Special." It was decorated to represent Shetland Mare, Supreme Champion "Hollydell Dixie," and was issued in a limited edition of 553 in August 1995. Both the Beswick and BCC backstamps appear on this model.

Designer: Amanda Hughes-Lubeck
Height: 5 ¼", 13.3 cm

Colourway	Finish	DA #	Intro.	Disc.	U.K. £	U.S. $	Can. $
Skewbald (BCC95)	Gloss	185	1995	Ltd. Ed.	150.00	225.00	350.00
Dapple grey	Gloss	185	1999	Current	45.00	N/A	N/A

Note: The Sheltand Pony model was transferred from the Royal Doulton backstamp (DA185) in September 1999.

SPIRIT OF WHITFIELD

This model of "Kruger" was commissioned by the Chatterley Whitfield Mining Museum. Only four models exist.

Designer: Graham Tongue
Height: 9", 22.9 cm

Colourway	Finish	Intro.	Disc.	U.K. £	U.S. $	Can. $
Brown	Matt	1987	1987		Auction Sale 1994, £2,750.00	

WARLORD'S MARE
"ANOTHER BUNCH"

Another Bunch, issued in a special edition of 1,500, was the second in a series of specially commissioned models for P. R. Middleweek & Co. from The John Beswick Studios. This photograph is of the original clay model.

Designer: Graham Tongue
Height: 6", 15.1 cm

Colourway	Finish	Intro.	Disc.	U.K. £	U.S. $	Can. $
Bay/brown with red, white and blue sash	Gloss	1997	Spec. Ed.	65.00	100.00	150.00

Note: See also the Dartmoor Family page 348.

WELSH MOUNTAIN PONY/
"CHAMPION WELSH MOUNTAIN PONY"

The Champion Welsh Mountain Pony was the 1999 Beswick Collectors Club "Special". A "Beswick" green rug with yellow binding has BCC99 on the corner, and a red rosette is on the bridle. The Champion Welsh Pony was issued in a limited edition of 580.

SERIES: Connoisseur

Welsh Mountain Pony   "Champion Welsh Mountain Pony"

Designer: Graham Tongue
Height: 8 ¼", 21.0 cm

Colourway	Finish	DA #	Intro.	Disc.	U.K. £	U.S. $	Can. $
Black (BCC99)	Gloss	247	1999	Ltd. Ed.	125.00	200.00	300.00
White	Gloss	247	1999	Current	110.00	N/A	N/A

Note: Model DA247 was transferred from the Royal Doulton backstamp in September 1999.

Wall Ornaments
- Horses

INDEX BY MODEL NUMBER

Photograph not
available at press time

Model No. 686
**HORSE'S HEAD LOOKING LEFT THROUGH A
HORSESHOE**
First Version - Flat back

Designer: Mr. Owen
Height: 7 ¼″ x 6″, 18.4 x 15.0 cm
Colour: 1. Brown - gloss
            2. Dark chestnut - gloss
Issued: 1938-1939
Varieties: 807

Colourway	U.K. £	U.S. $	Can. $
1. Brown	85.00	135.00	200.00
2. Dark chestnut	100.00	165.00	250.00

Photograph not
available at press time

Model No. 687
**HORSE'S HEAD LOOKING RIGHT THROUGH A
HORSESHOE**
First Version - Flat back

Designer: Mr. Owen
Height: 7 ¼″ x 6″, 18.4 x 15.0 cm
Colour: 1. Brown - gloss
            2. Dark chestnut - gloss
Issued: 1939-1939
Varieties: 806

Colourway	U.K. £	U.S. $	Can. $
1. Brown	85.00	135.00	200.00
2. Dark chestnut	100.00	165.00	250.00

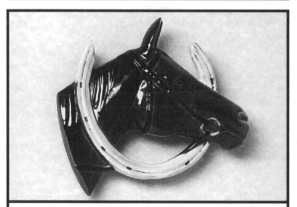

Model No. 806
**HORSE'S HEAD LOOKING RIGHT THROUGH A
HORSESHOE**
Second Version - Raised back

Designer: Mr. Owen
Height: 7 ¼″ x 6″, 18.4 x 15.0 cm
Colour: Brown - gloss
Issued: 1939-1968
Varieties: 687

Description	U.K. £	U.S. $	Can. $
Gloss	75.00	125.00	175.00

Model No. 807
**HORSE'S HEAD LOOKING LEFT THROUGH A
HORSESHOE**
Second Version - Raised back

Designer: Mr. Owen
Height: 7 ¼″ x 6″, 18.4 x 15.0 cm
Colour: Brown - gloss
Issued: 1938-1968
Varieties: 686

Description	U.K. £	U.S. $	Can. $
Gloss	75.00	125.00	175.00

Model No. 1382
HUNTER HEAD

Designer:	Arthur Gredington	
Height:	4" x 4", 10.1 x 10.1 cm	
Colour:	Brown - gloss	
Issued:	1955-1969	

Description	U.K. £	U.S. $	Can. $
Gloss	55.00	90.00	130.00

Model No. 1384
PALOMINO HEAD

Designer:	Arthur Gredington	
Height:	4"x 4", 10.1 x 10.1 cm	
Colour:	Palomino - gloss	
Issued:	1955-1969	

Description	U.K. £	U.S. $	Can. $
Gloss	70.00	115.00	165.00

Model No. 1385
ARAB HEAD

Designer:	Arthur Gredington	
Height:	4" x 4", 10.1 x 10.1 cm	
Colour:	Dark brown - gloss	
Issued:	1955-1969	

Description	U.K. £	U.S. $	Can. $
Gloss	65.00	110.00	150.00

Model No. 1505
HUNTSMAN

Designer:	Albert Hallam and James Hayward	
Height:	8 ½", 21.6 cm	
Colour:	1. Brown - gloss	
	2. Copper lustre	
Issued:	1958-1962	

Colourway	U.K. £	U.S. $	Can. $
1. Brown	150.00	250.00	350.00
2. Copper lustre	100.00	165.00	250.00

Model No. 1513
"TAKING OFF"

Designer:	Colin Melbourne
Height:	9", 22.9 cm
Colour:	1. Brown - gloss
	2. Copper lustre
Issued:	1958-1962

Colourway	U.K. £	U.S. $	Can. $
1. Brown	165.00	265.00	400.00
2. Copper lustre	125.00	200.00	300.00

Model No. 1514
"LANDING"

Designer:	Colin Melbourne
Height:	7 ¾", 19.7 cm
Colour:	1. Brown - gloss
	2. Copper lustre
Issued:	1958-1962

Colourway	U.K. £	U.S. $	Can. $
1. Brown	165.00	265.00	400.00
2. Copper lustre	125.00	200.00	300.00

Model No. 1515
"GOING OVER"

Designer:	Colin Melbourne
Height:	7 ½", 19.1 cm
Colour:	1. Brown - gloss
	2. Copper lustre
Issued:	1958-1962

Colourway	U.K. £	U.S. $	Can. $
1. Brown	165.00	265.00	400.00
2. Copper lustre	125.00	200.00	300.00

Model No. 2699
TROY

Designer:	Unknown
Height:	6", 15.0 cm
Colour:	Brown - matt
Issued:	1984-1989
Series:	Champions All

Description	U.K. £	U.S. $	Can. $
Matt	45.00	80.00	125.00

Model No. 2700
ARKLE

Designer:	Unknown
Height:	6″, 15.0 cm
Colour:	Bay - matt
Issued:	1984-1989
Series:	Champions All

Description	U.K. £	U.S. $	Can. $
Matt	45.00	80.00	125.00

Model No. 2701
THE MINSTREL

Designer:	Unknown
Height:	6″, 15.0 cm
Colour:	Chestnut - matt
Issued:	1984-1989
Series:	Champions All

Description	U.K. £	U.S. $	Can. $
Matt	45.00	80.00	125.00

Model No. 2702
RED RUM

Designer:	Unknown
Height:	6″, 15.0 cm
Colour:	Bay - matt
Issued:	1984-1989
Series:	Champions All

Description	U.K. £	U.S. $	Can. $
Matt	45.00	80.00	125.00

BESWICK
Connoisseur Range
COLLECTORS PIECES

JOHN BESWICK LTD., Gold Street, Longton, Stoke-on-Trent, ST3 2JP, England
Telephone Stoke-on-Trent 33041   Cables Beswere, Stoke-on-Trent

A MEMBER OF THE ROYAL DOULTON GROUP OF COMPANIES

Miscellaneous

INDEX BY MODEL NUMBER

Model No. 2093
OLD STAFFORDSHIRE LION

Designer:	Graham Tongue
Height:	5 ¾", 14.6 cm
Colour:	Grey, cream, green - gloss
Issued:	1967-1971

Description	U.K. £	U.S. $	Can. $
Gloss	250.00	400.00	600.00

Model No. 2094
OLD STAFFORDSHIRE UNICORN

Designer:	Graham Tongue
Height:	6", 15.0 cm
Colour:	Grey, cream, green - gloss
Issued:	1967-1971

Description	U.K. £	U.S. $	Can. $
Gloss	250.00	400.00	600.00

Photograph not
available at press time

Model No. 2137
T'ANG HORSE - Small

Designer:	Graham Tongue
Height:	8", 20.3 cm
Colour:	Green/bronze - gloss
Issued:	1967-1972

Description	U.K. £	U.S. $	Can. $
Gloss	275.00	450.00	675.00

Model No. 2182
HERALDIC UNICORN ON BASE

Designer:	Graham Tongue
Height:	8 ½", 21.6 cm
Colour.	Unknown
Issued:	Unknown

Description	U.K. £	U.S. $	Can. $
	300.00	475.00	700.00

Model No. 2205
T'ANG HORSE- Large
Designer: Graham Tongue
Height: 13", 33.0 cm
Colour: Green/bronze - gloss
Issued: 1968-1972

Description	U.K. £	U.S. $	Can. $
Gloss	350.00	575.00	825.00

Model No. 2222
LION (CAERNARVON 1969)
Designer: Mrs. Elliot
Height: 4", 10.1 cm
Colour: Cream, red lettering - matt
Issued: 1968-1969
Series: Pair with 2223

Description	U.K.£	U.S.$	Can.$
Matt		Only known example in the Beswick Museum	

Note: Issued to commemorate the investiture of Prince of Wales, Caernarvon, 1969.

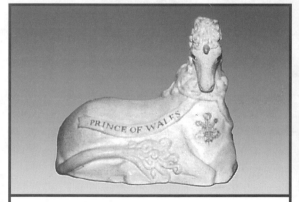

Model No. 2223
UNICORN (PRINCE OF WALES)
Designer: Mrs. Elliott
Height: 4", 10.1 cm
Colour. Cream, red lettering - matt
Issued: 1968-1969
Series: Pair with 2222

Description	U.K. £	U.S. $	Can. $
Matt		Only known example in the Beswick Museum	

Note: Issued to commemorate the Investiture of the Prince of Wales, Caernarvon, 1969.

Model No. 2514
"WHITE HORSE WHISKY"
Designer: Alan Maslankowski
Height: 6 ¾", 17.2 cm
Colour: White - gloss
Issued: 1974
Series: Advertising

Description	U.K. £	U.S. $	Can. $
Gloss	500.00	800.00	1,175.00

Model No. 3021   **UNICORN**

Designer: Graham Tongue
Height: 9″, 2.9 cm
Series: Britannia Collection

Colourway	Finish	Intro	Disc.	U.K. £	U.S. $	Can. $
Cream	Matt	1989	Unknown	225.00	350.00	525.00
Dark bronze	Gloss	1989	1992	125.00	200.00	300.00

Chapter Eight
WILD ANIMALS

The wild animals in this group have been produced by John Beswick for more than fifty years. Many are authentic and true to life in shape and colour, others are comical.

Beswick wild animals are very popular with collectors. They are less of a minefield for the inexperienced than some of the other series, as the animals are familiar and can be easily identified, since most carry the Beswick backstamp.

As you can see, Beswick produced these animals in a random order. It was not until the late 1930s that realism was created by the use of natural colours, instead of the very popular blue gloss used in earlier days. Around this time, the models were also refined to represent real animals.

The variety of animals is enormous and most animals are represented, ranging from the smallest mouse to the very large African elephant. The powerful bison, the gentle springbok and the elegant giraffe are just some of these superb pieces.

At the time of the introduction of the Connoisseur Series in 1967, most of the items were horses, and it was not until 1973 that three wild animals were absorbed into the series. These were the already existing versions of two elephants, numbers 998 and 1770, both free standing, and a puma on a rock, number 1702. As the name suggests, the Connoisseur Series comprises prestige models, and consequently were and are more expensive than the rest of the animals.

It is interesting to note that Arthur Gredington was the modeller responsible for the majority of the wild animals. Some collectors collect models from one particular designer or modeller, and these would make an excellent choice.

Many of the wild animals are avidly sought after. The search is a challenge, but well worth the effort if you can find your treasured piece.

INDEX BY MODEL NUMBER

Model No. 315
SQUIRREL - on pottery base

Designer:	Miss Greaves
Height:	8 ¾", 22.2 cm
Colour:	See below
Issued:	1935-by 1954

Colourway	U.K. £	U.S. $	Can. $
1. Blue - gloss	135.00	225.00	325.00
2. Blue/brown - satin	100.00	165.00	235.00
3. Cream - satin matt	100.00	165.00	235.00
4. Natural - satin	135.00	225.00	325.00

Model No. 368
FROG - on pottery base

Designer:	Miss Greaves
Height:	6 ¾", 16.5 cm
Colour:	See below
Issued:	1936-by 1954

Colourway	U.K. £	U.S. $	Can. $
1. Blue - gloss	135.00	225.00	325.00
2. Blue/brown - satin	100.00	165.00	235.00
3. Cream - satin matt	100.00	165.00	235.00
4. Gold		Rare	
5. Green - satin matt	100.00	165.00	235.00
6. Natural - satin	135.00	225.00	325.00

Model No. 316
RABBIT - on pottery base

Designer:	Miss Greaves
Height:	6 ¾", 17.2 cm
Colour:	1. Blue - gloss
	2. Blue/brown - satin
	3. Cream - satin matt
	4. Natural - satin
Issued:	1935-by 1954

Colourway	U.K. £	U.S. $	Can. $
1. Blue	135.00	225.00	325.00
2. Blue/brown	100.00	165.00	235.00
3. Cream	100.00	165.00	235.00
4. Natural	135.00	225.00	325.00

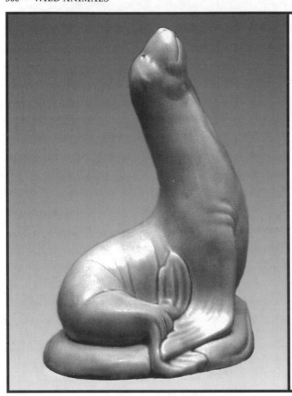

Model No. 383
SEAL - on pottery base

Designer: Mr. Owen
Height: 10", 25.4 cm
Colour: 1. Blue - gloss
2. Blue/brown - satin
3. Cream - satin matt
4. Natural - satin
Issued: 1936-by 1954

Colourway	U.K. £	U.S. $	Can. $
1. Blue	135.00	225.00	325.00
2. Blue/brown	100.00	165.00	235.00
3. Cream	100.00	165.00	235.00
4. Natural	135.00	225.00	325.00

Model No. 397
MONKEY - on pottery base

Designer: Mr. Owen
Height: 7", 17.8 cm
Colour: 1. Blue - gloss
2. Blue/brown - satin
3. Cream - satin matt
4. Natural - satin
Issued: 1936-by 1954

Colourway	U.K. £	U.S. $	Can. $
1. Blue	125.00	200.00	300.00
2. Blue/brown	100.00	165.00	235.00
3. Cream	100.00	165.00	235.00
4. Natural	125.00	200.00	300.00

Model No. 417
POLAR BEAR - on pottery base

Designer:	Mr. Owen
Height:	7", 17.8 cm
Colour:	1. Blue - gloss
	2. Cream - satin matt
	3. Natural - satin
Issued:	1936-by 1954

Colourway	U.K. £	U.S. $	Can. $
1. Blue	135.00	225.00	325.00
2. Cream	100.00	165.00	235.00
3. Natural	135.00	225.00	325.00

Model No. 455
RABBIT BOOKEND

Designer:	James Hayward
Height:	6 ¾", 17.2 cm
Colour:	1. Blue - gloss
	2. Various - satin matt
	3. White - matt
Issued:	1937-by 1954

Colourway	U.K. £	U.S. $	Can. $
1. Blue	85.00	135.00	200.00
2. Various	65.00	100.00	150.00
3. White	65.00	100.00	150.00

Note: Prices given are for single bookends.

Model No. 568/569
CHARACTER ELEPHANT

Designer:	Mr. Owen
Height:	1. Large - 9", 22.9 cm
	2. Small - 4 ¾", 12.1 cm
Colour:	1. Blue - gloss
	2. Cream - satin matt
Issued:	1938-by 1954

Colourway	U.K. £	U.S. $	Can. $
1. Blue - large	375.00	600.00	875.00
2. Cream - large	350.00	550.00	825.00
3. Blue - small	225.00	350.00	525.00
4. Cream - small	225.00	350.00	525.00

Model No. 663
ELEPHANT TOOTHBRUSH HOLDER

Designer:	Miss Catford
Height:	4 ½", 11.9 cm
Colour:	1. Blue - gloss
	2. Various - satin matt
	3. White - matt
Issued:	1938 -by 1954

Colourway	U.K. £	U.S. $	Can. $
1. Blue	150.00	250.00	350.00
2. Various	165.00	265.00	400.00
3. White	150.00	250.00	350.00

Model No. 664
FOX TOOTHBRUSH HOLDER

Designer:	Miss Catford
Height:	4 ¾", 12.1 cm
Colour:	1. Blue - gloss
	2. Various - satin matt
	3. White - matt
Issued:	1938-by 1954

Colourway	U.K. £	U.S. $	Can. $
1. Blue	135.00	225.00	325.00
2. Various	150.00	250.00	350.00
3. White	135.00	225.00	325.00

Model No. 665
RABBIT TOOTHBRUSH HOLDER

Designer:	Miss Catford
Height:	4 ¾", 12.1 cm
Colour:	1. Blue - gloss
	2. Various - satin matt
	3. White - matt
Issued:	1938-by 1954

Colourway	U.K. £	U.S. $	Can. $
1. Blue	135.00	225.00	325.00
2. Various	150.00	250.00	350.00
3. White	135.00	225.00	325.00

Model No. 692
ELEPHANT WITH HOWDAH

Designer:	Unknown
Height:	4 ¼", 10.8 cm
Colour:	Blue - gloss
Issued:	1939-by 1954

Colourway	U.K. £	U.S. $	Can. $
Blue	150.00	250.00	350.00

Model No. 696
DEER ON ROCK

Designer:	Arthur Gredington
Height:	8", 20.3 cm
Colour:	See below
Issued:	1939-1954
Set:	721

Colourway	U.K. £	U.S. $	Can. $
1. Blue - gloss	85.00	135.00	200.00
2. Brown - gloss	75.00	125.00	175.00
3. Cream - satin	65.00	100.00	150.00
4. Flambé - gloss	200.00	325.00	475.00

Model No. 697
HIPPOPOTAMUS

Designer:	Mr. Watkin
Height:	2 ¼", 5.7 cm
Colour:	1. Blue - gloss
	2. Cream - satin matt
Issued:	1939-by 1954
Series:	Fun Models

Colourway	U.K. £	U.S. $	Can. $
1. Blue	75.00	125.00	175.00
2. Cream	65.00	100.00	150.00

Model No. 698
GIRAFFE

Designer:	Mr. Watkin	
Height:	1. Large - 6", 15.0 cm	
	2. Small - 4", 10.1 cm	
Colour:	1. Blue - gloss	2. Cream - satin matt
Issued:	1939-by 1954	
Series:	Fun Models	

Colourway	U.K. £	U.S. $	Can. $
1. Blue - large	125.00	200.00	300.00
2. Cream - large	125.00	200.00	300.00
3. Blue - small	75.00	125.00	175.00
4. Cream - small	75.00	125.00	175.00

Photograph not
available at press time

Model No. 709
BEAVER

Designer:	Mr. Watkin
Height:	Unknown
Colour:	Unknown
Issued:	1939-Unknown

Description	U.K. £	U.S. $	Can. $
Beaver		Extremely Rare	

Note: Possibly not put into production.

Model No. 711
PANDA

Designer:	Mr. Watkin
Height:	4 ½", 11.9 cm
Colour:	1. Black and white - gloss
	2. Blue - gloss
	3. Cream - satin matt
Issued:	1939-by 1954

Colourway	U.K. £	U.S. $	Can. $
1. Black/white	85.00	135.00	200.00
2. Blue	135.00	225.00	325.00
3. Cream	85.00	135.00	200.00

Model No. 720
PANDA CUB

Designer:	James Haywood
Height:	3 ¾", 9.5 cm
Colour:	1. Black and white - gloss
	2. Blue - gloss
	3. Cream - satin matt
Issued:	1939-by 1954

Colourway	U.K. £	U.S. $	Can. $
1. Black/white	95.00	150.00	225.00
2. Blue	75.00	125.00	175.00
3. Cream	75.00	125.00	175.00

Model No. 721
DEER ON BASE

Designer:	Arthur Gredington
Height:	4 ½", 11.9 cm
Colour:	See below
Issued:	1939-by 1954
Set:	696

Colourway	U.K. £	U.S. $	Can. $
1. Blue - gloss	75.00	125.00	175.00
2. Brown - gloss	65.00	100.00	150.00
3. Green - matt	75.00	125.00	175.00
4. White - matt	75.00	125.00	175.00

Model No. 738
PANDA WITH BALL

Designer:	Mr. Watkin
Height:	4 ½", 11.9 cm
Colour:	1. Black and white - gloss
	2. Blue - gloss
	3. Cream - satin matt
Issued:	1939-by 1954

Colourway	U.K. £	U.S. $	Can. $
1. Black/white	85.00	135.00	200.00
2. Blue	125.00	200.00	300.00
3. Cream	85.00	135.00	200.00

Model No. 823
RABBIT - On haunches

Designer:	Arthur Gredington
Height:	3", 7.6 cm
Colour:	1. Blue - gloss
	2. Brown - gloss
Issued:	1940-1971
Set:	824, 825, 826

Colourway	U.K. £	U.S. $	Can. $
1. Blue	45.00	70.00	100.00
2. Brown	20.00	30.00	50.00

Model No. 824
RABBIT - Scratching ear

Designer:	Arthur Gredington
Height:	2 ¼", 5.7 cm
Colour:	1. Blue - gloss
	2. Brown - gloss
Issued:	1940-1971
Set:	823, 825, 826

Colourway	U.K. £	U.S. $	Can. $
1. Blue	40.00	65.00	95.00
2. Brown	15.00	25.00	35.00

Model No. 825
RABBIT - Crouching

Designer:	Arthur Gredington
Height:	1 ½", 3.8 cm
Colour:	1. Blue - gloss
	2. Brown - gloss
Issued:	1940-1971
Set:	823, 824, 826

Colourway	U.K. £	U.S. $	Can. $
1. Blue	30.00	50.00	70.00
2. Brown	15.00	25.00	35.00

Model No. 826
RABBIT - Seated

Designer:	Arthur Gredington
Height:	2", 5.0 cm
Colour:	1. Blue - gloss
	2. Brown - gloss
Issued:	1940-1971
Set:	823, 824, 825

Colourway	U.K. £	U.S. $	Can. $
1. Blue	30.00	50.00	70.00
2. Brown	15.00	25.00	35.00

Model No. 828
ELEPHANT

Designer: Mr. Owen
Colour: 1. Blue - gloss
            2. Cream - satin matt
            3. Pale grey - gloss
Issued: 1940-by 1954

Description	Colourway	Height	U.K. £	Price U.S. $	Can. $
Large	Blue	6", 15.0 cm	150.00	250.00	350.00
Large	Cream	6", 15.0 cm	125.00	200.00	275.00
Large	Pale grey	6", 15.0 cm	135.00	225.00	300.00
Medium	Blue	4 ½", 11.9 cm	125.00	200.00	275.00
Medium	Cream	4 ½", 11.9 cm	110.00	180.00	240.00
Medium	Pale grey	4 ½", 11.9 cm	115.00	190.00	250.00
Small	Blue	3", 7.6 cm	100.00	170.00	235.00
Small	Cream	3", 7.6 cm	70.00	110.00	170.00
Small	Pale grey	3", 7.6 cm	85.00	140.00	200.00

Model No. 830
LIZARD

Designer:	Miss Joachim
Height:	Unknown
Colour:	Green - gloss
Issued:	1940-Unknown

Colourway	U.K. £	U.S. $	Can. $
Green		Extremely Rare	

Model No. 841
LEOPARD - Seated

Designer:	Arthur Gredington
Height:	6 ¼", 15.9 cm
Colour:	Tan brown, black spots - gloss
Issued:	1940-by 1954

Colourway	U.K. £	U.S. $	Can. $
Tan brown/black	350.00	550.00	825.00

Model No. 845A
ZEBRA
First Version - Tan with black stripes

Designer:	Arthur Gredington
Height:	7 ¼", 18.4 cm
Colour:	Tan with black stripes - gloss
Issued:	1940-Unknown

Colourway	U.K. £	U.S. $	Can. $
Tan/black	300.00	500.00	750.00

Model No. 845B
ZEBRA
Second Version - White with black stripes

Designer:	Arthur Gredington
Height:	7 ¼", 18.4 cm
Colour:	White with black stripes - gloss
Issued:	Unknown-1969

Colourway	U.K. £	U.S. $	Can. $
White/black	100.00	175.00	250.00

Model No. 853
GIRAFFE - Small

Designer:	Arthur Gredington
Height:	7 ¼", 18.4 cm
Colour:	1. Natural - gloss
	2. Stone - satin finish
	3. White - gloss
Issued:	1940-1975

Colourway	U.K. £	U.S. $	Can. $
1. Natural	85.00	135.00	200.00
2. Stone	70.00	115.00	165.00
3. White	75.00	125.00	175.00

Model No. 954
STAG - Lying

Designer:	Arthur Gredington
Height:	5 ½", 14.0 cm
Colour:	Light brown - gloss
Issued:	1941-1975

Colourway	U.K. £	U.S. $	Can. $
Light brown	50.00	80.00	125.00

Model No. 974
ELEPHANT - Trunk stretching - small

Designer:	Arthur Gredington
Height:	4 ¾", 12.1 cm
Colour:	Grey - gloss or matt
Issued:	1. Gloss - 1943 -1996
	2. Matt - 1985-1988

Description	U.K. £	U.S. $	Can. $
1. Gloss	30.00	50.00	75.00
2. Matt	35.00	55.00	85.00

Model No. 981
STAG - Standing

Designer:	Arthur Gredington
Height:	8", 20.3 cm
Colour:	1. Light brown - gloss or matt
	2. Bronze with black shading - satin
Issued:	1a. Gloss - 1942-1997
	1b. Matt - 1985-1988
	2. Satin - 1989-1992
Series:	2. Britannia Collection

	Description	U.K. £	U.S. $	Can. $
1a.	Gloss	25.00	40.00	60.00
1b.	Matt	35.00	55.00	80.00
2.	Satin	40.00	65.00	95.00

Model No. 998
ELEPHANT - Trunk stretching - large

Designer:	Arthur Gredington
Height:	10 ¼", 26.0 cm
Colour:	Natural - gloss or satin matt
Issued:	1. Gloss - 1943-1975
	2. Satin matt - 1970-1973
Series:	Model in satin matt finish was transferred to Connoisseur Series in 1973.

	Description	U.K. £	U.S. $	Can. $
1.	Gloss	200.00	325.00	475.00
2.	Satin matt	225.00	350.00	525.00

Model No. 999A
DOE

Designer:	Arthur Gredington
Height:	6", 15.0 cm
Colour:	1. Light brown - gloss
	2. Light and dark brown - matt
Issued:	1. Gloss - 1943-1997
	2. Matt - 1985-1988

Description	U.K. £	U.S. $	Can. $
1. Gloss	20.00	30.00	50.00
2. Matt	25.00	40.00	60.00

Model No. 999B
DOE AND FAWN - on wooden plinth

Designer: Arthur Gredington
Height: 7", 17.8 cm
Colour: Light brown - gloss
Issued: 1993-1996

Colourway	U.K. £	U.S. $	Can. $
Light brown	35.00	55.00	80.00

Note: Doe is no. 999, Fawn is no. 1000.

Model No. 1000A
FAWN
First Version - tail up

Designer: Arthur Gredington
Height: 3 ½", 8.9 cm
Colour: Light brown - gloss
Issued: 1943-1955

Colourway	U.K. £	U.S. $	Can. $
Light brown	60.00	95.00	150.00

Model No. 1000B
FAWN
Second Version - tail down

Designer: Arthur Gredington
Remodelled: Mr. Orwell
Height: 3 ½", 8.9 cm
Colour: Light brown - gloss or matt
Issued: 1. Gloss - 1955-1997
        2. Matt - 1985-1988

Description	U.K. £	U.S. $	Can. $
1. Gloss	15.00	25.00	35.00
2. Matt	20.00	30.00	50.00

Model No. 1003
FAWNIE

Designer: Arthur Gredington
Height: 5 ¼", 13.3 cm
Colour: Grey-brown - gloss
Issued: 1944-1967
Series: Fun Models

Colourway	U.K. £	U.S. $	Can. $
Grey-brown	90.00	150.00	200.00

Model No. 1005
KANGARINE

Designer:	Arthur Gredington
Height:	5", 12.7 cm
Colour:	1. Blue with white markings - gloss
	2. Brown - gloss
Issued:	1944-1966
Series:	Fun Models

Colourway	U.K. £	U.S. $	Can. $
1. Blue	125.00	200.00	300.00
2. Brown	100.00	165.00	250.00

Model No. 1007
SQUIRREL - Standing

Designer:	Arthur Gredington
Height:	2 ¼", 5.7 cm
Colour:	Tan - gloss
Issued:	1944-c.1963
Set:	1008, 1009
Series:	Fun Models

Colourway	U.K. £	U.S. $	Can. $
Tan	40.00	65.00	95.00

Model No. 1008
SQUIRREL - Lying

Designer:	Arthur Gredington
Height:	1 ¾", 4.5 cm
Colour:	Tan - gloss
Issued:	1944-c.1963
Set:	1007, 1009
Series:	Fun Models

Colourway	U.K. £	U.S. $	Can. $
Tan	40.00	65.00	95.00

Model No. 1009
SQUIRREL - With Nut Cracker

Designer:	Arthur Gredington
Height:	4 ½", 11.9 cm
Colour:	Tan - gloss
Issued:	1944-c.1963
Set:	1007, 1008
Series:	Fun Models

Colourway	U.K. £	U.S. $	Can. $
Tan	50.00	80.00	125.00

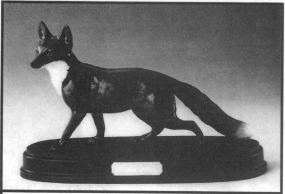

Model No. 1016A
FOX - Standing

Designer:	Arthur Gredington
Height:	5 ½", 14.0 cm
Colour:	Red-brown and white - gloss or matt
Issued:	1. Gloss - 1945-1997
	2. Matt - 1985-1988
Varieties:	1016B

Description	U.K. £	U.S. $	Can. $
1. Gloss	20.00	30.00	50.00
2. Matt	30.00	50.00	75.00

Model No. 1016B
FOX - Standing - on wooden plinth

Designer:	Arthur Gredington
Height:	6 ¾", 17.2 cm
Colour:	Red-brown and white - gloss
Issued:	1993-1996
Varieties:	1016A

Colourway	U.K. £	U.S. $	Can. $
Red-brown/white	30.00	50.00	75.00

Model No. 1017
FOX - Curled

Designer:	Arthur Gredington
Height:	1 ¾", 3.2 cm
Colour:	Red brown - gloss or matt
Issued:	1. Gloss - 1945 -1996
	2. Matt - 1985-1988

Description	U.K. £	U.S. $	Can. $
1. Gloss	15.00	25.00	50.00
2. Matt	30.00	50.00	75.00

Model No. 1019
BISON

Designer:	Arthur Gredington
Height:	5 ¾", 14.6 cm
Colour:	Dark brown - gloss
Issued:	1945-1973

Colourway	U.K. £	U.S. $	Can. $
Dark brown	100.00	165.00	250.00

Model No. 1021
STOAT

Designer:	Arthur Gredington
Height:	5 ½", 14.0 cm
Colour:	1. Tan (summer coat) - gloss
	2. White (winter coat) - gloss
Issued:	1945-1963

Colourway	U.K. £	U.S. $	Can. $
1. Tan	175.00	275.00	400.00
2. White	150.00	250.00	350.00

Model No. 1024
HARE - Running

Designer:	Arthur Gredington
Height:	5 ¼", 12.7 cm
Colour:	Tan - gloss
Issued:	1945-1963

Colourway	U.K. £	U.S. $	Can. $
Tan	300.00	500.00	700.00

Model No. 1025
HARE - Seated

Designer:	Arthur Gredington
Height:	7", 17.8 cm
Colour:	Tan - gloss
Issued:	1945-1963

Colourway	U.K. £	U.S. $	Can. $
Tan	200.00	325.00	500.00

Model No. 1038
KOALA BEAR

Designer:	Arthur Gredington
Height:	3 ½", 8.9 cm
Colour:	Grey - gloss
Issued:	1945-1971
Set:	1039, 1040

Colourway	U.K. £	U.S. $	Can. $
Grey	35.00	55.00	80.00

Model No. 1039
KOALA BEAR - On branch

Designer:	Arthur Gredington
Height:	2 ¼", 5.7 cm
Colour:	Grey - gloss
Issued:	1945-1973
Set:	1038, 1040

Colourway	U.K. £	U.S. $	Can. $
Grey	25.00	40.00	60.00

Model No. 1040
KOALA BEAR

Designer:	Arthur Gredington
Height:	2 ¼", 5.7 cm
Colour:	Grey - gloss
Issued:	1945-1973
Set:	1038, 1039

Colourway	U.K. £	U.S. $	Can. $
Grey	25.00	40.00	60.00

Model No. 1043
CAMEL FOAL

Designer:	Arthur Gredington
Height:	5", 12.7 cm
Colour:	Light and dark brown - gloss
Issued:	1946-1971
Set:	1044

Colourway	U.K. £	U.S. $	Can. $
Brown	60.00	95.00	145.00

Model No. 1044
CAMEL

Designer:	Arthur Gredington
Height:	7", 17.8 cm
Colour:	Light and dark brown - gloss
Issued:	1946-1973
Set:	1043

Colourway	U.K. £	U.S. $	Can. $
Brown	100.00	165.00	250.00

Model No. 1048
SPRINGBOK

Designer:	Arthur Gredington
Height:	7 ¼", 18.4 cm
Colour:	Tan and white - gloss
Issued:	1946-1963

Colourway	U.K. £	U.S. $	Can. $
Tan/white	250.00	400.00	575.00

Model No. 1049
CHIMPANZEE WITH PIPE

Designer:	Arthur Gredington
Height:	4 ¾", 12.1 cm
Colour:	Brown - gloss
Issued:	1946-1969

Colourway	U.K. £	U.S. $	Can. $
Brown	100.00	165.00	250.00

Model No. 1082
LEOPARD

Designer:	Arthur Gredington
Height:	4 ¾", 12.1 cm
Colour:	1. Golden brown with black markings - gloss
	2. Black - satin
Issued:	1946-1975

Description	U.K. £	U.S. $	Can. $
1. Gloss	100.00	165.00	250.00
2. Satin	90.00	145.00	225.00

Model No. 1089
KOALA BEAR - With fruit

Designer:	Miss Jones
Height:	3 ½", 8.9 cm
Colour:	Grey - gloss
Issued:	1947-1971

Colourway	U.K. £	U.S. $	Can. $
Grey	35.00	55.00	80.00

Model No. 1160
KANGAROO

Designer:	Arthur Gredington
Height:	5 ¾", 14.6 cm
Colour:	Brown - gloss
Issued:	1949-1966

Colourway	U.K. £	U.S. $	Can. $
Brown	100.00	165.00	250.00

Model No. 1255
MONKEY WITH DRUM

Designer:	Miss Granoska
Height:	2 ½", 6.4 cm
Colour:	Brown and green - gloss
Issued:	1952-1963
Set:	1256, 1257, 1258, 1259, 1260

Colourway	U.K. £	U.S. $	Can. $
Brown/green	125.00	200.00	300.00

Model No. 1256
MONKEY WITH TUBA

Designer:	Miss Granoska
Height:	2 ½", 6.4 cm
Colour:	Brown and green - gloss
Issued:	1952-1963
Set:	1255, 1257, 1258, 1259, 1260

Colourway	U.K. £	U.S. $	Can. $
Brown/green	125.00	200.00	300.00

Model No. 1257
MONKEY WITH FIDDLE

Designer:	Miss Granoska
Height:	2 ½", 6.4 cm
Colour:	Brown and green - gloss
Issued:	1952-1963
Set:	1255, 1256, 1258, 1259, 1260

Colourway	U.K. £	U.S. $	Can. $
Brown/green	125.00	200.00	300.00

Model No. 1258
MONKEY WITH SAXOPHONE

Designer:	Miss Granoska
Height:	2 ½", 6.4 cm
Colour:	Brown and green - gloss
Issued:	1952-1963
Set:	1255, 1256, 1257, 1259, 1260

Colourway	U.K. £	U.S. $	Can. $
Brown/green	125.00	200.00	300.00

Model No. 1259
MONKEY WITH GUITAR

Designer:	Miss Granoska
Height:	2 ½", 6.4 cm
Colour:	Brown and green - gloss
Issued:	1952-1963
Set:	1255, 1256, 1257, 1258, 1260

Colourway	U.K. £	U.S. $	Can. $
Brown/green	125.00	200.00	300.00

Model No. 1260
MONKEY WITH BANJO

Designer:	Miss Granoska
Height:	2 ½", 6.4 cm
Colour:	Brown and green - gloss
Issued:	1952-1963
Set:	1255, 1256, 1257, 1258, 1259

Colourway	U.K. £	U.S. $	Can. $
Brown/green	125.00	200.00	300.00

Model No. 1308
SKUNK

Designer:	Arthur Gredington
Height:	2 ¾", 7.0 cm
Colour:	Black and white - gloss
Issued:	1953-1963
Set:	1309, 1310

Colourway	U.K. £	U.S. $	Can. $
Black/white	75.00	125.00	175.00

Model No. 1309
SKUNK

Designer:	Arthur Gredington
Height:	1 ½", 3.8 cm
Colour:	Black and white - gloss
Issued:	1953-1963
Set:	1308, 1310

Colourway	U.K. £	U.S. $	Can. $
Black/white	45.00	70.00	100.00

Model No. 1310
SKUNK

Designer:	Arthur Gredington
Height:	2", 5.0 cm
Colour:	Black and white - gloss
Issued:	1953-1963
Set:	1307, 1309

Colourway	U.K. £	U.S. $	Can. $
Black/white	45.00	70.00	100.00

Model No. 1313
BEAR - Standing

Designer:	Arthur Gredington
Height:	2 ½", 6.4 cm
Colour:	Black or brown - gloss
Issued:	1953-1966
Set:	1314, 1315

Colourway	U.K. £	U.S. $	Can. $
1. Black	65.00	100.00	150.00
2. Brown	65.00	100.00	150.00

Model No. 1314
BEAR - On hind legs

Designer:	Arthur Gredington
Height:	4 ½", 11.9 cm
Colour:	Black or brown - gloss
Issued:	1953-1966
Set:	1313, 1315

Colourway	U.K. £	U.S. $	Can. $
1. Black	65.00	100.00	150.00
2. Brown	65.00	100.00	150.00

Model No. 1315
BEAR CUB - Seated

Designer:	Arthur Gredington
Height:	2 ¼", 5.7 cm
Colour:	Black or brown - gloss
Issued:	1953-1966
Set:	1313, 1314

Colourway	U.K. £	U.S. $	Can. $
1. Black	45.00	70.00	100.00
2. Brown	45.00	70.00	100.00

Model No. 1335
TORTOISE MOTHER WITH HAT

Designer:	Miss Granoska
Length:	2 ¾", 7.0 cm
Colour:	Brown - gloss
Issued:	1954-1973
Set:	1336, 1337

Colourway	U.K. £	U.S. $	Can. $
Brown	60.00	95.00	145.00

Model No. 1336
TORTOISE GIRL WITH BONNET

Designer:	Miss Granoska
Length:	1 ¾", 4.5 cm
Colour:	Brown - gloss
Issued:	1954-1973
Set:	1335, 1337

Colourway	U.K. £	U.S. $	Can. $
Brown	35.00	55.00	80.00

Model No. 1337
TORTOISE BOY WITH CAP

Designer:	Miss Granoska
Length:	1 ¾", 4.5 cm
Colour:	Brown - gloss
Issued:	1954-1973
Set:	1335, 1336

Colourway	U.K. £	U.S. $	Can. $
Brown	35.00	55.00	80.00

Model No. 1379
BUSH BABY - With mirror

Designer:	Mr. Orwell
Height:	2", 5.0 cm
Colour:	Grey-brown - gloss
Issued:	1955-1966
Set:	1380, 1381

Colourway	U.K. £	U.S. $	Can. $
Grey-brown	50.00	80.00	115.00

Model No. 1380
BUSH BABY - With candlestick

Designer:	Mr. Orwell
Height:	2", 5.0 cm
Colour:	Grey-brown - gloss
Issued:	1955-1966
Set:	1379, 1381

Colourway	U.K. £	U.S. $	Can. $
Grey-brown	50.00	80.00	115.00

Model No. 1381
BUSH BABY - With book

Designer:	Mr. Orwell
Height:	1 ½", 3.8 cm
Colour:	Grey-brown - gloss
Issued:	1955-1966
Set:	1379, 1380

Colourway	U.K. £	U.S. $	Can. $
Grey-brown	50.00	80.00	115.00

Model No. 1440
FOX - Standing

Designer:	Arthur Gredington
Height:	2 ½", 6.4 cm
Colour:	Red-brown and white - gloss or matt
Issued:	1. Gloss - 1956-1997
	2. Matt - 1985-1988

Description	U.K. £	U.S. $	Can. $
1. Gloss	12.00	20.00	30.00
2. Matt	15.00	25.00	35.00

Model No. 1486
TIGERESS

Designer:	Colin Melbourne
Height:	4 ¼", 10.8 cm
Colour:	Tan with black stripes and markings - gloss
Issued:	1957-1975

Colourway	U.K. £	U.S. $	Can. $
Tan/black	100.00	165.00	250.00

Model No. 1506
LION - Facing right

Designer:	Colin Melbourne
Height:	5 ¼", 13.3 cm
Colour:	Golden brown - gloss
Issued:	1957-1967
Set:	1507, 1508

Colourway	U.K. £	U.S. $	Can. $
Golden brown	75.00	125.00	175.00

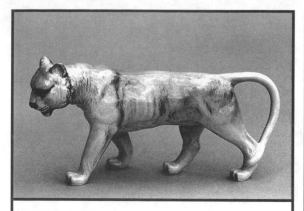

Model No. 1507
LIONESS - Facing left

Designer: Colin Melbourne
Height: 4 ¾", 12.1 cm
Colour: 1.   Black - satin
             2.   Golden brown - gloss
Issued: 1957-1967
Set: 1506, 1508

Colourway	U.K. £	U.S. $	Can. $
1. Black	50.00	80.00	125.00
2. Golden brown	75.00	125.00	175.00

Model No. 1508
LION CUB - Facing right

Designer: Colin Melbourne
Height: 4", 10.1 cm
Colour: Golden brown - gloss
Issued: 1957-1967
Set: 1506, 1507

Colourway	U.K. £	U.S. $	Can. $
Golden brown	45.00	70.00	100.00

Model No. 1532
HIPPOPOTAMUS

Designer: Colin Melbourne
Height: 3 ½", 8.9 cm
Colour: Dark grey with pink underneath - gloss
Issued: 1958-1966

Colourway	U.K. £	U.S. $	Can. $
Dark grey	175.00	275.00	400.00

Model No. 1533
POLAR BEAR

Designer: Arthur Gredington
Height: 4 ¾", 12.1 cm
Colour: 1.   Blue - gloss
             2.   White - gloss
Issued: 1958-1966

Colourway	U.K. £	U.S. $	Can. $
1. Blue	125.00	200.00	300.00
2. White	150.00	250.00	350.00

Model No. 1534
SEAL

Designer:	Arthur Gredington
Length:	5 ¾", 14.6 cm
Colour:	Grey - gloss
Issued:	1958-1966

Colourway	U.K. £	U.S. $	Can. $
Grey	125.00	200.00	300.00

Model No. 1551
CHAMOIS

Designer:	Pal Zalmen
Height:	4", 10.1 cm
Colour:	Fawn or grey - gloss
Issued:	1958-1971
Series:	Fun Models

Colourway	U.K. £	U.S. $	Can. $
1. Fawn	60.00	95.00	140.00
2. Grey	60.00	95.00	140.00

Model No. 1597
GIRAFFE

Designer:	J. Lawson
Height:	4 ¼", 10.8 cm
Colour:	Tan with dark patches - gloss
Issued:	1959-1971
Series:	Fun Models

Colourway	U.K. £	U.S. $	Can. $
Tan	65.00	100.00	150.00

Model No. 1615A
BABYCHAM
First Version - Large eyes

Designer:	Albert Hallam
Height:	4", 10.1 cm
Colour:	Yellow - gloss
Issued:	1960-1975
Series:	Fun Models

Description	U.K. £	U.S. $	Can. $
Large eyes	60.00	95.00	150.00

Model 1615B
BABYCHAM
Second Version - Small eyes, name on ribbon

Designer:	Albert Hallam
Height:	4", 10.1 cm
Colour:	Yellow - gloss
Issued:	Unknown
Series:	Fun Models

Description	U.K. £	U.S. $	Can. $
Small eyes	60.00	95.00	150.00

Model No. 1631
GIRAFFE - Large

Designer:	J. Lawson
Height:	12", 30.5 cm
Colour:	Light brown with dark brown patches - gloss
Issued:	1959-1975

Colourway	U.K. £	U.S. $	Can. $
Brown	150.00	250.00	350.00

Note: Pattern and colour varies.

Model No. 1678
MOUSE

Designer:	Albert Hallam
Height:	2 ½", 6.4 cm
Colour:	Grey - gloss
Issued:	1960-1997

Colourway	U.K. £	U.S. $	Can. $
Grey	20.00	30.00	50.00

Model No. 1688
REINDEER

Designer:	J. Lawson
Height:	3 ¾", 9.5 cm
Colour:	1. Fawn - gloss
	2. Grey - gloss
Issued:	1960-1971
Series:	Fun Models

Colourway	U.K. £	U.S. $	Can. $
1. Fawn	65.00	100.00	150.00
2. Grey	65.00	100.00	150.00

Model No. 1702
PUMA ON ROCK
Style One

Designer:	Arthur Gredington	
Height:	8 ½", 21.6 cm	
Colour:	1.	Black - gloss
	2.	Tawny - gloss or matt
Issued:	1.	Black
		a. Gloss - 1960-1973
Reissued:		b. Gloss - 1979-1983
Issued:	2.	Tawny
		a. Gloss - 1960-1975
		b. Matt - 1970-1973
		c. Satin matt - 1973-1989
Reissued:		d. Gloss - 1979-1983
Series:	2c.	Connoisseur Series

Colourway	U.K. £	U.S. $	Can. $
1. Black			
a. Gloss	140.00	225.00	325.00
b. Reissued	140.00	225.00	325.00
2. Tawny			
a. Gloss	125.00	200.00	300.00
b. Matt	125.00	200.00	300.00
c. Satin matt	125.00	200.00	300.00
d. Reissued	125.00	200.00	300.00

Model No. 1720
ELEPHANT AND TIGER

Designer:	Arthur Gredington
Height:	12", 30.5 cm
Colour:	Grey, tan with black stripes - gloss
Issued:	1960-1975

Description	U.K. £	U.S. $	Can. $
Gloss	650.00	1,000.00	1,500.00

Note: The elephant is the same model as used in 1770.

Model No. 1733
COMICAL FOX

Designer:	Harry Sales
Height:	3 ¼", 8.3 cm
Colour:	Red-brown and white - gloss
Issued:	1961-1968
Series:	Fun Models

Description	U.K. £	U.S. $	Can. $
Gloss	60.00	95.00	150.00

Model No. 1748
FOX - Seated

Designer:	Arthur Gredington
Height:	3", 7.6 cm
Colour:	Red-brown and white - gloss or matt
Issued:	1. Gloss - 1961-1997
	2. Matt - 1985-1988

Description	U.K. £	U.S. $	Can. $
1. Gloss	10.00	15.00	20.00
2. Matt	15.00	25.00	35.00

Model No. 1761
FOXY BANK

Designer:	Albert Hallam
Height:	8 ½", 21.6 cm
Colour:	Tan, brown and black on white - gloss
Issued:	1961-1967
Series:	Fun Models / Money bank

Description	U.K. £	U.S. $	Can. $
Gloss	75.00	125.00	175.00

Model No. 1770
ELEPHANT - Trunk in salute

Designer: Arthur Gredington
Height: 12", 30.5 cm
Colour: Grey - gloss or satin matt
Issued: 1. Gloss - 1961-1975
           2. Satin matt - 1970-1973

Description	U.K. £	U.S. $	Can. $
1. Gloss	225.00	375.00	525.00
2. Satin matt	250.00	425.00	575.00

Note: Satin matt transferred to Connoiseur Series in 1973. Elephant same model as used in 1720.

Model No. 1815
PANDA CUB

Designer: Albert Hallam
Height: 2 ¼", 5.7 cm
Colour: Black and white - gloss or matt
Issued: 1. Gloss - 1962-1997
           2. Matt - 1985-1988

Description	U.K. £	U.S. $	Can. $
1. Gloss	15.00	25.00	35.00
2. Matt	15.00	25.00	35.00

Model No. 1823
PUMA ON ROCK
Style Two

Designer: Arthur Gredington
Height: 6", 15.0 cm
Colour: 1. Black - gloss
           2. Tawny - gloss
Issued: 1. Black - 1962-1973
           2. Tawny - 1962-1975

Colourway	U.K. £	U.S. $	Can. $
1. Black	95.00	150.00	225.00
2. Tawny	115.00	185.00	275.00

Model No. 1943
BEAVER ON LOG - Facing left

Designer: Albert Hallam
Height: 2 ½", 6.4 cm
Colour: Tan - gloss
Issued: 1964-1967

Colourway	U.K. £	U.S. $	Can. $
Tan	175.00	275.00	400.00

Model No. 2089
LION - Facing left

Designer:	Graham Tongue
Height:	5 ½", 14.0 cm
Colour:	Golden brown - gloss
Issued:	1967-1984

Colourway	U.K. £	U.S. $	Can. $
Golden brown	50.00	80.00	125.00

Model No. 2090
MOOSE

Designer:	Arthur Gredington
Height:	6 ¼", 15.9 cm
Colour:	Dark brown - gloss or satin matt
Issued:	1967-1973

Description	U.K. £	U.S. $	Can. $
1. Gloss	350.00	650.00	825.00
2. Satin matt	350.00	650.00	825.00

Model No. 2096
TIGER

Designer:	Graham Tongue
Height:	7 ½", 19.1 cm
Colour:	Tan with black stripes - gloss or matt
Issued:	1. Gloss - 1967-1990
	2. Matt - 1985-1988

Description	U.K. £	U.S. $	Can. $
1. Gloss	85.00	135.00	200.00
2. Matt	75.00	125.00	200.00

Note: Example known in black satin matt - very rare.

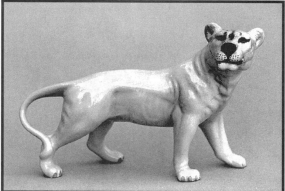

Model No. 2097
LIONESS - Facing right

Designer:	Graham Tongue
Height:	5 ¾", 14.6 cm
Colour:	Golden brown - gloss
Issued:	1967-1984

Colourway	U.K. £	U.S. $	Can. $
Golden brown	60.00	95.00	150.00

Model No. 2098
LION CUB - Facing left

Designer:	Graham Tongue
Height:	4", 10.1 cm
Colour:	Golden brown - gloss
Issued:	1967-1984

Colourway	U.K. £	U.S. $	Can. $
Golden brown	35.00	60.00	85.00

Model No. 2131
RABBIT

Designer:	Albert Hallam, Graham Tongue
Height:	3", 7.6 cm
Colour:	Light brown and white - gloss
Issued:	1967-1973
Series:	Fun Models

Colourway	U.K. £	U.S. $	Can. $
Brown/white	75.00	125.00	175.00

Model No. 2132
RABBIT WITH BABY

Designer:	Albert Hallam
Height:	3", 7.6 cm
Colour:	Light brown and white - gloss
Issued:	1967-1971
Series:	Fun Models

Colourway	U.K. £	U.S. $	Can. $
Brown/white	75.00	125.00	175.00

Model No. 2194
RACOON ON LOG

Designer:	Albert Hallam
Height:	4 ¼", 10.8 cm
Colour:	Dark grey - gloss
Issued:	1968-1972

Colourway	U.K. £	U.S. $	Can. $
Dark grey	175.00	300.00	450.00

Model No. 2195
BEAVER ON LOG - Facing right

Designer:	Albert Hallam
Height:	4 ½", 11.9 cm
Colour:	Brown - gloss
Issued:	1968-c.1973

Colourway	U.K. £	U.S. $	Can. $
Brown	175.00	300.00	450.00

Model No. 2237
BABYCHAM WALL PLAQUE

Designer:	Graham Tongue
Height:	3" x 6 ¼", 7.6 x 15.9 cm (Concave)
Colour:	Unknown - gloss
Issued:	c.1970-c.1975
Series:	Wall Plaques

Description	U.K. £	U.S. $	Can. $
Gloss	100.00	175.00	225.00

Model No. 2253
HEDGEHOG

Designer:	Harry Sales
Height:	3 ½" 8.9 cm
Colour:	1. Blue - gloss
	2. Brown - gloss
Issued:	1969-1971
Series:	Moda Range

Colourway	U.K. £	U.S. $	Can. $
1. Blue	125.00	200.00	300.00
2. Brown	125.00	200.00	300.00

Photograph not
available at press time

Model No. 2302
MOUSE

Designer:	Albert Hallam
Height:	1 ¾", 8.9 cm
Colour:	Unknown
Issued:	1969-Unknown

Description	U.K. £	U.S. $	Can. $
Mouse	Possibly not put into production.		

Model No. 2312
KANGAROO

Designer:	Albert Hallam
Height:	5", 12.7 cm
Colour:	Light and dark brown - gloss
Issued:	1970-1973

Description	U.K. £	U.S. $	Can. $
Gloss	125.00	200.00	300.00

Model No. 2348
FOX

Designer:	Graham Tongue
Height:	12 ½", 31.7 cm
Colour:	Red-brown and white - gloss
Issued:	1970-1984
Series:	Fireside Model

Description	U.K. £	U.S. $	Can. $
Gloss	250.00	375.00	575.00

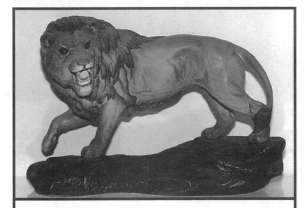

Model No. 2554A
LION ON ROCK

Designer:	Graham Tongue
Height:	8 ¼", 21.0 cm
Colour:	Golden brown - satin matt
Issued:	1975-1984
Varieties:	2554B (standing)
Series:	Connoisseur

Description	U.K. £	U.S. $	Can. $
Satin matt	150.00	250.00	350.00

Model No. 2554B
LION - Standing

Designer:	Graham Tongue
Height:	6 ¾", 17.2 cm
Colour:	Golden brown - gloss
Modelled:	1975
Issued:	1987-1995

Description	U.K. £	U.S. $	Can. $
Gloss	100.00	165.00	250.00

Model No. 2613
PANDA "CHI CHI"
First Version - With bamboo shoot

Designer:	Unknown		
Height:	3 ¾", 9.5 cm		
Colour:	Black and white - gloss		
Issued:	1978-c.1980		
Varieties:	2944		

Description	U.K. £	U.S. $	Can. $
Gloss		Rare	

Note: This model was produced for the London Natural History Museum.

Model No. 2629
STAG

Designer:	Graham Tongue		
Height:	13 ½", 34.3 cm		
Colour:	1. Golden brown - satin matt		
	2. Bronze with black shading - satin		
Issued:	1. 1978-1989	2. 1989-1992	
Series:	2. Connoisseur		

Colourway	U.K. £	U.S. $	Can. $
1. Golden brown	175.00	300.00	400.00
2. Bronze/black	150.00	250.00	350.00

Note: Transferred to (DA 32) 08/89, "Majestic Stag."

Model No. 2686
OTTER

Designer:	David Lyttleton		
Height:	2 ¼", 5.7 cm		
Colour:	Grey - matt		
Issued:	1985-1985		

Description	U.K. £	U.S. $	Can. $
Matt	35.00	60.00	85.00

Note: Part of a trial run in 1985 but never put into general production.

Model No. 2687
BADGER

Designer:	David Lyttleton		
Height:	3", 7.6 cm		
Colour:	Black - matt		
Issued:	1985-1985		

Description	U.K. £	U.S. $	Can. $
Matt	35.00	60.00	85.00

Note: Part of a trial run in 1985 but never put into general production.

Model No. 2693
SEAL

Designer:	Graham Tongue
Height:	3 ½", 8.9 cm
Colour:	Grey - matt
Issued:	1985-1985

Description	U.K. £	U.S. $	Can. $
Matt	35.00	60.00	85.00

Note: Part of a trial run in 1985 but never put into general production.

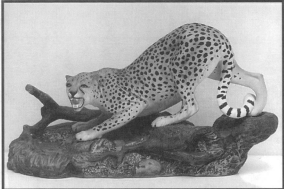

Model No. 2725
CHEETAH ON ROCK

Designer:	Graham Tongue
Height:	6 ½", 16.5 cm
Colour:	Pale brown with dark spots - satin finish
Issued:	1981-1989
Series:	Connoisseur

Description	U.K. £	U.S. $	Can. $
Satin finish	150.00	250.00	350.00

Note: Transferred to R.D. backstamp (DA 39) 08/89 later called "The Watering Hole."

Model No. 2944
PANDA "CHI CHI"
Second Version - Without bamboo shoot

Designer:	Unknown
Height:	3 ¾", 9.5 cm
Colour:	Black and white - matt
Issued:	1985-1985
Varieties:	2613

Description	U.K. £	U.S. $	Can. $
Matt	150.00	250.00	350.00

Note: Part of a trial run in 1985 but did not go into general production.

Model No. 3009
CHEETAH - Standing

Designer:	Graham Tongue
Height:	5", 12.7 cm
Colour:	Golden brown with dark spots - gloss
Issued:	1986-1995

Description	U.K. £	U.S. $	Can. $
Gloss	75.00	125.00	175.00

Model No. 3392
BADGER CUB

Designer: Amanda Hughes-Lubeck
Height: 2″, 5.0 cm
Colour: Black and white - gloss
Issued: 1992-1997
Set: 3393, 3394

Description	U.K. £	U.S. $	Can. $
Gloss	15.00	25.00	35.00

Model No. 3393
BADGER - Male

Designer: Amanda Hughes-Lubeck
Height: 2″, 5.0 cm
Colour: Black and white - gloss
Issued: 1992-1997
Set: 3392, 3394

Description	U.K. £	U.S. $	Can. $
Gloss	15.00	25.00	35.00

Model No. 3394
BADGER - Female

Designer: Amanda Hughes-Lubeck
Height: 2″, 5.0 cm
Colour: Black and white - gloss
Issued: 1992 -1997
Set: 3392, 3393

Description	U.K. £	U.S. $	Can. $
Gloss	15.00	25.00	35.00

Model No. 3397
HARVEST MOUSE

Designer: Martyn Alcock
Height: 2 ¼″, 5.7 cm
Colour: Brown - gloss
Issued: 1992-1997

Description	U.K. £	U.S. $	Can. $
Gloss	15.00	25.00	35.00

Model No. 3399
WOODMOUSE

Designer: Martyn Alcock
Height: 3 ¼", 8.3 cm
Colour: Brown - gloss
Issued: 1992-1997

Description	U.K. £	U.S. $	Can. $
Gloss	15.00	25.00	35.00

Model No. 3568
MEERKAT - Seated

Designer: Martyn Alcock
Height: 3", 7.6 cm
Colour: Grey and brown - gloss
Issued: 1996 in a limited edition of 1,250

Description	U.K. £	U.S. $	Can. $
Gloss	25.00	40.00	60.00

Model No. 3571
MEERKAT - Standing

Designer: Martyn Alcock
Height: 3 ½", 8.9 cm
Colour: Grey and brown - gloss
Issued: 1996 in a limited edition of 1,250

Description	U.K. £	U.S. $	Can. $
Gloss	25.00	40.00	60.00

Model No. G189
VIETNAMESE POT-BELLIED PIG

Designer:	Amanda Hughes-Lubeck
Length:	6", 15.2 cm
Colour:	Dark brown - gloss
Issued:	1999 to the present

Colourway	U.K. £	U.S. $	Can. $
Gloss	27.50	N/A	N/A

Note: Transferred from the Royal Doulton backstamp (DA189) in September 1999.

Model No. G213
VIETNAMESE POT-BELLIED PIGLET

Designer:	Warren Platt
Length:	3", 7.6 cm
Colour:	Grey - gloss
Issued:	1999 to the present

Colourway	U.K. £	U.S. $	Can. $
Gloss	11.50	N/A	N/A

Note: Transferred from the Royal Doulton backstamp (DA213) in September 1999.

Model No. G223
NIGERIAN POT-BELLIED PYGMY GOAT

Designer:	Amanda Hughes-Lubeck
Length:	5 ¼", 14.0 cm
Colour:	White with black patches - gloss
Issued:	1999 to the present

Colourway	U.K. £	U.S. $	Can. $
Gloss	27.50	N/A	N/A

Note: Transferred from the Royal Doulton backstamp (DA223) in September 1999.

Model No. SC1
FLY FISHING

Designer:	Andy Moss
Height:	3 ¼", 8.3 cm
Colour:	Green, slate, blue and black
Issued:	1998 in a limited edition of 1,500
Series:	Sporting Characters

Colourway	U.K. £	U.S. $	Can. $
Green/slate/blue	40.00	65.00	100.00

Note: Commissioned by Sinclairs.

Model No. SC2
LAST LION OF DEFENSE

Designer:	Andy Moss
Height:	4 ¼", 11.0 cm
Colour:	Red and white
Issued:	1998 in a limited edition of 1,500
Series:	Sporting Characters

Colourway	U.K. £	U.S. $	Can. $
Red/white	40.00	65.00	100.00

Note: Commissioned by Sinclairs.

Model No. SC3
IT'S A KNOCKOUT

Designer:	Andy Moss
Height:	4 ¼", 11.0 cm
Colour:	Red, white and black
Issued:	1998 in a limited edition of 1,500
Series:	Sporting Characters

Colourway	U.K. £	U.S. $	Can. $
Red/white/black	40.00	65.00	100.00

Note: Commissioned by Sinclairs.

Model No. SC4
SLOPING OFF

Designer:	Andy Moss
Height:	5 ¼", 13.3 cm
Colour:	White, black and yellow
Issued:	1999 in a limited edition of 1,500
Series:	Sporting Characters

Colourway	U.K. £	U.S. $	Can. $
White/black/yellow	40.00	65.00	100.00

Note: Commissioned by Sinclairs.

Model No. SC5
A ROUND WITH FOXY

Designer:	Andy Moss
Height:	6", 15.0 cm
Colour:	Green, yellow and brown
Issued:	2000 in a limited edition of 1,500
Series:	Sporting Characters

Colourway	U.K. £	U.S. $	Can. $
Green/yellow/brown	40.00	65.00	100.00

Note: Commissioned by Sinclairs.

Model No. SC6
OUT FOR A DUCK

Designer:	Andy Moss
Height:	5 ½", 14.0 cm
Colour:	Cream
Issued:	2000 in a limited edition of 1,500
Series:	Sporting Characters

Colourway	U.K. £	U.S. $	Can. $
Cream	40.00	65.00	100.00

Note: Commissioned by Sinclairs.

WILD ANIMAL
WALL PLAQUES

Model No. 2933
LION'S HEAD

Designer:	Graham Tongue
Height:	6", 15.0 cm
Colour:	Golden brown - matt
Issued:	1985-1989

Description	U.K. £	U.S. $	Can. $
Matt	50.00	85.00	125.00

Model No. 2934
TIGER'S HEAD

Designer:	Arthur Gredington
Height:	6", 15.0 cm
Colour:	Tan - matt
Issued:	1985-1989

Description	U.K. £	U.S. $	Can. $
Matt	50.00	85.00	125.00

Model No. 2936
STAG'S HEAD

Designer:	Graham Tongue
Height:	6", 15.0 cm
Colour:	Light brown - matt
Issued:	1985-1989

Description	U.K. £	U.S. $	Can. $
Matt	50.00	85.00	125.00

Chapter Nine

THE CM SERIES

This unique series of models, all created by Colin Melbourne, evokes great emotion amongst collectors; it is either loved or hated there are no half measures here. The models were called "contemporary" when they were in production during the late 1950s. They reflected the mood of the time, both in style and in decoration. None of the decorations are realistic, and all are stylized, some to a greater extent than others.

The decoration for the models in this section fall into two categories:

Series 1. Issued 1956-1962

This series is sub-divided in three groups:

1. Colour combinations—charcoal grey/red/white gloss
2. Spotted colour combinations—yellow/shaded charcoal/black
3. Solid colours—grey/brown/green blue/white

Series 2. Issued 1962-1966

This was called the chalk design. The background colour was white and the decorations in geometric shapes or floral designs appeared in a variety of colourways.

INDEX BY MODEL NUMBER

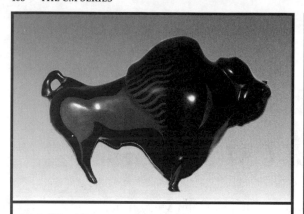

Model No. 1409
BISON - Large

Designer:	Colin Melbourne
Length:	7 ½" x 10 ½", 19.1 x 26.7 cm
Colour:	For colour combinations and varieties see page 393
Issued:	1956-by 1963

Description	U.K. £	U.S. $	Can. $
Series 1	135.00	225.00	325.00
Series 2	175.00	275.00	400.00

Model No. 1410
COW

Designer:	Colin Melbourne
Height:	5", 12.7 cm
Colour:	For colour combinations and varieties see page 393
Issued:	1956-by 1963

Description	U.K. £	U.S. $	Can. $
Series 1	135.00	225.00	325.00

Model No. 1411
HORSE

Designer:	Colin Melbourne
Height:	8 ½", 21.6 cm
Colour:	For colour combinations and varieties see page 393
Issued:	1956-by 1966

Description	U.K. £	U.S. $	Can. $
Series 1	135.00	225.00	325.00
Series 2	200.00	325.00	500.00

Model No. 1412
CAT - Large

Designer:	Colin Melbourne
Height:	9 ½", 24.0 cm
Colour:	For colour combinations and varieties see page 393
Issued:	1956-by 1966

Description	U.K. £	U.S. $	Can. $
Series 1	150.00	250.00	350.00
Series 2	175.00	275.00	400.00

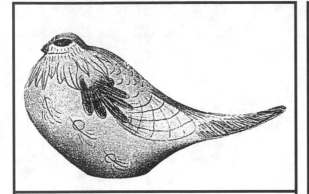

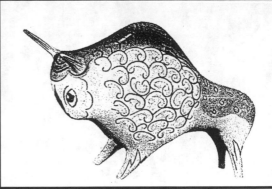

Model No. 1413
DOVE

Designer:	Colin Melbourne
Height:	9", 22.9 cm
Colour:	For colour combinations and varieties see page 393
Issued:	1956-by 1965

Description	U.K. £	U.S. $	Can. $
Series 1	115.00	185.00	275.00
Series 2	135.00	225.00	325.00

Model No. 1414
BISON - Medium

Designer:	Colin Melbourne
Length:	5 ½" x 8 ¾", 14.0 x 22.2 cm
Colour:	For colour combinations and varieties see page 393
Issued:	1956-by 1966

Description	U.K. £	U.S. $	Can. $
Series 1	135.00	225.00	325.00
Series 2	150.00	250.00	350.00

Model No. 1415
BIRD

Designer:	Colin Melbourne
Height:	5 ¼", 13.3 cm
Colour:	For colour combinations and varieties see page 393
Issued:	1956-by 1965

Description	U.K. £	U.S. $	Can. $
Series 1	115.00	185.00	275.00
Series 2	135.00	225.00	325.00

Model No. 1416
COCK - Small

Designer:	Colin Melbourne
Height:	5", 12.7 cm
Colour:	For colour combinations and varieties see page 393
Issued:	1956-by 1965

Description	U.K. £	U.S. $	Can. $
Series 1	135.00	225.00	325.00
Series 2	175.00	275.00	400.00

Model No. 1417
CAT

Designer:	Colin Melbourne
Height:	5 ½", 14.0 cm
Colour:	For colour combinations and varieties see page 393
Issued:	1956-by 1966

Description	U.K. £	U.S. $	Can. $
Series 1	75.00	125.00	175.00
Series 2	150.00	250.00	350.00

Model No. 1418
FOX - Small

Designer:	Colin Melbourne
Length:	2" x 8", 5.0 x 20.3 cm
Colour:	For colour combinations and varieties see page 393
Issued:	1956-by 1966

Description	U.K. £	U.S. $	Can. $
Series 1	90.00	145.00	200.00
Series 2	135.00	225.00	325.00

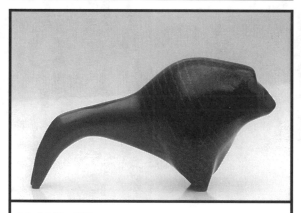

Model No. 1419
LION

Designer:	Colin Melbourne
Height:	4 ¾", 12.1 cm
Colour:	For colour combinations and varieties see page 393
Issued:	1956-by 1963

Description	U.K. £	U.S. $	Can. $
Series 1	135.00	225.00	325.00

Model No. 1420
OWL - Small

Designer:	Colin Melbourne
Height:	4 ¾", 12.1 cm
Colour:	For colour combinations and varieties see page 393
Issued:	1956-by 1965

Description	U.K. £	U.S. $	Can. $
Series 1	115.00	185.00	275.00
Series 2	135.00	225.00	325.00

Model No. 1462
OWL - Large

Designer:	Colin Melbourne
Height:	8 ¼″, 21.0 cm
Colour:	For colour combinations and varieties see page 393
Issued:	1956-by 1965

Description	U.K. £	U.S. $	Can. $
Series 1	135.00	225.00	325.00
Series 2	150.00	250.00	350.00

Model No. 1463
BULLDOG

Designer:	Colin Melbourne
Height:	Unknown
Colour:	For colour combinations and varieties see page 393
Issued:	1956-1970

Description	U.K. £	U.S. $	Can. $
Series 1	110.00	175.00	250.00

Model No. 1465
ZEBRA

Designer:	Colin Melbourne
Height:	6″, 15.0 cm
Colour:	For colour combinations and varieties see page 393
Issued:	1956-by 1966

Description	U.K. £	U.S. $	Can. $
Series 1	175.00	275.00	400.00
Series 2	200.00	325.00	500.00

Model No. 1467
COCK - Large

Designer:	Colin Melbourne
Height:	11 ¾″, 29.8 cm
Colour:	For colour combinations and varieties see page 393
Issued:	1956-by 1963

Description	U.K. £	U.S. $	Can. $
Series 1	175.00	275.00	400.00
Series 2	225.00	350.00	525.00

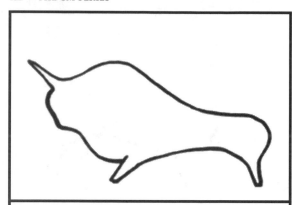

Model No. 1468
BISON - Small

Designer:	Colin Melbourne
Height:	Unknown
Colour:	For colour combinations and varieties see page 393
Issued:	1956-by 1966

Description	U.K. £	U.S. $	Can. $
Series 1	135.00	225.00	325.00
Series 2	175.00	275.00	400.00

Model No. 1469
DACHSHUND

Designer:	Colin Melbourne
Length:	7″, 17.8 cm
Colour:	For colour combinations and varieties see page 393
Issued:	1957-1970

Description	U.K. £	U.S. $	Can. $
Series 1	90.00	145.00	200.00
Series 2	135.00	225.00	325.00

Model No. 1470
CLOWN ON HORSE - Small

Designer:	Colin Melbourne
Height:	5 ¾″, 14.6 cm
Colour:	For colour combinations and varieties see page 393
Issued:	1957-by 1966

Description	U.K. £	U.S. $	Can. $
Series 1	150.00	250.00	350.00
Series 2	200.00	325.00	500.00

Model No. 1471
GOOSE

Designer:	Colin Melbourne
Height:	3 ½″, 8.9 cm
Colour:	For colour combinations and varieties see page 393
Issued:	1957-by 1962

Description	U.K. £	U.S. $	Can. $
Series 1	110.00	175.00	250.00

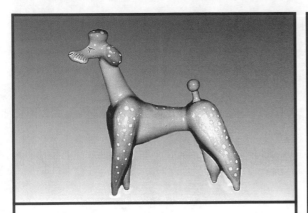

Model No. 1472
POODLE

Designer:	Colin Melbourne
Height:	5 ¾", 14.6 cm
Colour:	For colour combinations and varieties see page 393
Issued:	1957-1962

Description	U.K. £	U.S. $	Can. $
Series 1	150.00	250.00	350.00

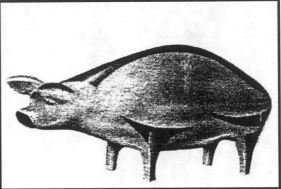

Model No. 1473
PIG

Designer:	Colin Melbourne
Length:	2 ½" x 6", 6.4 x 15.0 cm
Colour:	For colour combinations and varieties see page 393
Issued:	1957-by 1965

Description	U.K. £	U.S. $	Can. $
Series 1	110.00	175.00	250.00
Series 2	135.00	225.00	325.00

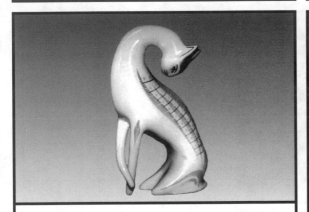

Model No. 1474
CAT

Designer:	Colin Melbourne
Height:	5 ¼", 13.3 cm
Colour:	For colour combinations and varieties see page 393
Issued:	1957-by 1966

Description	U.K. £	U.S. $	Can. $
Series 1	135.00	225.00	325.00
Series 2	150.00	250.00	350.00

Model No. 1475
FOX - Large

Designer:	Colin Melbourne
Length:	10 ½", 26.7 cm
Colour:	For colour combinations and varieties see page 393
Issued:	1957-by 1966

Description	U.K. £	U.S. $	Can. $
Series 1	135.00	225.00	325.00
Series 2	150.00	250.00	350.00

Model No. 1476
CLOWN ON HORSE - Large

Designer:	Colin Melbourne
Height:	8 ½", 21.6 cm
Colour:	For colour combinations and varieties see page 393
Issued:	1957-by 1966

Description	U.K. £	U.S. $	Can. $
Series 1	250.00	400.00	600.00
Series 2	300.00	475.00	750.00

Model No. 1481
REINDEER

Designer:	Colin Melbourne
Height:	5 ½", 14.0 cm
Colour:	For colour combinations and varieties see page 393
Issued:	1957-by 1966

Description	U.K. £	U.S. $	Can. $
Series 1	150.00	250.00	350.00
Series 2	175.00	275.00	400.00

Model No. 1482
PEACOCK

Designer:	Colin Melbourne
Height:	3 ½", 8.9 cm
Colour:	For colour combinations and varieties see page 393
Issued:	1957-by 1965

Description	U.K. £	U.S. $	Can. $
Series 1	135.00	225.00	325.00
Series 2	150.00	250.00	350.00

Chapter Ten

LITTLE LIKEABLES

INDEX BY MODEL NUMBER

LL1
FAMILY GATHERING™
(Hen and Two Chicks)

Designer:	Diane Griffiths
Height:	4 ½", 11.9 cm
Colour:	White hen and chicks with yellow beaks and gold comb on hen - gloss
Issued:	1985 - 1987

Description	U.K. £	U.S. $	Can. $
Gloss	50.00	80.00	125.00

LL2
WATCHING THE WORLD GO BY™
(Frog)

Designer:	Robert Tabbenor
Height:	3 ¾", 9.5 cm
Colour:	White frog, black and green eyes - gloss
Issued:	1985-1987

Description	U.K. £	U.S. $	Can. $
Gloss	50.00	80.00	125.00

LL3
HIDE AND SEEK™
(Pig and Two Piglets)

Designer:	Robert Tabbenor
Height:	3 ¼", 8.3 cm
Colour:	White pigs with pink noses, ears and tails - gloss
Issued:	1985-1987

Description	U.K. £	U.S. $	Can. $
Gloss	50.00	80.00	125.00

LL4
MY PONY™
(Pony)

Designer:	Diane Griffiths
Height:	7 ¼", 18.4 cm
Colour:	White pony with blue highlights in mane and tail - gloss
Issued:	1985-1987

Description	U.K. £	U.S. $	Can. $
Gloss	50.00	80.00	125.00

LL5
ON TOP OF THE WORLD™
(Elephant)

Designer:	Diane Griffiths
Height:	3 ¾", 9.5 cm
Colour:	White elephant with black eyes and gold nails - gloss
Issued:	1985-1987

Description	U.K. £	U.S. $	Can. $
Gloss	50.00	80.00	125.00

LL6
TREAT ME GENTLY™
(Fawn)

Designer:	Diane Griffiths
Height:	4 ½", 11.9 cm
Colour:	White fawn with black and brown eyes, black nose and gold hoof - gloss
Issued:	1985-1987

Description	U.K. £	U.S. $	Can. $
Gloss	50.00	80.00	125.00

LL7
OUT AT LAST™
(Duckling)

Designer:	Robert Tabbenor
Height:	3 ¼", 8.3 cm
Colour:	White duck with black and brown eyes and gold beak - gloss
Issued:	1985-1987

Description	U.K. £	U.S. $	Can. $
Gloss	50.00	80.00	125.00

LL8
CATS CHORUS™
(Cats)

Designer:	Robert Tabbenor
Height:	4 ¾", 12.1 cm
Colour:	Two white cats with black and green eyes, black nose, pink ears and mouth - gloss
Issued:	1985-1987

Description	U.K. £	U.S. $	Can. $
Gloss	50.00	80.00	125.00

Chapter Eleven
STUDIO SCULPTURES

The series of Studio Sculptures made a very brief appearance, most for a maximum of two years, and some for only six months, between 1984 and 1985. When the collection was launched, Harry Sales, Beswick's Design Manager, explained "The new bonded ceramic body gives us endless opportunities to capture every minute detail of the subject and bring the sculptures to life."

The models in this new medium formed four groups, of which two are relevant to this book. These are: the "Countryside Series" which consists of fourteen models and includes birds, a squirrel, dogs, and rabbits, and the "Young Friends Series" which contained four different models, two of which are in two colourways, of pet cats and dogs. None of the models were "free standing" for the model incorporated a base, and some had an additional wooden plinth.

The Studio Sculptures were completely different in style and detail because of the different medium used. They were also different in price! In 1985 their prices ranged from £13.95 to £59.00 and they were considerably more than models in earthenware. For example the Studio Sculpture Wren "Early Bird" retailed at £15.95 whilst the Beswick Wren (993) was £4.95 quite a difference. Therefore it was not too surprising to find that overall the series was not the expected commercial success and so it was not listed in the 1986 price list.

INDEX BY MODEL NUMBER

For other figurines in the Studio Sculpture Series see *The Charlton Standard Catalogue of Royal Doulton Beswick Storybook Figurines.*

Beatrix Potter Series- SS1, SS2, SS3, SS4, SS11, SS26, SS27

Thelwell Series - SS7, SS12; SS23-25 not allocated.

SS5
PUPPY LOVE (Two puppies)

Designer:	Unknown
Height:	4 ½", 11.9 cm
Colour:	1. One brown/white, one black/white - satin matt
	2. One black/white, one white with black patches - satin matt
Issued:	1984-1986
Series:	Young Friends

Colourway	U.K. £	U.S. $	Can. $
1. Brown/black	45.00	70.00	100.00
2. Black/white	45.00	70.00	100.00

SS6
I SPY
(Two kittens)

Designer:	Unknown
Height:	4 ½", 11.9 cm
Colour:	1. Two white cats - satin matt
	2. One tabby, one ginger - satin matt
Issued:	1984-1986
Series:	Young Friends

Colourway	U.K. £	U.S. $	Can. $
1. White	45.00	70.00	100.00
2. Tabby/ginger	45.00	70.00	100.00

SS8
CONTENTMENT
(Dutch Rabbits)

Designer:	Unknown
Length:	4 ¾", 12.1 cm
Colour:	1. Brown and white - satin matt
	2. Black and white - satin matt
Issued:	1984-1986
Series:	Countryside

Colourway	U.K. £	U.S. $	Can. $
1. Brown/white	30.00	50.00	70.00
2. Black/white	30.00	50.00	70.00

SS9
BRIGHT EYES
(Dutch Rabbit)

Designer:	Unknown
Length:	4 ½", 11.9 cm
Colour:	1. Brown and white - satin matt
	2. Black and white - satin matt
Issued:	1984-1986
Series:	Countryside

Colourway	U.K. £	U.S. $	Can. $
1. Brown/white	30.00	50.00	70.00
2. Black/white	30.00	50.00	70.00

SS10
MIND HOW YOU GO
(Goose and goslings)

Designer:	Unknown
Length:	5 ¼", 13.3 cm
Colour:	White goose and yellow goslings - satin matt
Issued:	1984-1986
Series:	Countryside

Description	U.K. £	U.S. $	Can. $
Satin matt	65.00	100.00	150.00

SS13
HAPPY LANDINGS
(Swan on wooden base)

Designer:	Unknown
Height:	5", 12.7 cm
Colour:	White - satin matt
Issued:	1984-1986
Series:	Countryside

Description	U.K. £	U.S. $	Can. $
Satin matt	65.00	100.00	150.00

SS14
THE CHASE
(Dogs on wooden base)

Designer:	Unknown
Height:	4", 10.1 cm
Colour:	Shaded brown and white - satin matt
Issued:	1984-1986
Series:	Countryside

Description	U.K. £	U.S. $	Can. $
Satin matt	65.00	100.00	150.00

SS15
HIDE AND SEEK
(Dogs on wooden base)

Designer:	Unknown
Height:	4 ½", 11.9 cm
Colour:	Shaded brown - satin matt
Issued:	1984-1986
Series:	Countryside

Description	U.K. £	U.S. $	Can. $
Satin matt	65.00	100.00	150.00

SS16
MENU FOR TODAY
(Spaniel puppy with kitten)

Designer:	Unknown
Height:	3 ½", 8.9 cm
Colour:	1. Brown puppy, white kitten - satin matt
	2. Brown puppy, tabby kitten - satin matt
Issued:	1984-1986
Series:	Young Friends

Colourway	U.K. £	U.S. $	Can. $
1. Brown/white	45.00	70.00	100.00
2. Brown/tabby	45.00	70.00	100.00

SS17
SHARING
(German Shepherd puppy with kitten)

Designer:	Unknown
Height:	3 ½", 8.9 cm
Colour:	Black and brown dog, white kitten - satin matt
Issued:	1984-1986
Series:	Young Friends

Description	U.K. £	U.S. $	Can. $
Satin matt	50.00	80.00	125.00

SS18
PLANNING AHEAD
(Squirrel)

Designer:	Unknown
Height:	3", 7.6 cm
Colour:	Red - satin matt
Issued:	1984-1986
Series:	Countryside

Description	U.K. £	U.S. $	Can. $
Satin matt	35.00	55.00	80.00

SS19
EARLY BIRD
(Wren)

Designer:	Unknown
Height:	2 ½", 6.4 cm
Colour:	Dark and light brown - satin matt
Issued:	1984-1986
Series:	Countryside

Description	U.K. £	U.S. $	Can. $
Satin matt	35.00	55.00	80.00

Photograph not
available at press time

SS20
GOLDEN RETRIEVER - on wooden base

Designer: Unknown
Height: 5", 12.7 cm
Colour: Golden brown - satin matt
Issued: 1984-1986
Series: Countryside

Description	U.K. £	U.S. $	Can. $
Satin matt	50.00	80.00	125.00

Photograph not
available at press time

SS21
POINTER - on wooden base

Designer: Unknown
Height: 5", 12.7 cm
Colour: White and brown - satin matt
Issued: 1984-1986
Series: Countryside

Description	U.K. £	U.S. $	Can. $
Satin matt	50.00	80.00	125.00

Photograph not
available at press time

SS22
ENGLISH SETTER - on wooden base

Designer: Unknown
Height: 5", 12.7 cm
Colour: White and liver - satin matt
Issued: 1984-1986
Series: Countryside

Description	U.K. £	U.S. $	Can. $
Satin matt	50.00	80.00	125.00

SS28
ROBIN

Designer: Unknown
Height: 3", 7.6 cm
Colour: Brown and red - satin matt
Issued: 1985-1986
Series: Countryside

Description	U.K. £	U.S. $	Can. $
Satin matt	35.00	55.00	80.00

SS29
BLUE TIT

Designer:	Unknown
Height:	2 ½", 6.4 cm
Colour:	Yellow, green and white - satin matt
Issued:	1985-1986
Series:	Countryside

Description	U.K. £	U.S. $	Can. $
Satin matt	35.00	55.00	80.00

SS30
CHAFFINCH

Designer:	Unknown
Height:	2 ¼", 5.7 cm
Colour:	Brown, ochre, grey, black - satin matt
Issued:	1985-1986
Series:	Countryside

Description	U.K. £	U.S. $	Can. $
Satin matt	35.00	55.00	80.00

Chapter Twelve

WHISKY FLASKS

INDEX BY MODEL NUMBER

Model No. 2051
LOCH NESS MONSTER (NESSIE)

Designer: Albert Hallam
Height: 3", 7.6 cm
Colour: Grey-green - gloss
Issued: 1965-1986

Description	U.K. £	U.S. $	Can. $
1. Head stopper	25.00	40.00	50.00
2. Base stopper	25.00	40.00	50.00

Model No. 2104
EAGLE

Designer: Graham Tongue
Height: 4", 10.1 cm
Colour: Brown - gloss
Issued: 1967-1986

Description	U.K. £	U.S. $	Can. $
Gloss	15.00	25.00	30.00

Model No. 2281
EAGLE

Designer: Graham Tongue
Height: 11", 27.9 cm
Colour: Brown - gloss
Issued: 1969-1984

Description	U.K. £	U.S. $	Can. $
Gloss	85.00	135.00	200.00

Note: Model no. 2281 was remodelled in 1980 with a removable head stopper.

Model No. 2350
HAGGIS BIRD

Designer: James Haywood
Remodelled: Albert Hallam
Height: 2 ½", 6.4 cm
Colour: Brown - gloss
Issued: 1971-1986

Description	U.K. £	U.S. $	Can. $
Gloss	15.00	25.00	30.00

Model No. 2561
GROUSE

Designer:	David Lyttleton
Height:	9", 22.9 cm
Colour:	Brown and red - gloss
Issued:	1976-1984

Description	U.K. £	U.S. $	Can. $
Gloss	65.00	100.00	150.00

Note: Model no. 2561 was remodelled with a removable head stopper.

Model No. 2583
OSPREY

Designer:	David Lyttleton
Height:	7 ¾", 19.7 cm
Colour:	Browns and white - gloss
Issued:	1977-1986

Description:	U.K. £	U.S. $	Can. $
Gloss	50.00	80.00	125.00

Model No. 2636
SQUIRREL

Designer:	David Lyttleton
Height:	3 ½", 8.9 cm
Colour:	Red-brown - gloss
Issued:	1978-1986

Description	U.K. £	U.S. $	Can. $
Gloss	15.00	25.00	30.00

Model No. 2639
KESTREL

Designer:	Graham Tongue
Height:	6 ½", 16.5 cm
Colour:	Dark grey and white - gloss
Issued:	1979-1986

Description	U.K. £	U.S. $	Can. $
Gloss	50.00	80.00	125.00

Model No. 2640
BUZZARD

Designer:	Graham Tongue
Height:	6 ½", 16.5 cm
Colour:	Dark brown and grey - gloss
Issued:	1979-1986

Description	U.K. £	U.S. $	Can. $
Gloss	65.00	100.00	150.00

Model No. 2641
MERLIN

Designer:	Graham Tongue
Height:	6 ½", 16.5 cm
Colour:	Dark grey and white - gloss
Issued:	1979-1986

Description	U.K. £	U.S. $	Can. $
Gloss	65.00	100.00	150.00

Model No. 2642
PEREGRINE FALCON

Designer:	Graham Tongue
Height:	6 ½", 16.5 cm
Colour:	Dark grey and white - gloss
Issued:	1979-1986

Description	U.K. £	U.S. $	Can. $
Gloss	65.00	100.00	150.00

Model No. 2678
EAGLE

Designer:	Graham Tongue
Height:	10 ½", 26.7 cm
Colour:	Light and dark brown - gloss
Issued:	1980- 1987

Description	U.K. £	U.S. $	Can. $
Gloss	65.00	100.00	150.00

Model No. 2686
OTTER

Designer:	David Lyttleton
Height:	2 ¼", 5.7 cm
Colour:	Grey and brown - gloss
Issued:	1981-1986

Description	U.K. £	U.S. $	Can. $
Gloss	15.00	25.00	30.00

Model No. 2687
BADGER

Designer:	David Lyttleton
Height:	3", 7.6 cm
Colour:	Black and white - gloss
Issued:	1981-1986

Description	U.K. £	U.S. $	Can. $
Gloss	15.00	25.00	30.00

Model No. 2693
SEAL

Designer:	Graham Tongue
Height:	3 ½", 8.9 cm
Colour:	Grey - gloss
Issued:	1980-1986

Description	U.K. £	U.S. $	Can. $
Gloss	15.00	25.00	30.00

Model No. 2781
TAWNY OWL

Designer:	Graham Tongue
Height:	6 ¼", 15.9 cm
Colour:	Brown - gloss
Issued:	1982-1987

Description	U.K. £	U.S. $	Can. $
Gloss	65.00	100.00	150.00

Model No. 2798
GROUSE

Designer:	David Lyttleton
Height:	9 ½", 24.0 cm
Colour:	Brown and red - matt
Issued:	1982-1987

Description	U.K. £	U.S. $	Can. $
Gloss	65.00	100.00	150.00

Model No. 2809
BARN OWL

Designer:	Graham Tongue
Height:	6 ¾", 17.2 cm
Colour:	Tan-brown and white - gloss
Issued:	1983-1987

Description	U.K. £	U.S . $	Can. $
Gloss	65.00	100.00	150.00

Model No. 2825
SHORT-EARED OWL

Designer:	Graham Tongue
Height:	6 ¾", 17.2 cm
Colour:	Dark and light brown - gloss
Issued:	1983-1987

Description	U.K. £	U.S. $	Can. $
Gloss	65.00	100.00	150.00

Model No. 2826
SNOWY OWL

Designer:	Graham Tongue	
Height:	1.	6 ½", 16.5 cm
	2.	5 ¾", 14.6 cm
Colour:	White - gloss	
Issued:	1983-1987	

Description	U.K. £	U.S . $	Can. $
1. Large	65.00	100.00	150.00
2. Small	50.00	80.00	125.00

Chapter Thirteen
COMMISSIONED
MODELS

During the early 1990s Beswick used some of its current freestanding models and now attached them to either a ceramic or wooden base.

Various companies, including British Coal, one of the major home shopping networks and a direct mail corporation, seem to be the largest commissioners of these items.

Little is known about these models, for they are not listed in the Beswick product line.

INDEX BY MODEL NUMBER

Model No. 818
"HORSES GREAT AND SMALL" - on ceramic base

Designer: Arthur Gredington
Height: 10", 25.4 cm
Colour: Dark brown and white - gloss
Issued: Unknown

Description	U.K. £	U.S. $	Can. $
Gloss	95.00	175.00	225.00

Model No. 967
COCKER SPANIEL "HORSESHOE PRIMULA"

Designer: Arthur Gredington
Height: 6 ¾", 17.1 cm
Colour: Golden brown - gloss
Issued: Unknown

Description	U.K. £	U.S. $	Can. $
Gloss	85.00	150.00	200.00

Model No. 1436/1460
"SHARING" - on ceramic base

Designer: Arthur Gredington and Colin Melbourne
Height: 4 ¾", 12.1 cm
Colour: Grey cat, brown dog - gloss
Issued: Unknown

Description	U.K. £	U.S. $	Can. $
Gloss	75.00	125.00	175.00

Model No. 1558/1678
"WATCH IT" - on ceramic base

Designer:	Albert Hallam and Pal Zalmen
Height:	8 ¾", 22.2 cm
Colour:	Chocolate point cat, grey mouse - gloss
Issued:	Unknown

Description	U.K. £	U.S. $	Can. $
Gloss	75.00	125.00	175.00

Model No. 1867
"PERSIAN CAT" - on brass plate

Designer:	Albert Hallam
Height:	9 ½", 24.0 cm
Colour:	Ginger - gloss
Issued:	Unknown

Description	U.K. £	U.S. $	Can. $
Gloss	90.00	150.00	225.00

Model No. 1886/3093
"PLAYTIME" - on ceramic base

Designer:	Albert Hallam
Height:	5", 12.7 cm
Colour:	White kitten with pink or lemon ball of wool - gloss
Issued:	Unknown

Description	U.K. £	U.S. $	Can. $
Gloss	55.00	100.00	150.00

Model No. 2221
ST. BERNARD "CORNA GARTH STROLLER"
- on ceramic base

Designer:	Albert Hallam
Height:	6 ¾", 17.1 cm
Colour:	Dark brown, tan and white - gloss
Issued:	Unknown

Description	U.K. £	U.S. $	Can. $
Gloss	95.00	150.00	225.00

Model No. 2590/1436
"GOOD FRIENDS" - on ceramic base

Designer:	Colin Melbourne
Height:	6", 15.2 cm
Colour:	White and tan dog, ginger kitten - gloss
Issued:	Unknown

Description	U.K. £	U.S. $	Can. $
Gloss	75.00	125.00	175.00

Model No. 4677
SOLID FRIENDSHIP - on wooden plinth

Designer:	Albert Hallam and Warren Platt
Height:	5 ½", 14.0 cm
Colour:	White mouse, black and white cat, and white dog with brown patches - gloss
Issued:	1993

Description	U.K. £	U.S. $	Can. $
Gloss	75.00	125.00	175.00

Note: This model was a special commission for British Coal.

INDEX OF MODEL NUMBERS

ALPHABETICAL INDEX

ROYAL DOULTON IS OUR SPECIALITY!

We Buy ♦ We Sell ♦ We Appraise

Colonial House Features the Largest Selection of Current and Discontinued Items in the Following Lines:

+ OLD & NEW ROYAL DOULTON
FIGURES & CHARACTER JUGS
+ HUMMELS
+ DAVID WINTER COTTAGES
+ DEPT. 56 COTTAGES AND
SNOWBABIES

+ ROYAL WORCESTER
+ WEE FOREST FOLK
+ WALT DISNEY CLASSICS
+ SWAROVSKI CRYSTAL
+ LLADRÓ
+ LILLIPUT LANE

WE DO MAIL ORDER WORLDWIDE

Send for our latest product catalogue!

Colonial House Of Collectibles
We carry Current & Discontinued Beanie Babies!

**Monday to Saturday
10 am to 5 pm
or by appointment**

**182 Front Street,
Berea, OH 44017
Tel: (440) 826-4169 or
(800) 344-9299
Fax: (440) 826-0839
Email: yworrey@aol.com**

448

Specialising in rare and discontinued Royal Doulton, Beswick and Wade

The Potteries Antique Centre

Open seven days

Browse amongst a wide variety of Royal Doulton, Beswick, Wade, Moorcroft, Crown Derby, Shelley, Minton, Clarice Cliff, Crown Devon, Coalport, Royal Worcester, Paragon, Charlotte Rhead, Royal Winton and lots more!
****

Our huge inventory includes:
Character & Toby Jugs, Figurines, Animals, Dinner & Tea Ware, Plaques & Plates,
David Hands, Colin Melbourne, Wind in the Willows, Disney, Series ware,
Stoneware, Flambé, Kitty MacBride, and more.....
****

Come and see our excellent and extensive range of collectable pottery in the New Collectable Room:
A direct retail outlet for LJB Ceramics, Carlton Ware, The Old Chintz Company, Moorland, Bairstow Manor, Peggy Davies, Kevin Francis, plus many more......
New releases in Bunnykins, Wade, Beswick, Beatrix Potter and Royal Doulton.

The Potteries Antique Centre
271 Waterloo Road, Cobridge, Stoke-on-Trent, Staffordshire. ST6 3HR
Tel: 01782 201455 Fax: 01782 201518 E-mail: potteries.antiques@virgin.net
Visit our on-line shopping page on our website!
www.potteriesantiquescentre.com

Potteries Specialist Auctions

Hold auctions of mainly 20th Century British pottery every month which include approximately 600 lots of rarities and discontinued pieces from many of the well known manufacturers, the company also hold regular specialist auctions amongst which are Carltonware, Wade and Kevin Francis. For further information regarding entries, commission rates, estimates etc. or to order a catalogue contact
Steve Anderson on 01782 286622.